When [in Mark 9:14-29] Jesus challenged the father's belief, we hear the man's agonising cry, "Lord, I believe; help thou mine unbelief." In the Good News this is translated, "I do have faith, but not enough. Help me to have more!" Or in the New English Bible, "I have faith," cried the boy's father; "help me where faith falls short."

These translations are certainly clear and concise, but they lack the glorious poetic drama of the King James Version. Somehow the passion of the father's cry is diminished. . . .

"I believe; help thou mine unbelief" is matchless, and needs no help or explanation.

— actor Alec McCowen, commenting
on his performances of Mark's Gospel
in his book *Personal Mark*

Help My Unbelief

FLEMING RUTLEDGE

WILLIAM B. EERDMANS PUBLISHING COMPANY
GRAND RAPIDS, MICHIGAN / CAMBRIDGE, U.K.

© 2000 Wm. B. Eerdmans Publishing Co.

All rights reserved

Wm. B. Eerdmans Publishing Co.
255 Jefferson Ave. S.E., Grand Rapids, Michigan 49503 /
P.O. Box 163, Cambridge CB3 9PU U.K.
www.eerdmans.com

Printed in the United States of America

05 04 03 02 01 00   7 6 5 4 3 2 1

ISBN 0-8028-3895-2

"Mrs. Hamer, Mrs. Durr, Brother Will, and the Word of Faith"
first appeared in the *Virginia Seminary Journal,* July 1999.

To my mother
Alice Dabney Parker

and in memory of my father
John C. Parker

through whom I came to know the unfailing love of God
and from whom I learned to follow the truth
come where it may
cost what it will

Contents

Contents

Contents

Contents

Preface

This collection of sermons has been designed for the man or woman who wonders about faith. We might call such a person a "faithful doubter" or even an "unbelieving believer." As I write sermons, it is this person whom I often have in mind. Sometimes he or she is a loyal church member who nevertheless admits, "I don't think I have enough faith," or "I wish I had as much faith as my wife [husband, mother, brother, friend, pastor] does," or even "I think I am losing my faith." This person has a nagging feeling of inferiority, isolation, or unworthiness in comparison to others whom he imagines to be more accomplished. There is thought to be a standard of belief or certainty that one must attain in order to function as a fully acceptable member of the community of faith.

There are more of these doubting believers in the pews on Sunday morning than is usually acknowledged, since frequently there is a tacit agreement among churchgoers that they will not inflict their uncertainties upon one another. Many opportunities are thereby lost, because congregational life deepens and grows when we acknowledge our struggles as a necessary part of Christian discipleship. Those who envy the apparent confidence of their fellows might be reassured to know that their questioning presence among the faithful adds seasoning and maturity to what might otherwise become a vapid enterprise. The introductory sermon in this collection — based on the New Testament text "I believe; help my unbelief" (Mark 9:24) — is therefore addressed not only to those who feel they are on the verge of giving up but also to those whose faith seems unshakeable. Those who suppress or rarely experience doubt will benefit from acknowledging its presence in others as part of the journey that all are embarked upon together.

The doubting churchgoer is not the only person in view here. There is a second type of doubting seeker, the person who almost never goes to church but nevertheless is sometimes heard saying, "I'm not very religious, but sometimes I would like to believe more." A variant on this is the person who is curious about faith. He or she takes a world religion course, mulls over the big questions, browses in the "spiritual" section at the actual or virtual bookshop. This person muses, "Jesus must have been just one of many religious figures," "I don't suppose the Bible is really trustworthy," or "I wonder why religion seems to be a big factor in many people's lives." This person will sometimes read a sermon or listen to one on the radio, even if he or she will not go to a church service.

Yet another type of person has pushed what faith he has into a closet and closed the door, embarrassed into hiding by the incredulity of friends and associates. I have a vivid recollection of a New Yorker of many accomplishments, a sophisticated man with a wide acquaintance who spoke to me once at a gathering of the cultural elite. Knowing I was ordained, he leaned over and said, "I'm a Christian, but I don't ever say so in this crowd." He meant it to sound insouciant and self-mocking, but I could tell he was sincere by the way he glanced around as though he truly feared to be overheard. A few years later he died prematurely, and his traditional Episcopal funeral was attended by many of that same group. Afterwards, as I left the church, I heard one well-known writer saying disdainfully, "Well! that was very *religious!*" The deceased man had borne his witness after all from beyond the grave, but what a pity that he could not have done it more wholeheartedly in this life as well. I often think of him. These sermons are offered with him in mind, and others like him. It is my hope that, if the Lord pleases, some readers might hereby be encouraged to grow openly in faith without being intimidated into silence by those who "sit in the seat of the scoffers" (Ps. 1:1).

Negative Capability

When doubters respond to the preached Word, it is the action of the Holy Spirit blowing on tiny sparks of faith, warming the embers that lie hidden but alive under cold heaps of ashes. Luke tells us that

> The apostles said to the Lord, "Increase our faith!" And the Lord said, "If you had faith as a grain of mustard seed, you could say to this sycamine tree, 'Be rooted up, and be planted in the sea,' and it would obey you." (Luke 17:5-6)

By means of hyperbole, Jesus is saying to them that even the tiniest amount of faith will suffice for great things when God is present. It is *his own presence* that "increases faith." The first sermon in this collection shows what happens when a doubter says to Jesus, "Help my unbelief." It is not our own faith that we trust, but the faithfulness of the Lord himself.

Flannery O'Connor, who wrote about faith as well as anyone has, referred to "help my unbelief" as "the foundation prayer of faith." Writing a letter to a friend who was in the process of rejecting the church (and, we gather, rather proud of doing so), she warned, "Some people when they lose their faith in Christ, substitute a swollen faith in themselves." The humility of faith, she knew, lies in the recognition that faith is given by God and cannot be identified as a human achievement. Precisely because it is beyond human competence, it must be received as a gift, not summoned up by an act of human will. Nor can it be claimed as though it were a finished product. O'Connor wrote further, "Let me tell you this: faith comes and goes. It rises and falls like the tides of an invisible ocean. If it is presumptuous to think that faith will stay with you forever, it is just as presumptuous to think that unbelief will."[1] Faith comes to us as pure grace from the faithful One who "raises the dead and calls into existence the things that do not exist" (Rom. 4:17) — most assuredly including faith where no faith exists.

Because faith is given only by grace, not by works (Rom.

4:16), the preacher is engaged in a task that is paradoxically humble and bold at the same time. It is humble because only God can use the sermon to elicit faith, but it is bold as well, because God has promised that his "word . . . shall not return to me empty, but it shall accomplish that which I purpose" (Isa. 55:11). Resting in this promise, grounded in the faithfulness of God, the preacher is granted confidence of a truly ultimate nature, because God's living Word penetrates the human words and endows them with power that does not come from ourselves. In this confidence Paul writes, "My speech and my message were not in plausible words of human wisdom, but in demonstration of the Spirit and of power, that your faith might not rest in the wisdom of human beings but in the power of God" (1 Cor. 2:4-5).

This paradox of humility and confidence is embodied in the sermon. The same Paul who declares that the gospel was given him by a revelation of Jesus Christ himself (Gal. 1:12) also writes, "I was with you in weakness and in much fear and trembling" (1 Cor. 2:3). The gospel announcement, though it is made with boldness, is not handed down directly from on high, untouched by human imperfection. The preacher must struggle in the pulpit. John Keats coined the phrase "negative capability." He defined it in a letter to a friend this way: "*Negative Capability,* that is when man is capable of being in uncertainties, Mysteries, doubts, without any irritable reaching after fact & reason." One of Keats' biographers comments, "This ability to 'remain content with half knowledge' — what today is called 'tolerance for ambiguity' was, as Keats saw it, essential to the poet insofar as he above all men explores the frontiers of human experience and struggles with its endless diversity and contradictions."[2] A preacher without negative capability cannot lead the people of God with integrity. The preacher speaks from within the same "uncertainties, Mysteries, and doubts" as they. The Scriptures are filled with references to God's "alien work" (Isa. 28:21) and with questions like "O Lord, why dost thou forget our affliction and oppression?" (Ps. 44:23-24), "Why does the way of the wicked prosper?" (Jer. 12:1), and "How long, O Lord? Wilt thou hide thyself for ever?" (Ps. 89:46). There is no "answer" to these questions.

There is only the "answer" given to Job, which is no answer at all, but a radical disclosure of the reality and power of God in spite of everything. This "in spite of" encompasses both the humility and the confidence of the preaching task.

The Plan of This Book

Many readers of this book will notice right away that the grouping of sermons under various headings is somewhat artificial. I readily admit this. Not a single one of these sermons was originally prepared to answer a specific question or to address a specific issue. They were written, as all sermons should be written, as expositions of Biblical texts in specific situations. In some cases the reader may find that the assignment of a sermon to a particular section in the Table of Contents seems arbitrary. Some may appear unnecessarily forced into one category or another, with the undesirable result of reducing their meaning. Most of the sermons, in fact, could have been grouped under several headings or no heading at all.

Nevertheless, over the years it has occurred to me that I am always thinking, as I prepare, about the questions that people have. Even though the sermons were not written in response to particular problems, those problems have frequently seemed to form part of the context for the sermons' delivery. Various people have responded to them in ways that encouraged me to present them in a format that might help people to live faithfully in the midst of specific doubts and uncertainties. I hope that readers will recognize and forgive the limitations of the way in which the sermons have been categorized, so that there will be space and possibility for them to speak in other ways and to other issues if that should be the Spirit's leading.

I do not pretend that this collection addresses every question. There are many important issues of faith that are not identified in the Table of Contents, though readers will sense their presence between the lines. Nor is it claimed that questions and problems are addressed adequately. Sermons do not work that way. They are not logical exercises or theological treatises. They do not seek to persuade, but to reveal. They do not present arguments; they demonstrate. They point beyond themselves to the One whose Word creates and sustains faith. Here again is an observation from one of Flannery O'Connor's letters: "You arrive at enough certainty to be able to make your way, but it is making it in darkness. Don't expect faith to clear things up for you. It is trust, not certainty."[3] We may say, following this line of thought, that sermons have the immediate, situational character of *witness*. They may be likened to the narrow beams of a flashlight shining briefly in first one dark place, then another. They are not floodlights, nor will they endure for long, but if these offerings provide momentary illumination along the way of any traveler, I shall be very grateful.

Acknowledgments

There have always been a certain number of writers who find that the juices flow most freely when they work in public. Virtually all these sermons were written in either a coffeehouse, a tea shop, or a public library. The proprietors of these estimable institutions deserve our undying thanks, not only for providing the services (in the case of the libraries) and the atmosphere (in the case of the coffee and tea shops) but also for leaving us keyboard-pounders and page-turners alone for uncounted hours. I am particularly grateful to the cozy, homelike libraries of Stockbridge and Lenox, Massachusetts; Essex, Connecticut; Rye, New York; and especially the Scoville Library in Salisbury, Connecticut. Other places that have nourished this writer's spirit are Bagel Best in Rye; the Riga Mountain Roast in Lakeville, Connecticut; Sally Lunn's tea shop in Princeton; the Still Perkin' coffee shop in the Garden District of New Orleans; and the Red Lion Inn in Stockbridge. A very special mention must be made of Mary, the mistress of the Chaiwalla tea shop in Salisbury, Connecticut, who not only has the best tea in the United States but also has allowed me far more plugged-in laptop time than I deserve.

And now a word about the house of Eerdmans. As the spring

and fall catalogs come out from Grand Rapids each year, there is quiet rejoicing among all those who care about the future of generous orthodoxy in the Body of Christ. In a time when all of the headlines focus on trendy, sensation-seeking assaults upon Nicene Christianity and most of the revenue derives from uncritical mass-market "spirituality," Eerdmans continues faithfully to serve the one, holy, catholic and apostolic church with a remarkable range of books from various perspectives and traditions. Without sacrificing scholarly standards or critical judgment, this publishing house is steadfastly committed to providing the church with theologically responsible resources for the unprecedented challenges that we face. Yet it would be a mistake to call Eerdmans "conservative." They represent the very best of critical orthodoxy today — politically imaginative and pastorally liberal, exegetically adventurous and theologically progressive, yet always committed to the church's foundation in the Word of God, incarnate and written. I am very thankful for their vocation and ministry among us, and am proud to be an Eerdmans author.

Finally, my chief acknowledgment must be to my husband Dick. His unflagging commitment to our Lord's church, to the radical gospel, and to my vocation has been for many years my rock and shield. His love for the preached Word continues to be my nearest proof that God's Word will not return empty to the Giver.

INTRODUCTION

Help My Unbelief

CHRIST'S CHURCH, SHEFFIELD, MASSACHUSETTS

> *I believe; help my unbelief!*
>
> (MARK 9:24)

How much do you have to believe to be a *bona fide* Christian? What *is* a believer? What is an unbeliever? Which are you? Don't jump to conclusions too quickly; just because a person is sitting in a church pew doesn't necessarily mean that he or she is a person of great faith. A lot of people are hanging on by the thinnest of threads.

There used to be more certainty about the content of Christian faith than there is today. Children used to learn their catechisms and memorize Scripture. These days, it seems as though "believers" can be just about anything, making it up as they go along. Vaguely general ideas of religion and "spirituality" threaten to replace orthodoxy. Political candidates used to speak of churches and synagogues; now they say "faith-based organizations," because that takes in the whole spectrum. It is part of the climate of our times; most people in the mainline churches have been trained not to offend people of other faiths, so we try to avoid saying anything too concrete.[1] A few months ago I heard a sermon in which the preacher exhorted us for fifteen minutes to have faith without ever saying a single word about what we were supposed to have faith in. Surely, however, we

[3]

cannot avoid the issue indefinitely. And so the question becomes, faith in what? Belief in what? And does it matter?

One of the most common remarks made to clergy is "I wish I had as much faith as you do." This usually is an expression of genuine longing. Other versions of the same idea, however, can come across as thinly veiled sarcasm, "Well, of course you're way out ahead of the rest of us." This is a way of saying, "You're just too good to be true; I can't relate to you at all." Yet another group tends toward a note of hopelessness. "I don't think I'm ever going to have enough faith." This third group interests me especially, because a lot of people dear to me are in it. It can be very frustrating to talk to them. They have this idea that a certain specific amount of faith is required, and they are convinced that whatever the necessary amount is, they don't have it and they aren't ever going to have it. Sometimes it seems as though they have deified their unbelief; their very doubts have become articles of faith.

Clergy are often tempted to preach about faith. My homiletics professor, the distinguished Lutheran preacher Edmund Steimle, warned us not to do it. He said, "You can never get a person to believe by talking to him about faith. If you want your child to make friends with the child down the street, you can talk to her about friendship till you're blue in the face and it gets you nowhere. What you can do is arrange a meeting where friendship might occur. Or it might not. It is no longer in your hands."[2]

In Mark's Gospel, chapter 9, Jesus has just come down off the Mount of Transfiguration where Peter, James and John "beheld his glory, glory as of the only Son from the Father" (John 1:14). Our Lord wastes no time soaking up these divine rays, however. Before you know it they are all coming down off the mountain and Jesus is plunged into the midst of yet another controversy. He finds his disciples in the midst of a large crowd, contending with the established teachers of religion. This happened to Jesus virtually every day; his entire ministry was conducted on a battlefield. If he left his disciples unattended for a few hours, the struggle moved to them. Here in our reading, we learn that a number of curious people have gathered around them and the scribes, to see the fireworks. As Jesus approaches, many of these spectators break away from the knot of arguing people and come to greet him with awe and wonder. Mark is showing us that the very person of Jesus causes amazement, before he even says or does anything. His very presence calls forth reactions, for and against.

Jesus asks the disputants, "What are you discussing?" (Mark 9:16). One of the men present promptly speaks up and takes responsibility for setting off the conflict. "Teacher," he said, "I brought my son to you, for he has a dumb spirit; and wherever it seizes him, it dashes him down; and he foams and grinds his teeth and becomes rigid; and I asked your disciples to cast it out, and they were not able" (vv. 16-18). This is the immediate cause of the controversy; the official teachers of the Law are heaping scorn upon the disciples of Jesus for presuming to wield the power of exorcism — driving away demons — and then for failing at it. Because the disciples' ministry is an extension of Jesus' own, we can see right away that the Master's authority is now in question. We are meant to feel the tension in the situation as everyone looks at Jesus to see what he will do.

His response is remarkable. Remember, he has just come down from the Mount of Transfiguration where he has communed with the great and faithful spirits of Moses and Elijah, where he has heard his own Father say, "This is my beloved Son; listen to him" (Mark 9:7). Now he is back down on this darkling plain where pain and demonic possession consort with ignorance and official enmity. "O faithless generation, how long am I to be with you? How long am I to bear with you?" (v. 19). This very unusual outburst offers an extraordinary insight into the depth of our Lord's loneliness and isolation among us on earth. It has become apparent to him that not even his closest friends understand him. Jesus does not speak here with ordinary human impatience; he speaks as the only One who has perfect faith in the midst of an unfaithful world.[3] These words of our Lord encompass the laments of all the prophets of Israel and of God the Father himself. "Jesus stands at God's side, grieving with God at the distress caused by such unbelief."[4] The Father and the Son together are mourning for the "faithless generation" —

which does not mean the people of Jesus' time only, but all the people of all time, including you and me. He is saying, "How am I to endure this rejection of my love?"[5] Here is the essence of Jesus' suffering — to know that his outpouring of himself has found no channel for its power. He must do it all alone. And so, shouldering the burden, he says, "Bring the boy to me."

Let us join in envisioning this scene. Jesus is surrounded by many people, none of them really dependable and most of them outright hostile. His disciples have misapprehended their own vocation; they think that their proximity to Jesus guarantees magical powers to them, extensions of their own egos to be exercised at will, almost mechanically, without the necessary abandonment of themselves to the sole sovereignty of God.[6] Because of their failure, the crowd is now wondering if Jesus himself isn't bogus, too. In particular, the father of the possessed boy has just seen his hopes dashed and his confidence badly shaken. But we are getting ahead of the story; let us return to the moment when Jesus says, "Bring the boy to me." We are told that when they did so, the evil spirit "saw Jesus," and "immediately it convulsed the boy, and he fell on the ground and rolled about, foaming at the mouth" (Mark 9:20). We today would say that this was epilepsy, and indeed, most commentators have long agreed on that diagnosis. However, we are being told something different here, something revelatory: the epilepsy is distinct from the boy. There is an enemy at work in him. I am vividly reminded of a famous *New Yorker* magazine article from about twenty years ago, the story of the Creedmoor psychiatric hospital and a severely afflicted schizophrenic named Sylvia Frumkin. Her mother came to see her at the hospital and found her in a straitjacket. Sylvia said, "It's not me, Ma. It's the illness. The illness is stronger than I am."[7]

And so, we are to understand, we are not dealing here with a story of a person being healed by some sort of psychological suggestion. The problem is not within the boy, but external to him; the demon is, as we might say today, "ego-alien." Jesus never says a word to the boy at all. The boy is lying on the ground writhing and foaming as the drama goes on above him. The only active characters

are the father, the demon, and the Lord. This is a pitched battle between the Messiah and the ancient Enemy of humankind. The en-
gagement is taking place on two levels at once — the particular local level, and the apocalyptic level where the power of God
confronts and unmasks the forces of evil. We, the readers of Mark's
Gospel, already know something about Jesus that the father does
not know; in earlier chapters, Mark has let us in on the secret that
Jesus has absolute power over the demons and they are terrified of
him. But the father is not aware of this cosmic drama. He is like any
frightened parent of a sick child; he is bewildered, helpless, desperate. He has brought his son to Jesus' disciples hoping for help, but
their failure has caused him to lose most of that hope. His words to
Jesus clearly show that he isn't expecting much at this stage. He
says, "[The evil spirit] has often cast him into the fire and into the
water, *to destroy him;* but *if you can do anything,* have pity on us and
help us" (Mark 9:22). From these words, we see that we are looking
at a human life about to be obliterated by an evil power, and we are
aware that the father is very doubtful of Jesus' ability to do anything about it. The outcome hangs here, on this point. Heaven and
earth hold their breath. The demon has already deployed his weapons; the boy is thrashing about in a terrifying fashion. Jesus, we already know, can vanquish the evil power with a mere word. But he
delays. The disciples have failed, the teachers of the Law look on
scornfully, the crowd hangs back in bemusement, no longer certain
what to expect as the Master draws out the dialogue with the father
by repeating his own doubtful words back to him: "'If you can do
anything!' All things are possible to him who believes." And immediately the father of the boy cried out and said, "I believe; help my
unbelief!" (vv. 23-24).

In a split second the father has been seized by hope. He has
been seized by life. He has been seized by the power of God. And
the father's own corresponding action is to grasp with all his might
at the giver of hope and life and healing power. He puts himself
into Jesus' hands totally. In words that have been called the greatest
cry of faith in the entire Bible, he places himself under the mercy
and mastery of the Lord. "I believe; help my unbelief!" The instant

is electric. The crowd, sensing the critical moment, surges forward. Jesus utters the command with the most emphatic possible stress on his own unique authority: "Thou dumb and deaf spirit, I charge thee, come out of him, and enter into him no more" — whereupon the demon, uttering a terrible cry of rage and defeat, convulsed the boy terribly and fled from him. "The boy lay there like a corpse; so that most people standing round said, 'He is dead.' But Jesus took him by the hand and lifted him up, and he arose" (vv. 25-27).

"All things are possible to him who believes." Believes what? Believes that all things are possible? Believes in faith healing? Believes in belief? No. All commentators agree: the faith which is evoked by Jesus' dialogue with the father is not assent to any theological proposition. It is not agreement with any religious principle. It is not acquiescence in any spiritual program. It is radical trust in the person of Jesus, the One "who calls into existence the things that do not exist" (Rom. 4:17), the One who creates faith where there is no faith.

St. Mark's little church was looking at the very real possibility of persecution and death for its confession of Christ as Lord. The evangelist wrote with this in mind. "Most people" did not place their trust in Jesus.[8] "Most people," looking at a little congregation like Mark's, like the one we are in today, will say, "It's got no future." "Most people," faced with incurable illness will say, "It's hopeless." "Most people" will say of a corpse, "He's dead." But here is something wonderful. The words used by Mark to describe the healing of the boy are these: "Jesus took him by the hand and lifted him up, and he arose." This is the Easter affirmation.[9] Mark is telling us that "even in the case where God's power is most likely to be thwarted (the case of death itself), that is precisely the point at which the power of God in the Resurrection manifests itself through those who believe."[10]

Dear people of God, through the retelling of this story, Jesus Christ the Lord has arranged a meeting between himself and you. It is out of my hands. It is in his hands. He is not waiting for you to figure it all out. He is not lying back observing to see if you have enough faith. He is not withholding his approval pending your successful application. He has come forward to meet you, in word and sacrament. The only person with perfect faith is Jesus Christ. When he says "All things are possible to him who believes," there is a sense in which he speaks first of himself. It is by *his* faith, *his* faithfulness, that we receive our own faith.[11] There is no foundation more certain than that. And listen to this. Remember how he burst out, "O faithless generation . . . how long am I to bear with you?" We know the answer to that now, don't we? He bore with us. He bore with us to the end. He bore with us all the way to the Cross. "Love bears all things" (1 Cor. 13:7). "Surely he has borne our griefs and carried our sorrows" (Isa. 53:4). "He himself bore our sins in his body on the tree" (1 Pet. 2:24).

Are you a believer or an unbeliever? No matter how troubling your doubts may be, no matter how inadequate you may feel compared to others, no matter how often you may feel that you are just going through the motions, you would not be here this morning if you did not have some germ of faith, however small. That is the Holy Spirit of Christ already at work in you. It is enough. Trust the Lord of faith to make it grow. We need never say again, "I wish I had more faith." Instead, we have the infinite privilege of praying, "Lord, I believe; help thou mine unbelief," knowing that in the fullness of time he will speak the word that will banish the enemy forever.

AMEN.

THE NATURE OF GOD

Moses *and* Monotheism: *A Response to Dr. Freud*

HARVARD MEMORIAL CHURCH, CAMBRIDGE, MASSACHUSETTS

And the Lord said to Moses, I AM WHO I AM.

(EXOD. 3:14)

You don't actually believe in God here at Harvard, do you? A certain professor wrote in *The New Yorker* about three years ago that "I'm religious, but I try to keep quiet about it. In Cambridge, where I work, religiosity is accounted one of those conditions that suggest some lapse of hygiene on the part of those afflicted, as with worms or lice."[1] Richard Rorty has recently declared himself exhilarated because "in the final stages of democracy we won't need religion any more."[2] Six weeks ago, Salman Rushdie told *New York Times* readers that his hope for the third millennium is that we would "finally outgrow our need for religion."[3] These sorts of observations are so commonplace among the high priests of our culture that they scarcely merit mention. Here is a rather more piquant comment on religious faith, from a letter of English novelist Virginia Woolf. Writing to her sister Vanessa about a visit with T. S. Eliot, she reports,

> I have had a most shameful and distressing interview with poor dear Tom Eliot, who may be called dead to us from this day for-

ward. He has become an Anglo-Catholic, believes in God . . . and goes to church. I was really shocked. A corpse would seem to me more credible than he is. I mean, there's something obscene in a living person sitting by the fire and believing in God.[4]

Well, in spite of all, as your preacher today I identify myself with some words that Paul once wrote: "I am not ashamed of the gospel" (Rom. 1:16). Thanks be to God, the Reverend Dr. Gomes isn't either.[5] So, feeling myself in good company in spite of the prevailing Cambridge ethos, I propose to call in the big guns and match them up: Moses and Freud.

I confess that I cheated a little bit with the sermon title this morning. At the end of his life, Freud did publish a work called *Moses and Monotheism,* but it is of little use for the student of the Bible.[6] I just borrowed the title. The real place to look for Freud's views on religion is his great essay *The Future of an Illusion.* You may cite Voltaire, Nietzsche, Darwin, the Bloomsbury group, Richard Rorty, or anyone else that you choose, but for my money, when it comes to making mincemeat of religion, Freud is the main man. As far as I know, *The Future of an Illusion* is the most devastating argument ever mounted against religious faith. Every time I read it I feel rather like a fool for continuing to be a believer.[7]

Let us be clear straightway that we are not going to be trashing Freud this morning. In fact, Freud is one of my intellectual heroes. Like all great men he made some great mistakes, but the more I read him the more I admire him. True lovers of the Judeo-Christian tradition should worry more about free-floating generic "spirituality" than about Freud's scrupulous and principled atheism. Freud's life's work, insofar as it was granted to him, was the unmasking of illusions. He would be offended to hear it, but others before me have observed that the enmity of Freud was more constructive for Christianity than the friendship of Jung.[8]

The last illusion, Freud believed, is religion. Because it is the most tenacious self-deception, it is therefore most deserving of the truth-seeker's implacable hostility. "Religious ideas . . . are illusions," he wrote, because they are "fulfilments of the oldest, strongest, and most urgent wishes of mankind. The secret of their strength lies in the strength of those wishes." And again, "[Religious ideas are] born from man's need to make his helplessness tolerable." And again, he insists, wherever religious notions and practices appear among peoples, they are "merely the products of their own mental activity. . . . What is characteristic of illusions is that they are derived from human wishes."⁹

One of the great merits of Dietrich Bonhoeffer's *Letters and Papers from Prison,* fragmentary and undigested though they are, is that Bonhoeffer, in his Nazi prison cell, was attempting to articulate a Biblical theology that was "religionless." This was an act of great intellectual courage, analogous to his physical courage in defying Hitler. Even with the SS and the hangman at his very door, he continued to renounce the convenience of ready answers and the consolations of conventional piety. We might wish that Bonhoeffer had lived long enough to come to terms with Freud, but even though that did not happen, we can see what he was aiming at when he wrote that Christianity could not be dependent upon "human self-expression" and said that he was drawn "more to the religionless people than the religious."¹⁰

And so, speaking of irreligion, we come now to Moses, that colossal figure towering over the Old Testament and Jewish history. This has been a Moses year: DreamWorks animated him, the religion departments of the newsmagazines had a field day with him, and *Time* put him on the cover.¹¹ We have just read the Biblical story of the event in Moses' life that introduces the God of Israel by name for the first time.¹² Let us join Moses as he goes about his chores as a shepherd in the inhospitable Midianite desert. It is important to understand that we are not meeting up with some super-spiritual person here. Indeed, there is hardly a mention of anything religious in the saga of Moses up to this point. How *irreligious* it is, in fact, with its discussions of demographics, construction projects, slave labor, class distinctions, economic calculations, and ethnic cleansing. The Biblical atmosphere of worldly reality is a radical departure from that of Near Eastern religion.¹³ You will hear a great deal in comparative religion classes about the borrowings of the Hebrews from surrounding cultures, but these borrowings undergo such a transformation in the process that only the most superficial points of comparison remain.

So here is Moses, herding his father-in-law's sheep. What a dreary situation he finds himself in, after all the excitement of being a prince of Egypt! Remember, Moses at this point does not know who he is. Is he Egyptian or Hebrew, aristocrat or shepherd, urbanite or nomad? Where does he come from and where is he going? Who are his gods, those of Egypt or those of the trackless wilderness? If he has any thoughts about these things, we are not told. What we are told is this: he sees a fire in the desert. What a strange sight! It is an eerie thing to imagine, because there isn't much in a desert to burn, only a few scattered shrubs, nothing to start a real brushfire. The light of the sun reflecting on sand and rock is already blinding and the heat is ferocious, so an untended fire is a true oddity. "Moses looked, and behold, the bush was burning, yet it was not consumed. And Moses said, 'I will turn aside and see this great sight, why the bush is not burnt'" (Exod. 3:2-3). Moses approached the blaze with mere human curiosity, but as he drew near something happened that lifted the occasion entirely out of the category of freaks of nature. A voice spoke to Moses, calling his name. "Moses, stand back!" Not an inch closer! "Draw not nigh hither: put off thy shoes from off thy feet, for the place whereon thou standest is holy ground" (v. 5). I hope this makes you feel at least some vestige of a shiver. Can you see how this is presented? It is not a vision that Moses had. It is an act of God. The subject of the story is not Moses at all. It is God. "God called unto Moses out of the midst of the bush" (v. 4).

Now Freud would say that all of this is nothing more than a projection of human wishes and human longings. Okay, but let us suspend disbelief for a moment. The important thing to understand is that the Bible forbids us to think about the text this way. If we rewrite the story by saying that Moses *imagined* that God spoke to him, it changes into something else altogether. You may not believe a word of the Bible, but it isn't fair to recast it in terms other than its own. With rather staggering audacity, it presents us with something we could not have imagined: a God who discloses himself *over against* human religious fantasies, saying, "I am the God of thy father, the God of Abraham, the God of Isaac, and the God of Jacob. And Moses hid his face; for he was afraid to look upon God" (v. 6). Here is a God who strikes fear and awe for an entirely different reason than the usual divinities of ancient religion. "Israel's God was of a type absolutely unique in the ancient world."[14] Here is no sun god or moon god or fertility god. This God has entered history and bound himself up with identifiable human beings with specific names. In his best-selling book *The Gifts of the Jews,* Thomas Cahill writes,

> [Here is] the God beyond the mountain, the God beyond the sky, the unknowable God whose purposes are hidden from human intelligence, who cannot be manipulated. . . . This God is the initiator; he encounters [human beings], they do not encounter him. . . . This God is profoundly different from them, not their projection or their pet, not the usual mythological creature whose intentions can be read in auguries or who can be controlled by human rituals. . . . this God who is beyond all our amulets and scheming, the God who rains on picnics, the God who allows human beings to be inhuman, who has sentenced us all to death. . . . All the other gods are figments, sorry projections of human desires.[15]

Cahill, though, as good as he is, is not careful enough to be consistent throughout his book that the Bible presents God always as the prime mover, never Moses or any other human being. One could easily come away from *The Gifts of the Jews* thinking that the patriarchs and prophets were religious geniuses who invented it all.[16] However, interpreting the Bible on its own terms — unfashionable though that is in high academic circles nowadays — requires that we acknowledge the *intention* of the various Biblical writers even if we do not acquiesce in it. Their intention is to bear witness to the reality, presence, and power of a God who was there *before Moses thought of him,* a God who said, mysteriously, I AM WHO I am. Freud wrote that "Philosophers . . . give the name of 'God' to some vague abstraction which they have created for themselves."[17] To which God himself replies, "I am not a vague abstraction, I am not what you think, I am not what you would like me to be, I am not a projection of your wishes, I have not been created by anyone; on the contrary, I AM the Creator of all that is." God is who he is in himself. The burning bush is an ineffable symbol of "the transcendent, awesome, and unapproachable Divine Presence," self-generated, self-perpetuating, absolute and underived, unaffected by anything outside itself.[18]

Now, let us be fair to Dr. Freud. He has already thought of all this. He writes, "It does not help much to have it asserted that [religious doctrine] originates from divine revelation, for this assertion is itself one of the doctrines whose authenticity is under examination, and no proposition can be a proof of itself." This is a compelling argument. Personally, I prefer the intellectual rigor of Freud to the feel-good religiosity that surrounds us these days. A Biblical theologian can readily agree with almost everything that Freud says about religion. Over against his penetrating analysis I would put this affirmation: the faith of Biblical Israel *is not religion,* because it is not projected out of human wishes.[19] The Bible is a human document, with all the marks of that humanness, but it is at the same time a genuine miracle, because it is the unique testimony to the God who stands over against human imagination and calls all of us into question.[20]

God in the burning bush presents himself as the fire that burns yet does not burn out, the fire that is not consumed by its own activity, the fire that in its energy does not destroy. This is the One Being whose essence derives from himself alone. He only can say I AM WHO I AM. Yet he visited a lowly bush and set it ablaze without consuming it.[21] This is not a philosophical statement about God's *essence,* but a wondrous sign of what God *does.* The theophany at the burning bush testifies to a God who is not just being-in-itself, but being-in-action.[22] The self-revelation of God in the burning bush is not to convey information, as though God were giving Moses a lecture in divinity. Rather, it is an invitation to us as it was a commission to Moses — an invitation to trust, a commission to follow, a summons to participate in God's mighty work of liberation.[23] The proper interpretation of the divine name, much disputed, means one thing for sure: most especially it means "God's presence with Moses and the people *in the event of the redemption from bondage.*"[24] In other words, God is not a mystical entity to contemplate at leisure. God is not known fully as YHWH until the deliverance at the Red Sea.[25] God is out there on the barricades with disreputable people like Moses and Paul and, who knows, maybe even Al Sharpton.[26] Our God is marching on.

And so the Lord is the one who says, "I have seen the affliction of my people who are in Egypt. . . . I know their sufferings, and I have come down to deliver them" (Exod. 3:7-8). The God who is really God, the God who parts the waters of the Red Sea and thunders from Mount Sinai is the One who appears in the world to take the part of the refugees, to defend the defenseless, to come alongside those who suffer and make their case his own. There is nothing like this in "religion." We may indeed share Freud's passion for the unmasking of illusions, for truly, something other than illusion is here. This "subversive narrative"[27] comes to its climax two thousand years later on a hill outside Jerusalem, where, in an identifiable historical year under an identifiable Roman governor, God allows himself, as Bonhoeffer wrote, to be "pushed out of the world onto the Cross" for the deliverance of those who have been sentenced to death.[28] And so, Paul declares, "While we were still helpless, Christ died for the ungodly" — for the irreligious and impious (Rom. 5:6).

Who is Moses? An ungodly man who was commandeered by God. Who am I? One who in spite of herself has been impressed into God's service. Who are you? You are one who has been drawn into God's presence by the power of his living Word, the fire that burns but does not consume. May his fire set us, too, ablaze with great things that never were but are coming into being, for this is not religion.

This is revolution.

Re-imagining and Revelation

GRACE CHURCH IN NEW YORK

> *Then the Lord answered Job out of the whirlwind:*
> *"Who is this that darkens counsel by words without*
>   *knowledge?*
> *Gird up your loins like a man,*
> *I will question you, and you shall declare to me."*

(JOB 38:1-3)

Some of you have probably been following the news story about the Reform Jewish synagogue in Cincinnati that applied for membership in the Union of American Hebrew Congregations even though its members had eliminated from their liturgy all references to God. What interested me especially were the various reasons that were given for these God-less prayers. The leader of the Beth Adam synagogue, Rabbi Robert Barr, said that the omissions were made "out of respect for . . . the varying concepts of God that are held by his congregation." Well, exactly. There are a million and one concepts of God in the world. We are surrounded by a veritable smorgasbord of gods. Many churches and synagogues today are indeed bending over backwards to accommodate these various gods. For instance, one of the members of the Cincinnati congregation stated that she could no longer accept the God of the Reform liturgy that she had grown up with: "It called upon a God that was a very male person. It was the kind of god that answers prayers and intervenes in the order of the universe. It wasn't a God concept that I hold." Even the liberal Reform Jews drew the line at this. When the Union of American Hebrew Congregations cast its votes, the synagogue of a thousand gods and no God was resoundingly refused membership. As one rabbi said, "Reform Judaism cannot be everything, or it will be nothing."

John Calvin wrote almost four hundred years ago that the human mind is a perpetual factory of idols. The people of God have been susceptible to foreign gods ever since they built a golden calf in the Sinai desert. It has been many a long day, however, since there has been so much rethinking of God within the churches. The Channel 13 news hour devoted a large chunk of time on a recent Thursday night to the controversial "Re-Imagining [God]" conference held last November in Minneapolis. My Presbyterian friends tell me that they cannot remember when their denomination has been in such turmoil. The Presbyterian General Assembly gathered last week and apparently met with some success in reaffirming the Scriptures and the creeds while at the same time calling for humility in seeking for theological truth and affirming *the role of imagination* in theology.

It was this last reference to imagination that caught my attention. All of us know and enjoy Strawberry Fields in Central Park, especially the evocative medallion in the pavement with John Lennon's single word, *Imagine.* Imagination is particularly important in the lives of children, and there is reason to be worried that their imaginations are being stunted by too much passive television watching and too many pop-up books that do all the work for them. Poetry is the ultimate channel for the human imagination; since many Americans today never read poetry, there is genuine cause for reaffirming the role of imagination.

On the other hand, with regard to God, there can be such a thing as too much imagination. One doesn't have to be a conservative Presbyterian to think that the "Re-Imagining" conference went too far. If God is truly God, then he is not a product of human thought.

One of the major themes of the Hebrew Bible is the over-powering message, pervading the Scripture from end to end, that there is *only one God* and *he is who he is in himself* regardless of what we may imagine him to be. This is a theme of the book of Job. It is popularly thought that Job is an attempt to explain the problem of undeserved suffering. If that is what it is, it is a very unsatisfactory and even offensive failure. The book of Job will always be something of a mystery, far bigger than our attempts to encompass it, but it was not written to explain suffering. A Jewish commentator, N. H. Tur-Sinai, states that the author-poet's intention is to demonstrate, not only to Jewish readers and hearers but also to Gentiles (among whom the Jews were exiled at the time), that Yahweh is truly God.[1]

Chapters three through thirty-seven of the book of Job are composed of human attempts to circumscribe God. Job's so-called friends are sure that they can get a fix on God. Their speeches go on interminably. A lot of what they say sounds good; you could pick it up and put it down somewhere else in the Bible and hardly know the difference. Other sections, though, are spun out of human presumption, human imagining. Job himself gets so wrapped up in his recital of his own innocence and virtue that he ends up passing judgment on God. In order to justify himself, he is ready to accuse God. Instead of throwing himself on the divine mercy, he has insisted on an explanation.

Our lesson from Job this morning is taken from the climax of the book. Job and his friends have exhausted themselves with words. They have described God at length and in every way that they can think of. Human resources are at an end. It is at this point that God speaks to Job out of the whirlwind.

Then the Lord answered Job out of the whirlwind:
"Who is this that darkens counsel by words
    without knowledge?
Gird up your loins like a man,
I will question you, and you shall declare to me.
Where were you when I laid the foundation of the earth? . . .

Who laid its cornerstone,
When the morning stars sang together,
    and all the sons of God shouted for joy? . . .
Have you entered into the springs of the sea,
Or walked in the recesses of the deep?
Have the gates of death been revealed to you,
Or have you seen the gates of deep darkness?
Have you comprehended the expanse of the earth?
Declare, if you know all this."

(38:1-7, 16-18)

Note the remarkable fact that God has nothing to say about Job's suffering. He passes over it with sublime disregard as though it had never happened. He gives no answer to Job's passionate questions. Instead, God declares that he is the questioner and Job is the one called into question ("I will question you, and you will declare to me"). God grants complete human dignity to Job as a matter of course ("Gird up your loins like a man"), but he charges him with the ultimate presumption: "Shall a faultfinder contend with the Almighty? . . . Will you even put me in the wrong? Will you condemn me that you may be justified?" (40:2, 8). Instead of answers and explanations, God grants a revelation of himself in his pure being. Job, in the inevitable self-centeredness that comes with misery, had forgotten that God exists entirely apart from Job's need for him. God's divine address to Job blows Job's mind, as we say; he is raised above his troubles to the self-forgetful contemplation of God's majesty:

Then Job answered the Lord:
"I know that thou canst do all things,
And that no purpose of thine can be thwarted. . . .
I had heard of thee by the hearing of the ear,
But now my eye sees thee;
Therefore I despise my words,
And repent in dust and ashes."

(42:1, 5-6)

If we are right in our interpretation, the book of Job reveals the God who is really God against the presumptions and imaginations of human beings. It is a prodigious declaration of the reality and being of God.

In his essay, *The Future of an Illusion,* Sigmund Freud argues with great forcefulness that religious faith in general and Judeo-Christian faith in particular are "born from man's need to make his helplessness tolerable." Human beings "give the name of 'God' to some vague abstraction which they have created for themselves . . . and even boast that they have recognized a higher purer concept of God, notwithstanding that their God is now nothing more than an insubstantial shadow and no longer the mighty personality of religious doctrines."[2]

Well, then, is the book of Job right? Or is it, too, a projection of man's need for a powerful protector and vindicator? Is the Bible a product of human mental activity as Freud says it is? If we are to be Christians into the next millennium, we need to meet these challenges squarely. It is far better to look disbelief straight in the face than to make up a god to suit ourselves. It is far more dangerous for theistic faith to allow made-up gods into the synagogue and church than it is to carry on a conversation with an atheist who warns against creating gods in our own image.

I had an odd experience this morning. I was praying to God about my sermon as I usually do, and I was praying somewhat mechanically in the terms that I usually pray — Heavenly Father, Dear Lord, and so forth. Suddenly the words of God speaking out of the whirlwind came to me. It's true that I had been thinking about these words all week, but only as a subject for a sermon. This morning they seemed to come to me *directly:* "Who is this that darkens counsel by words without knowledge?" As a sermon-writer putting words together, I felt what the Old Testament calls the fear of the Lord, and I remembered that the Old Testament says three times in three different places that the fear of the Lord is the beginning of wisdom. Was I, too, putting together "words without knowledge"? How could I ever be sure? What right does a preacher have to stand in in the pulpit and proclaim God?

The witness of the Bible is that every other god under the sun is a product of human consciousness except only the God of the Old and New Testaments. Whether we believe this or not, we must admit that it is an awesome claim. I am more convinced than ever that the Scriptures set before us something, or rather some One, who is far beyond anything the unassisted human imagination could dream up. Freud understands the Bible very well in certain respects. He knows what he is up against. He courageously refuses to believe in anything that emerges as a projection of human needs and wishes, but he does not fail to see that the God proclaimed in the Bible is no "vague abstraction," no "insubstantial shadow," but a "mighty personality." The author of the book of Job has anticipated Freud's objection. Is the God of the Bible a god that we have created for ourselves? Job was written, at least in part, to give a resounding "no" to that question. God does not respond to Job's wishes and needs; on the contrary, he seems to be completely independent of them. God's reply to Job is no reply at all; it is a disclosure of radical divine autonomy.

I have been living and wrestling with the Old and New Testaments for more than half a century of my life. There are not many challenges to that Scripture that I have not heard and considered. Every time I think I am losing my faith, the Biblical story seizes me yet again with a life all its own. No other religious document has this power. I remain convinced in spite of all the arguments that God really does inhabit this text. With Job, I say yet again, "I had heard of thee with the hearing of the ear, but now my eye sees thee; therefore I despise my words, I melt away in dust and ashes" (42:5-6).

Some witty modern-day atheist said that the Christian who loses her faith in God leaves him high and dry without a God not to believe in. That's a mistake I, for one, am not going to make. The God we proclaim to you today is not the "vague abstraction" of the philosophers or the "insubstantial shadow" of the New Agers, but the "mighty personality" who speaks to Job from the storm. He is the living God. He upset my neatly packaged prayer this morning as he will upset yours, but he offers something infinitely better than we could have imagined: the vision of himself as the Creator of the universe who, ultimately, is on our side. "Hear, O Israel, the Lord our God, the Lord is one" (Deut. 6:4).

And now let us say together, "I believe in God the Father almighty, maker of heaven and earth . . ."

AMEN.

The Trinity in the Last Ditch

ST. JAMES CHURCH, DALLAS

The grace of the Lord Jesus Christ and the love of God and the fellowship of the Holy Spirit be with you all.

(2 COR. 13:14)

I magine for a moment that you are the parent of a child, or young person, who appears to be on the verge of destroying himself, or herself. Maybe he is hooked on drugs and failing in school, maybe she is anorexic and starving herself, maybe he has run away from home. You are like most parents — you would do anything, anything at all, to reverse the situation. You would spend huge amounts of money for professional help; you would fly across the country; you would pay a ransom, mortgage the house, go without sleep, neglect your own health, jeopardize your standing in the community, throw yourself on the mercy of anyone you thought might intervene. You are desperate. You would make a complete fool of yourself if you thought it might get your child's attention.

This is the position in which the Apostle Paul finds himself at the end of his second letter to the Christians in Corinth. The Corinthian church has gone completely off the rails and, furthermore, is on the verge of rejecting him as their leader and teacher. He is planning a trip to Corinth, but trips in those days took months, and he knows that by the time he gets there it might be too late. In desperation he writes an impassioned, erratic letter to the congregation, trying first one tack and then another. The last four chapters of Second Corinthians form the most agonized portion of the New Testament. One commentator called it almost too painful to read. It is crabbed, tumultuous, disjointed, wildly uneven.[1] If I came across a letter like this written by a person I loved, I might delete parts of it, because I wouldn't want the author to look bad for posterity. Indeed, it is rather surprising that some of these chapters were saved by the church. Very little of 2 Corinthians appears in our lectionary, and it is rarely taught in its entirety.

So, frankly, it is amazing to find chapter 13 turning up in the lectionary for Trinity Sunday, one of the glory days of the Christian year. It seems a most peculiar choice. I would be curious to know if any of you noticed, as it was read, that it has a very strange tone, very unlike the Paul that many of us know and some of us love. "Examine yourselves to see whether you are holding to your faith. Test yourselves. Mend your ways." We don't think of Paul barking orders like this. It sounds uncharacteristically brusque and didactic. Paul of all people knows that commands of this sort are problematic, for as he wrote to the church in Rome, "the very commandment which promised life proved to be death to me" (Rom. 7:10). What's actually going on, however, is that he is trying first one approach and then another. Appeals to the Corinthians' better nature alternate with sarcasm: "Do you not realize that Jesus Christ is in you? — unless indeed you fail to meet the test." He continues, "We seem to have failed." By "we" he means "we apostles"; the Corinthians have turned away to "false apostles . . . disguising themselves as apostles of Christ" (2 Cor. 11:13). The Corinthians are dazzled by these interlopers, calling them "super-apostles"; they are leaders who have more charisma and glamor than Paul.[2] Like a parent agonizing because a child has fallen in with a fast crowd, Paul will try almost any argument to see if he can somehow rebuild trust and affection. Some of what he says doesn't even seem to make sense; as he dictates the letter, he jumps from one point to another, interrupting himself with exclamations about his own foolishness. This portion of 2 Corinthians is a helter-skelter, last-ditch effort to bring the Corinthian church back into the fold. He even does the thing he hates most of all and seeks to avoid at all costs — he is driven to defend himself by touting his own credentials as an apostle, even though he recognizes that in doing so he is "speaking as a fool" (11:21).

So what in the world does all this have to do with Trinity Sunday? Well, theoretically, this lesson was chosen for today because of the benediction at the end. When Paul signs off, he does so with a Trinitarian formula that is well known to us all: "The grace of the Lord Jesus Christ and the love of God and the fellowship of the Holy Spirit be with you all" (13:14). This threefold blessing is the reason for the text being read on this day. However, the passage still seems like a poor selection. The blessing seems tacked on almost as an afterthought. There are several other passages from the Epistles that would have been happier choices. How can we find something profitable in this reading when the surrounding context is so full of frustration and pain?

Sometimes it is more rewarding to struggle with problem passages than it is to try to find something new in the best-beloved ones. Over and over preachers have learned that wrestling with the text, like Jacob's wrestling with the angel, brings an unexpected blessing. Let us see where Paul's agonized letter takes us.

We're going to have to go back a few verses. Look at 13:3: "You desire proof that Christ is speaking in me," Paul says. Apparently the Corinthians, with a high degree of spiritual arrogance, are now questioning the credentials of their own founder! If that happened to me, I think I would have washed my hands of the ingrates and transferred my loving attention to some other church where I would be appreciated. But you see, Paul does not do that. He is hanging tough. He *will not* let them go. He is with them to the last ditch. He is willing to forego his own reputation in order to win them back. The super-apostles have apparently referred to Paul as weak. This seems unlikely to us, but we know from other places in the Corinthian correspondence that Paul was not an electrifying personality.[3] He was not one of those professors that gets voted most popular year after year. I remember a situation similar to this in my former parish. We had a layman in the congregation who often taught our large Bible study group. He later went on to become a New Testament scholar of world reputation. His Bible studies were by far more substantive and more artful than anyone else's, but many people in our congregation preferred other teachers who told jokes, were less subtle, and had a more scintillating style. In comparison to the super-apostles, Paul probably did seem lacking in razzle-dazzle. What Paul had, though, in full measure, was apostolic devotion. He was ready to die for his churches. Even more difficult than dying, he was ready to suffer for them. In this way he was truly conformed to Christ, his crucified Lord. Listen to this: "[Christ] is not weak in dealing with you, but is powerful in you. For he was crucified in weakness, but lives by the power of God. For we [true apostles] are weak in him, but in dealing with you we shall live with him by the power of God" (13:3-4).

Now let us return to Paul's benediction at the end of his painful letter. "The grace of the Lord Jesus Christ and the love of God and the fellowship of the Holy Spirit be with you all." At first glance it sounds a bit tired and formulaic to us, because we have heard it so many hundreds of times. However, we need to compare this benediction at the end of 2 Corinthians with those in his other letters. The one that we read today is the longest, richest, and fullest of all his valedictory blessings.[4] Usually he says, "The grace of our Lord Jesus be with you" (1 Cor. 16:23). Even to his best-beloved Philippians he says simply "the grace of our Lord Jesus Christ be with your spirit" (Phil. 4:23). Now, therefore, we are ready to see that Paul was not being perfunctory after all. The church that was breaking his heart is the one that gets the full Trinitarian blessing.[5]

Here we begin to move into the heart of the Trinity. We spoke yesterday about the unique nature of our three-personal God as self-giving love. That is what it means to believe in Father, Son, and Holy Spirit. The inmost being of God is a dynamic interrelatedness that pours itself out for the other without ceasing. It is not dependent on the worthiness of the other, or the response of the other, or the tractability of the other. God's love spends itself to the very last drop of the blood of the Son. As Paul wrote to the Corinthians in one of his previous letters, the love of God "bears all things, believes all things, hopes all things, endures all things" (1 Cor. 13:7).

And so now I ask you to reflect on your own life. Think about those people who have borne with you. Think of that person, or those people, who have loved you and stuck with you in spite of everything. Think of that person, or those people, who did not seem to care about themselves at all as they poured all their resources into you, even if you were ungrateful and unresponsive. Think of how, when you were at your very worst, there was someone who cared about you in spite of it all, someone who would not let you go, someone who was willing to make a fool of himself or herself if only it would help you. For many of us, this was our parents, but not for all of us; some of us will have had parents who failed us. Some of you will think of an aunt, a brother, a grandmother, a teacher, a youth leader, a spouse. That person has conveyed to you a measure of the love of God in three persons. It is only a small measure, for the love of one human being for another is only a hint of the perfect love of God, but it is the most important hint that we have in this fallen world. Human love is a glimmer of the full radiance of God's love. As the Father loves the Son and the Son loves the Father and the Holy Spirit pours forth from that love, so God loves you. This is our God, of whom the Psalmist says,

> Whither shall I go from thy spirit?
>   or whither shall I flee from thy presence?
> If I ascend up into heaven, thou art there:
>   if I make my bed in hell, behold, thou art there also.
> If I take the wings of the morning,
>   and dwell in the uttermost parts of the sea;
> Even there shall thy hand lead me,
>   and thy right hand shall hold me fast. (Psalm 139:7-10)

And so, dear people of God, you have drawn together this morning to offer worship and praise not to a vaguely imagined Something but to the Someone who is eternal and inexhaustible, yet personal, relational, and intimately loving, the God who pursues us even beyond the grave with his Resurrection power. The God whom we adore on Trinity Sunday is the Three-Personed God whose own inner core of being is love, and whose nature it is to give that love to his creatures without restraint, without measure, without calculation, without ceasing. As the Second Person of the Blessed Trinity says himself in today's Gospel, "Lo, I am with you always, even unto the end of the world" (Matt. 28:20). This is no dry scholarly doctrine that we celebrate today. Nor is this a vague, romanticized version of human love. This is the love that upholds the universe, the love that has become incarnate in history through Jesus Christ, the love that persists in breaking through our resistance, the love that is with us even into the last ditch of our messed-up lives. And so I may leave you today with renewed confidence and trust in our God who is truly God, invoking with renewed faith the apostolic blessing, "The grace of the Lord Jesus Christ and the love of God and the fellowship of the Holy Spirit be with you all."

AMEN.

GUILT AND INNOCENCE: JUSTIFICATION BY GRACE THROUGH FAITH

Christ vs. Adam: Kosovo and Beyond

ST. JOHN'S, ESSEX, CONNECTICUT

If, because of one man's trespass, death reigned through that one man, much more will those who receive the abundance of grace and the free gift of righteousness reign in life through the one man Jesus Christ. Then as one man's trespass led to condemnation for all men, so one man's act of righteousness leads to acquittal and life for all men. For as by one man's disobedience many were made sinners, so by one man's obedience many will be made righteous.

(ROM. 5:17-19)

Last Tuesday I was sitting at a picnic table overlooking Middle Cove in Essex. As the snowy egrets made their stately way across the shimmering sheet of water, I went through my file of clippings about Kosovo. A pull-quote from one of the articles caught my eye. "Macedonia's camps are sweltering caldrons of hate," it read. This is a snapshot of human life on our planet; a minority of us are living and working in idyllic circumstances while the vast majority around the world are suffering from every kind of inhumanity and deprivation. "Violence and destruction!" cries the prophet Jeremiah in today's Old Testament lesson, "Violence and destruction!" (20:8). For most of the world's population, life is hell. That is the situation to which Paul addresses himself in the Epistle to the Romans.

Every three years, the church reads Romans for sixteen weeks, from June to September. It's the best of all possible reasons to be in church these summer Sundays, because many people think that Romans is the most important book in the Bible. Certainly it is the one that has most often been the source for revolutionary and transforming ideas. The latest issue of *The New York Review of Books* contains a groundbreaking new essay about the fourth-century bishop Augustine of Hippo, whose reading of Romans remains to this day, on the eve of the third millennium, a fertile field for the Western imagination.[1] Augustine found Paul's writings to be a precise account of the human condition, at all times and in all places.

Paul the apostle, like Jeremiah the prophet before him, looks about him and sees a vast landscape of evil and godlessness. Indeed, Jesus himself warns of apocalyptic horrors in today's Gospel. Attractive surroundings do not mask the seriousness of the situation. The human condition is grave. Let us return to the matter of the Kosovar refugees in Macedonia. I think it is fair to say that most of us have had enormously sympathetic reactions to the plight of the million ethnic Albanians who have been treated with such ferocious inhumanity. Every night we look at televised scenes of heartbroken refugees returning to their destroyed homes where relatives were murdered and we think how awful that would be. With a typical human tendency to sentimentalize, we have viewed the Kosovar refugees as entirely innocent victims and have not cared to think further than that. However, the Bible teaches us something quite different about human nature; Jeremiah says, "The heart is deceitful above all things, and desperately corrupt, who can understand it?" (Jer. 17:9). In other words, human nature is never innocent.

The article about the Macedonian refugee camp tells a shocking tale. It describes a "terrifying and chaotic" event that took place two weeks ago. It seems that a Gypsy family had been in the camp for several weeks, along with the Albanians who were arriving every hour. Gypsies are the most despised minority in the world today, to begin with; in addition, they have been suspected of collaborating with the Serbs. A group of fifteen or twenty Albanian men assaulted two Gypsy men and beat them savagely. The Gypsies were rescued by aid workers and taken to the Catholic Relief building for safety. The mob of Albanians, growing in numbers by the minute, "tore down a chain-link fence, ripped bars from the windows, kicked in the front door and used a metal gutter as a battering ram." The terrified relief workers tried desperately to stop the attack but failed, and the Gypsy men were beaten again, almost to the point of death. The mob, "screaming for blood," had grown to *several thousand* by this time. When they discovered a seven-year-old Gypsy boy whom the aid workers were attempting to protect, they seized him and attempted to tear him limb from limb. Literally. Ed Joseph of the Catholic Relief Service, who days later was still shaken, said that they had attempted to rip the boy's arms off. Literally. Several aid workers including Mr. Joseph were somehow able to snatch the boy from the mob, and by a miracle the Red Sea parted. The arrival of several hundred Macedonian riot police and the American Ambassador finally put a stop to the nightmare, but it had lasted for four hours. As an unnerved Ed Joseph said later, "Any Serb still left [in Kosovo] when the refugees return had better be packing his bags."[2]

What we see illustrated here is that victims can become victimizers in a blink. Thus it has been throughout the millennia. In the refugee camps, there are gatherings in the evening where adults respond enthusiastically as children recite poems they have memorized about Serbian atrocities. Thus one generation after another teaches the children whom to despise. But this is just ancient Balkan hatred, isn't it? We Americans wouldn't do anything like that, would we? Well, I wonder. What would you and I do? Imagine that an armed horde came into this beautiful village of Essex and burned down the houses, made a special point of defacing the churches, rounded up the young men and shot them, and then rampaged through the streets trashing everything in sight just for the fun of it. What if they then gave us and our grandparents and young children ten minutes to get out, taking away all our personal documents, birth certificates, and family photos, then sending us off with no medicine, food, or water through mountains more rugged than the Adirondacks with nothing on the other side except depressed towns inhabited by people several notches down the socioeconomic scale from us? What attitude would you and I have then? And suppose further that we are sitting around idle in refugee camps which have become "sweltering caldrons of hate" where there is nothing useful to do except commiserate about what the enemy has perpetrated upon us. Can any of us be sure that, in such a context, we would step forward, risking our own lives, to save a collaborator from our own countrymen? A lot depends on circumstances, doesn't it? You and I have never been in a situation like that, so how do we know what we would do?

Paul, in Romans, paints one of the most comprehensive pictures of human wickedness that we have in the Bible. No one is excluded, he explicitly says: "All human beings, both Jews and Greeks, are under the power of sin, as it is written [in the Psalms], 'None is righteous, no, not one'" (Rom. 3:9-10). All of us are part of the human mob. This is a phenomenon to which Paul assigns the name of "Adam." Whether you believe that Adam was a real person or not makes no difference; the point is that somehow God's good creation has gone terribly wrong and the entire human race is implicated. Paul wants to make sure we understand this; in our text for this morning, he says it in five different ways. "Many died through one man's [Adam's] trespass . . . the judgment following one trespass [Adam's] brought condemnation . . . because of one man's trespass, death reigned through that one man [Adam]. . . . one man's trespass led to condemnation for all men . . . by one man's disobedience many were made sinners" (5:15-19). So you see that "Adam" is the name Paul gives to a development in human existence whereby we have all been taken captive by a power greater than we are, the power of sin and death. It is this power that motivates us, generation after generation, to hate black people or Serbs or Yankees or Tutsi or Jews or homosexuals or whatever. As one exhausted refugee said, "When will it ever end?"

The Biblical answer to that question is that it can never, ever end unless there is an intervention from beyond this world order altogether. In Psalm 69, the Psalmist understands the desperate predicament he is in; he cries out to God: "Rescue me from sinking in the mire; let me be delivered from my enemies and from the deep waters. Let not the flood sweep over me, or the deep swallow me up, or the pit close its mouth over me" (Ps. 69:14-15). The trespass of Adam, Paul writes, has made captives of us all and the result is condemnation for all human beings. There is no hope of our race improving itself in any definitive way except by the mercy of God. We all hope for good things to happen in the new millennium; some of these things are genuinely possible, like a cure for cancer, but human nature being what it is, it is also possible that our grandchildren will contract smallpox in a bioterrorist attack.[3] Such is our world as Paul describes it for us.[4]

Now, in forty years of teaching the Bible, I have made a discovery about my fellow Americans. There is a much-loved American theology that offers an answer to all these problems. The American answer to every theological and ethical dilemma is "freedom of the will." By making right choices, we believe, we can move out of the dominion of sin. The implication of this is, *I have moved out of the grip of sin; why haven't *you?*

Hmmm. Looking ahead in Romans to chapter 7, we move from the universal to the particular. Speaking no longer of the human race as a whole but of the individual human being, Paul writes, "I do not understand my own actions. For I do not do what I want, but I do the very thing I hate. . . . So then it is no longer I that do it, but sin which dwells within me . . . I can will what is right, but I cannot do it. For I do not do the good I want, but the evil I do not want is what I do. Now if I do what I do not want, it is no longer I that do it, but sin which dwells within me" (Rom. 7:16-20). This is one of the passages that sheds light on Augustine's struggle to control his own unwelcome desires. It describes the conflict within the human heart that should be familiar to us all. Paul continues, "When I want to do right, evil lies close at hand. For I delight in the law of God, in my inmost self, but I see in my members another law at war with the law of my mind and making me captive to the law of sin."[5]

When William Faulkner won the Nobel Prize, he said in his acceptance speech that the central human drama was "the human heart in conflict with itself." Paul's urgent message to us in Romans is that *the law of sin* is much stronger than we are. Even with the best will in the world we still make the same bad choices over and over, even if we have gotten as far as the White House. All of us are captive to sin in some form. More pernicious still is the form of sin that goes unacknowledged. The man who is clearly an alcoholic refuses to face up to it; the couple whose marriage has broken down doesn't admit it even to themselves; the woman who has been involved with one unsuitable man after another refuses to get counseling. Most pathetic of all, we relish every opportunity to cluck our tongues and roll our eyes at *somebody else's* behavior, giving not a thought to our own. We spend our lives trying to deny the existence of the strife that goes on within our own souls.

In last Sunday's *Times* magazine, Mark Edmundson, a scholar who specializes in Gothic themes in popular culture, explains what is still important about the work of Sigmund Freud: "Despite outward appearances and despite our wishes to the contrary, we are not unified beings. . . . Because we both wish and oppose our own desires, our inner lives are in a constant state of civil war." The great danger, Edmundson believes, is that we will not acknowledge "the push and pull of our desires," thereby becoming intolerably self-righteous.[6] This is precisely what Paul is talking about. There is nothing as unbearable as a self-righteous religious person. Such a person will not acknowledge "the war that rages inside." Such a person will seem unattractive and unreal to other people, who will feel themselves put down in some way. Self-righteous religiosity separates the spiritual from the unspiritual in a way that Paul says is the opposite of the gospel.

The Epistle to the Romans is addressed to suffering humankind as a whole. "Adam" is our collective name. We do terrible things to each other, and half the time we do not even realize that we are doing it. The Kosovars who are trying to dismember a child, the President who can't control his impulses, the Foxwoods addict[7] who gambles away his family's livelihood, the grown man who has no patience with his senile father, the enraged mother whom I saw yesterday dragging her screaming tot across the supermarket parking lot by one tiny arm — all of us are born into Adam, and our case is terminal. But now listen to Paul:

> The free gift [of God] is not like the trespass [of Adam]. For if many died through one man's [Adam's] trespass, much more have the grace of God and the free gift in the grace of that one man Jesus Christ abounded for many. . . . If, because of one man's trespass, death reigned through that one man [Adam], much more will those who receive the abundance of grace and the free gift of righteousness reign in life through the one man Jesus Christ.
>
> Thus, as one man's trespass led to condemnation for all men, so one man's act of righteousness leads to acquittal and life for all men. For as by one man's disobedience many were made sinners, so by one man's obedience many will be made righteous. (Rom. 5:15, 17-18)

I hope with all my heart that you hear this announcement today as the electrifying, world-transforming news that it is. God's action in the death and resurrection of our Lord Jesus Christ has reversed the sin of Adam, undone the reign of sin, loosed the grip of death, broken through our prison walls with righteousness and life. "Christ died for the *ungodly*" (Rom. 5:6), the victims *and* the victimizers, the sufferers *and* the perpetrators, the penitent sinners *and* the smugly self-righteous alike. "For as by one man's disobedience many were made sinners, so by one man's obedience many will be made righteous."

Now, just one more story. In November 1983 an all-white jury in Clayton County, Georgia, took forty minutes to convict an African-American man named Calvin Johnson of raping a white woman. The jury ignored the testimony of four black witnesses who supported his alibi, choosing instead to believe the ambivalent testimony of the white victim. Standing before the judge who had just sentenced him to life in prison, Mr. Johnson said, "With God as my witness, I have been falsely accused. . . . I just pray in the name of

Jesus Christ that the truth will eventually be brought out." Sixteen years later, June 15, 1999, holding a small New Testament in his hand, Calvin Johnson stood before another judge who signed an order to set him free. DNA tests had shown conclusively that he could not have committed the crime.[8]

Sixteen years as a lifer in a Georgia prison! The mind reels. What was Mr. Johnson's attitude about those who had done him wrong? His faith in Christ had gotten him through each day of those sixteen years, he said, never allowing him to despair. He said he held no lasting enmity toward the prosecutor, the victim, the jury, or the legal system. He said, "Bitterness will destroy you. Now I just need a job."

One story about Adam, one story about Christ. My dear fellow Christians of St. John's, by virtue of your baptism you do not belong to Adam. You belong to Christ. Hear again the gospel message: "As the trespass of one person led to condemnation for all people, so one person's act of righteousness leads to acquittal and life for all people. For as by one man's disobedience we were made sinners, so by one man's obedience we will be made righteous."

Now we are ready to hear our Lord Jesus say, "Let your light so shine before everyone, that they may see your good works and glorify your Father who is in heaven" (Matt. 5:16).

AMEN.

Death Sentence, Life Sentence

ST. JOHN'S, ESSEX, CONNECTICUT

As one man's trespass led to condemnation for all men, so one man's act of righteousness leads to acquittal and life for all men.

(ROM. 5:18)

Do you not know that all of us who have been baptized into Christ Jesus were baptized into his death? We were buried therefore with him by baptism into death, so that as Christ was raised from the dead by the glory of the Father, we too might walk in newness of life.

(ROM. 6:3-4)

Here is the front page of Thursday's Hartford paper. The banner headline reads "Rizzo Gets Death Penalty." Down at the bottom of the page is the story that would have been the lead story on most any other day, about the biggest fire in Hartford in fifty years. It would be interesting to know what sort of discussion they had at the newspaper about which story to feature at the top that day. Apparently the death penalty sells a lot of papers.

We are reading the Epistle to the Romans this summer, for sixteen weeks, a longer period than any other book of the Bible except the four Gospels, as befits its importance. Last Sunday we heard about Adam and Christ. "Adam" is the name Paul gives to sinful humanity. We are born into Adam whether we like it or not; as Paul puts it in chapter 5: "Because of one man's trespass, death reigned through that one man [Adam]. . . By one man's [Adam's] disobedience many were made sinners. . . . The judgment following [Adam's] trespass brought condemnation" (Rom. 5:16-17, 19). Paul draws a picture of sin and its companion, death, as an enslaving power ruling over everybody without exception. This isn't so easy for us to grasp. We are used to thinking in terms of individuals doing right or doing wrong, not just one big mass of guilty humanity. Paul, however, points people in unusual directions. I have a good friend who is both a Christian theologian and a trained psychoanalyst. A few months ago I was complaining because I had jury duty. She said, laughing, "I never get picked for juries. I tell them I don't believe in guilt and innocence, and that's the end of that."

You may remember from last week that the point Paul is making in his passage about Adam is that none of us is innocent of sin because we were all born in bondage to it. Recently a listener reminded me of a wonderful saying from the old days not so long ago when people really knew the Bible. When a person exhibited bad behavior, someone would say, "That's the old Adam in him." The implication is that all of us have to struggle with the "old Adam."

Projecting innocence onto another person or group, as though they were free of the old Adam, can actually be a very harmful thing to do. The news accounts from the Balkans this week confirm what we were saying last Sunday, that under certain conditions the Kosovar Albanians are capable of acting just as inhumanely as the Serbs. Another news story this week illustrates the slippery nature of innocence from a different perspective. It's an unusually good story, discerning and subtle, about the Tibetans who live in exile in northern India. Apparently the town of Dharmsala is enduring a great influx of tourists who have a romantic notion of Tibetans. These Western visitors come to soak up the supposed spiritual "aura" of Tibetans, the "ancient yoga of the inner light." They are looking for "the direct awakening of the unconditional state beyond the psychological self." Well, it doesn't take much knowledge of the

New Testament to know that there isn't any route through the psychological self to an unconditional state. There isn't anything down in there but just some more of "the old Adam." In case you don't believe me, here's what a leader of the Tibetan exiles has to say:

> [The visitors see us Tibetans as] creatures from another planet . . . [but] deep inside, every one of us is carrying a very heavy load in spite of our smiling faces and dignified appearance. As human beings, it is natural that we feel anger [toward the Chinese] and frustration [about our situation in exile] and even hatred.[1]

In other words, we can only maintain a romantic innocence if we really are "creatures from another planet." Everybody on *this* planet is born into Adam. That Tibetan leader probably doesn't know much about the Epistle to the Romans, but he knows that it can be exhausting to try to live up to the idealistic illusions of others. Paul the apostle understood that very well. That's why he always did his best to direct attention away from himself to the Lord. He writes, "not I, but Christ in me" and "Let him who boasts, boast of the Lord." As soon as we start putting ourselves at the center — *our* faith, *our* spirituality, *our* goodness — we're in trouble. Paul's preaching is radical because he levels the playing field so that no one has a spiritual advantage. You sometimes hear that Paul has taken the simple teachings of Jesus and made them into something outrageous. Well, they're outrageous, all right. We'll just have to live with that. But what about Jesus? Why was he killed? Why did all the religious people turn against him? Well, listen to today's Gospel again: Jesus says, "Do not think that I have come to bring peace on earth; I have not come to bring peace, but a sword" (Matt. 10:34). He says further that families will be divided because of his presence and message. That doesn't sound like the nonthreatening Jesus we all think we know and love, does it? Our Lord knew almost from the beginning of his ministry that he was on a collision course with the religious authorities, and the basic reason for that is that he treated everyone the same, making no distinctions. He did not grant any advantages to the good religious folk. They were in bondage to sin just like the prostitutes and tax collectors who came flocking to Jesus, but they were actually in greater danger because, unlike those "sinners," they did not recognize their own situation.

Let's go back to Tibet for a minute. I have had a passion for Tibet all my life, and I have a whole bunch of books about it. I have seen both of the Dalai Lama movies and I admire him. But he keeps saying these baffling things. Yesterday I was flipping through a magazine at a friend's house because I saw a headline about Tibet. It told a story about two Scottish trekkers in Nepal who saved the lives of some Tibetan monks and nuns who were fleeing the Chinese. The Dalai Lama praised the rescuers, saying that their heroic actions had proved what he always believed, that human nature was basically kind and gentle.[2] This seems a strange thing to say after what the Chinese have done to his country. The other Tibetan leader, the one who spoke about anger and hatred, was closer to the truth. Well, there have always been these two contrasting ways of understanding human nature. Either we are basically good and sin is just an aberration, or we are all sinners and goodness is a miraculous gift of God. If human nature is basically kind and gentle, then we don't need a Savior, we can just "be religious" and we'll do fine.

Most people, I think, take this "kinder and gentler" position.[3] But we need to understand that it's not Biblical. Perhaps you will remember the verse from last week's reading of Romans 5: "As one man's trespass led to condemnation for all men, so one man's act of righteousness leads to acquittal and life for all men" (v. 18). Two men, Adam and Christ. Two lines of development, one leading to condemnation and death, one leading to acquittal and life. The "old Adam" in us is so strong that only a far greater power can undo his effects; we cannot do it ourselves by "free will" or any other way. The important thing that Paul wants us to see, which he explains in three powerful chapters at the beginning of his letter, is this. "All human beings, both Jews and Greeks, are under the power of sin, as it is written: 'None is righteous, no, not one'" (3:9-10) and "There is no distinction; since all have sinned and fall short of the glory of God" (3:22-23).

When we have really grasped this assessment of our human condition, then we will hear Paul's words today with new ears:

> Do you not know that all of us who have been baptized into Christ Jesus were baptized into his death? We were buried therefore with him by baptism into death, so that as Christ was raised from the dead by the glory of the Father, we too might walk in newness of life. (Rom. 6:3-4)

As we say in the Eucharist, he has brought us "out of death into life." The old Adam has died and been buried with Christ. Jesus is the representative human being who has in every respect assimilated our sinfulness to his righteousness, thereby putting the old Adam to death and in its place bringing to life a new human being, a "new creation" (2 Cor. 5:17). This movement from death into life is the foundation for Christian ethics. In today's reading, for example, we see it clearly: "The death he died he died to sin, once for all, but the life he lives he lives to God. So you also must consider yourselves dead to sin and alive to God in Christ Jesus" (Rom. 6:10-11).

In March, an editorial in *Time* magazine stated that the strongest argument against the death penalty was that you might execute the wrong person.[4] In last week's sermon, we heard about a man who was on death row for sixteen years before it was discovered through his DNA that he didn't do what he was convicted of doing. Indeed, England revoked the death penalty in 1965 largely because of just such a case.[5] But that isn't the strongest reason, not for a Christian. This man Rizzo is guilty as hell. There is no doubt about it. He killed a man just to see what it felt like, and he has shown no remorse whatever. We have to have a better reason.

In last week's reading from Romans 5 we heard these words: "As one man's trespass led to condemnation for all men, so one man's act of righteousness leads to acquittal and life for all men" (5:18). Before God, we all deserve a death sentence. In Christ, we have all received a life sentence. Yes, a life sentence; "We were buried therefore with him by baptism into death, so that as Christ was raised from the dead by the glory of the Father, we too might walk in newness of life" (6:4).

When good things happen, that is not a sign that *human nature* is good. It is a sign that *God* is good and that he uses us to be his agents in the world. When we do good things, that points beyond ourselves to Christ. It is not *our* righteousness, it is *his* righteousness. There isn't anything in the Bible about spiritual "auras." What there is in the Bible is the glory of God in Jesus Christ.

Now I am going to say something about dentists. If there are any dentists in the congregation this morning, please don't take this personally. It could just as well be lawyers, or doctors, or clergy. It just happens that a front-page feature in *The New York Times* yesterday was about dentists. It seems that one of the greatest discrepancies between the affluent and the poor in America is children's dental care; tooth decay is the most prevalent childhood disease in America. Medicaid pays for some dental work, but most dentists will not treat patients on Medicaid. The article quoted a dentist who said that one patient like that would empty his waiting room. "They're not compliant," he said. "They have terrible hygiene. Why don't they take baths?"[6] Is that Adam speaking, or is that Christ? What does this say about human nature? Before you answer, think about what you or I would do. Are you and I innocent of such thoughts? If *we* were dentists, would *we* take poor patients? Are you sure?

A well-known "thrill killing" was recently in the news. Two pizza delivery men were asked to deliver pizzas to a remote house where they were ambushed and killed. There is no doubt about the guilt of the defendants, who planned the whole thing in cold blood. When one of them (Thomas Koskovich) was tried in New Jersey, the mother of one of the victims was called to testify about the anguish of the family. She did so, in moving detail. Then she was asked by the defense lawyer if she wanted the jury to return a death sentence. This is what she said:

> My whole family, my husband and my daughters, coming from a
> family of Christian faith, would most like to see Thomas

Koskovich take the evil that he's done, turn his life over to Christ, and become a strong witness to all those kids that are out there that might think that this is like the greatest thing to do to get attention, or whatever their motives are. . . . You have one death already, and multiplying it by two doesn't solve anything.

She concluded by asking the jury to consider "how they feel they have to answer to their God."[7]

Is that Adam speaking, or is that Christ?

Ethical decisions are not always easy. A lot depends on the thinking that goes into them. Sometimes making such decisions can mean "taking up a cross," as Jesus says in today's Gospel (Matthew 10:38). Taking up the Cross means dying to the old Adam, pointing beyond ourselves to Christ. But whoever you are and whatever condition you are in, whatever you are able to do for our Lord, be assured that there is good news today. You are not in Adam. You are in Christ. You have not received a death sentence. You have received a sentence to eternal life. "For if we have been united with him in a death like his, we shall certainly be united with him in a resurrection like his" (Rom. 6:5). "For as in Adam all die, even so in Christ shall all be made alive" (1 Cor. 15:22).

AMEN.

Flying First Class

CHRIST CHURCH, GREENVILLE, SOUTH CAROLINA, PARISH WEEKEND

(This sermon was written for a congregation that included children and youth.)

And the veil of the temple was torn in two, from top to bottom.

(MARK 15:38)

Therefore, brethren, since we have confidence to enter the sanctuary by the blood of Jesus, by the new and living way which he opened for us through the curtain . . . let us consider how to stir up one another to love and good works, not neglecting to meet together . . . but encouraging one another . . . all the more. . . .

(HEB. 10:19-20, 25)

Ever since the world began, human beings have divided each other up into categories. This is the technique we use for feeling better about ourselves than we deserve. Whatever group we belong to, that is the best one. We're not satisfied with being the best, though; we have to make others into the worst. We begin making these kinds of distinctions very early in life. Young people have all sorts of bad names for each other. Some of them are so bad that I can't say them from the pulpit. What are some names that we can say in church? I asked my young niece last week to give me an example and she said "dork." When we call another person a "dork," it sets them apart in another, less desirable category from us. When we use names, we are trying to push that other person away. We are saying that other person is really not good enough to associate with us. People said that to Jesus all the time; they complained that he was sitting at the table with all the wrong people. The good religious people thought that Jesus ought to give his preference to them. Jesus was in trouble almost every day of his life because he seemed to like the company of poor, troubled people as much as or better than the company of successful, prominent people.

Believe me, grown-ups do this just as much as kids, though sometimes we try to be more subtle about it. We speak about someone "making the cut," or not "making the cut," as the case may be. Without realizing what we are doing, we judge some people fit to associate with us and some not. Often the criteria that we use to make such determinations are entirely unrelated to the substance of the person. Some are "in" and some are "out" based on street address, blood lines, type of job, labels in clothes, club memberships, size of stock portfolio and other essentially superficial categories.

God, however, *is no respecter of persons.* I did not make that up. Those exact words are in the Bible. We find them in the King James Version of the book of Acts (10:34). In the Revised Standard Version it reads, "God shows no partiality." God is not partial to one person over another. That really is very hard for us to accept. We are fair-minded people, or try to be; we go around saying that we believe all people are created equal, and so forth, but way down deep we like to be preferred, or we like for our group to be preferred. For instance, we like for the Americans to win at the Olympics. Many people don't watch the Olympic events that have no Americans in them. We think that America is the best country. You know that the U.S. government was thinking about sending some bombers over to Iraq. What do the politicians talk about when they are trying to decide whether to go to war or not? They talk about how many American lives might be lost. They don't talk much about Iraqi lives, just American lives. You would think that Americans were more important than other people.

When one country declares war on another, one of the first things that happens is that they start making distinctions. They start calling each other bad names. In World War II almost all Americans referred to the Japanese as "Japs." Now it is considered very rude to call a Japanese person a "Jap," and most people don't do it. We change the names according to the enemy of the moment. In the Vietnam war, American soldiers often called Vietnamese people "geeks" or "slopes." When you are calling another person a name, it is easier to think he isn't really a person at all, so it's all right to kill him. God doesn't like that at all, because *God is no respecter of persons.* With God, there is no distinction between Vietnamese and Americans, Iraqis and Americans, Japanese and Americans. When God's son Jesus was on earth, he treated heathen Gentiles and ostracized Samaritans as though they were just as good as his own Jewish people. That was a religious scandal, and it brought him to the Cross.

One of the great problems of the Christian life is that, even though we know it is wrong to make these kinds of distinctions, we go on doing it anyway. We bow and scrape to the altar of inclusiveness and brotherly or sisterly love, and then we go right back to our restricted clubs and our exclusive neighborhoods and our white congregations. I don't know what the answer is to this problem. I confess to you that I love first-class treatment myself. I love to be taken to good restaurants and I love good seats at the opera. There have been two or three occasions when my husband has gotten me a Frequent Flyer upgrade to first class, and I loved every minute. I was thrilled to settle back in that big wide seat and be served a drink while in back of me I knew that the lower orders of mankind were fighting for spaces in the overhead bins and hitting each other over the head with their luggage. And of course, as you know, there is that curtain. The curtain divides the first class from all the other classes. And the seductive thing about it all is, if you sit on the first-class side of that curtain long enough, *you start thinking that you are entitled to it.*

Now I would like to describe to you something that happened when Jesus was crucified. This is what Mark's Gospel says: "Jesus uttered a loud cry, and breathed his last. And the curtain of the temple was torn in two, from top to bottom" (15:37-38).

In order to understand the significance of this, we need to

know something about the Jerusalem temple. It was constructed somewhat like those Russian dolls with a little doll inside a medium-size doll inside a big doll, only the Temple was shaped like a series of boxes within boxes; it was a series of courts within courts. The largest one was called the Court of the Gentiles. Anyone at all could come through the gate and mill around in the Court of the Gentiles. If you were not a Jew, though, you couldn't go any further. Only Jews could enter the Women's Court. Any Jew, male or female, could go into that. The hitch was that Jewish women couldn't go any farther; they had to stay there. The Men's Court was inside the Women's Court; that was available to all Jewish men. Beyond that, things got a lot more exclusive. Only priests could go inside the Priest's Court. Inside of that was the most sacred of all the areas, the inmost sanctuary, the Holy of Holies. Inside *that* was the mercy seat where forgiveness and restoration was to be had. No one at all could go into that except the High Priest, and he couldn't go in but once a year, on the Day of Atonement (Yom Kippur). And guess what closed off the Holy of Holies from the rest of the Temple? As you can guess, it was a curtain, called the veil of the temple.

So you see, there was a hierarchy of religious access. If you wanted to get close to God, if you wanted to be "in," if you wanted to be one of the chosen, if you wanted to be first class, you had to be the High Priest, or at least a priest. Certainly not a woman or a pagan. The whole setup was based on distinctions that separated groups from one another and restricted access to the mercy seat. But something happened. *The veil of the temple was torn in two from top to bottom.* In the moment that Jesus died on the Cross, distinctions came to an end. There was no longer any separation between the godly and the ungodly. There was no longer any curtain separating first class from second class. All the fun of looking down on others was gone. "There is no distinction," writes Paul to the Romans. "While we were still helpless, Christ died for the *ungodly*" (Rom. 3:22; 5:6). That's the heart of the gospel, right there. It's the most radical utterance ever uttered, because it does away with religious attainment altogether. "While we were still helpless" — that verse countermands the beloved American scripture, "God helps those who help themselves." The gospel is quite different: "While we were still helpless, Christ died for the ungodly." This is so revolutionary that it is hard to describe. Everything we believe about religion and God would have led us to believe that Christ would die for the righteous, the godly, the "spiritual." No, says the Lord himself, "I did not come to call the righteous, but sinners" (Mark 2:17). He died for those on the wrong side of the curtain, the wrong end of the temple, the wrong side of the tracks. This is why Paul wrote, "There is neither Jew nor Greek, there is neither slave not free, there is neither male nor female; [there is neither first class nor second class;] all are one in Christ Jesus" (Gal. 3:28).

There is a sense in which this might be heard as bad news for us. What fun is it to sit at the best table in the fancy restaurant if all the tables are alike? What thrill would you get from being ushered into the dance club if there wasn't that rope separating you from the rejected unfashionables? What fun is it to smoke a twenty-five dollar cigar if all the peons are smoking them too? Half the pleasure of smoking a premium cigar is knowing that you, unlike the peons, can afford it. What pleasure is there in traveling first class if there isn't going to be a curtain separating us from the luckless riffraff in the back? Where is the good news?

Here's the gospel. Here's the reason it's good news, not bad. If God were going to have a class system based on human merit, you and I might not make it. We might not. A Mexican strawberry-picker might make it and we might not. The black washerwoman down the road might make it and we might not. I read an interview with Donald Trump in which he made an uncharacteristically revealing comment. He said, "I'm not the happiest person in the world." Well, who could be the happiest person in the world if he is always looking over his shoulder to make sure nobody else is catching up? Who could be the happiest person if life consists of collecting things that other people can't afford? Who could be the happiest person if she always needs to be alert to keep undesirable people at a safe distance?

I said earlier that I really didn't know what the answer was to the problem we have with all this. But yes, I do know. I do know what the answer is. The answer is to keep telling the Jesus story. The answer is to keep in training by (as the Epistle to the Hebrews says in today's lesson) "not neglecting to meet together" (Heb. 10:25). The answer is to keep in touch with the Christian community where the story is kept alive even though the community itself is full of hypocrites and sinners like you and me. We keep on telling the story. *The veil of the temple was torn in two from top to bottom.* The way to the mercy seat of the Lord is open for all human beings. "Christ died for the ungodly" — that's you and me.

And God's promise is that, if we keep telling each other the story, we will quit sitting in judgment. Maybe we'll be satisfied with twenty-dollar bottles of wine instead of hundred-dollar bottles. Maybe we won't give away every cent of our money the way St. Francis did, but maybe we will give away more of it than we used to. And maybe we will start being happy, not because we have things that other people don't have, not because we have managed to lock ourselves up behind security gates, not because we have achieved a partnership or a colossal bonus, but because we aren't going to be envious of others anymore, because we aren't going to be selfish anymore, because we aren't going to be undercutting one another anymore. We aren't going to be envious or selfish or undercutting anymore because as we see other people sharing in the riches of Jesus Christ we are going to be thrilled for them. We are going to forget all about getting ahead of other people. It's just not going to be important to us anymore. We are going to forget about it because the most real thing in our lives is going to be the story of the Lord — the Lord who sacrificed his life for each and every one of us ungodly souls in order that the curtain might be torn down forever.

AMEN.

Access to Power

TRINITY CATHEDRAL, COLUMBIA, SOUTH CAROLINA

Nathan said to David, Thou art the man.

(2 SAM. 12:7)

A few days ago I read an article in the newspaper saying that the preachers in the American churches have been strangely silent about the troubles in the White House. All across the country, in conservative churches and liberal churches, sermons have conspicuously avoided the subject of President Clinton's difficulties. The reporter wondered why that was.

If this is true, I think I know at least one reason: it's just too embarrassing. We wish this had not happened. We wish it had never come to light. We really don't want to talk about it in church. Jay Leno plays the role of national exorcist every night, permitting us to let off some of our tension in explosions of somewhat nervous laughter. I for one find it much easier to laugh about it all than to address it seriously. But on the other hand I find the challenge of the news article too great to pass up. I would hate for the journalists to be the only moralists in the country.

You will probably be relieved to hear that this is not going to be a sermon about the President — not directly, anyway. I'm taking off from another newspaper column sent me by my sister. It was written by the syndicated columnist Cal Thomas, who seems to know something about Christianity and about the Bible. He writes about the appearance of Billy Graham on the "Today" show. Mr. Graham said that he forgives the President because he knows the frailty of human nature.[1]

I recall an article a few years back about Pope John Paul II. He was paying one of his visits to a Latin American country. A complaint was brought to him about a priest in one of the rural villages. It was well known that the priest had a mistress and several children. Everyone expected the pope to express shock and indignation. Instead, he said quietly, "Human frailty," and moved the conversation along to other, larger topics such as poverty and oppression.[2]

Anyone who has any knowledge of the Bible at all will be aware that it is populated from beginning to end by bad characters who are pressed into God's service to do great things. The mighty theme of the Scriptures is God's continual overriding of our failures to accomplish his purpose for good. Bad characters are the only kind of characters God has to work with; there are X marks over against everybody in one column or another. Human frailty cannot prevent God from recapturing the world that he loves. "For I know the plans I have for you," says the Lord to his disobedient people, "Plans for welfare and not for evil, to give you a future and a hope" (Jer. 29:11).

So, fellow bad characters, there is absolutely nothing that you can do that is so terrible that God cannot overcome it. His purpose toward you is gracious. His purpose toward you is merciful. His purpose toward you is unconditionally loving. That is the foundation on which we stand. The Eucharistic prayer of Thomas Cranmer has comforted me all my life as we express our confidence that God is "not weighing our merits, but pardoning our offences."

Nobody understands this better than Billy Graham, and I get the impression from Cal Thomas's column that Mr. Thomas understands it too. However, he brings several important questions to our most famous, most justly admired preacher. What exactly, he asks, is Mr. Graham forgiving the president for, since the president has not confessed to anything?[3] And how can Mr. Graham be the forgiver since he is not the one sinned against? And how can he forgive someone who has not repented? It is confusing when Billy Graham says on national television, "*I* forgive the President," because we can't tell from what he says that the forgiveness comes, not from the world-famous evangelist, but from the only person that can forgive sins committed against others — the Son of God himself.

Cal Thomas quotes more from the Bible in this one column than many Episcopalians do in a year. One of his references is to the prophet Nathan. We have just heard the reading from the Old Testament book of 2 Samuel. King David has committed adultery with Bathsheba, a married woman. She sends a message to the king that she is pregnant. David, like various presidents of the United States, contrives to cover up his sin. He summons her husband, Uriah, home from the battlefield so that it will seem as though he is the baby's father. Imagine David's frustration when Uriah, who seems to be a man of utmost integrity, says to the king, "The other commanders are camping out in the field with the foot soldiers, undergoing all sorts of privation and discomfort; how can you expect me to go home and take a shower and eat a nice dinner and sleep with my wife in my own bed? I will not do it" (11:11). David tries another tactic; he sits Uriah down and pours him cocktails until Uriah is loopy. Still Uriah will not go home to his wife, because as a consecrated soldier he is supposed to be celibate during the time of his military service. David is completely thwarted by this nobility of Uriah and, in fear and desperation, he dispatches him to the front lines where he is predictably killed. David promptly arranges to marry Bathsheba and thereby to legitimate his illicit paternity. It is clear from the narrative that David, up to this point, thinks he has gotten away with the whole sordid mess. He even says to a subordinate who is troubled by Uriah's death, "Don't worry about it; these things happen" (v. 25). There the story would seem to end. However, the narrator adds, ominously, "This thing that David had done displeased the Lord" (v. 27).

Close by there lived a prophet of the Lord named Nathan. He went to pay a call on David, and he told David a story:

There were two men in a certain city, the one rich and the other poor. The rich man had very many flocks and herds; but the poor man had nothing but one little ewe lamb, which he had bought. And he brought it up, and it grew up with him and with his children; it used to eat of his morsel, and drink from his cup, and lie in his bosom, and it was like a daughter to him. Now there came a traveler to the rich man, and he was unwilling to take one of his own flock or herd to prepare for the wayfarer who had come to him, but he took the poor man's lamb, and prepared it for the man who had come to him. (2 Sam. 12:1-4)

When David heard this story, we are told,

David's anger was greatly kindled against the man; and he said to Nathan, "As the Lord lives, the man who has done this deserves to die; and he shall restore the lamb fourfold, because he did this thing, and because he had no pity."

And Nathan said to David, "You are the man." (vv. 5-7)

In his newspaper column Cal Thomas asks, "For what exactly is Billy Graham forgiving the President? Is it blanket forgiveness . . . or is it limited immunity? At what point would Graham point his finger and . . . say, 'Thou art the man'?"

Another king, another prophet, several centuries later: "King Ahab looked up and saw the prophet Elijah approaching, and he said, 'Is it you, O troubler of Israel?' And Elijah said, 'I have not troubled Israel, but you have . . . because you have forsaken the commandments of the Lord and followed the Ba'als'" (1 Kings 18:17-18). Ahab's archetypally wicked wife Jezebel sends a message to Elijah that he is going to sleep with the fishes, so Elijah flees for his life. While he is in hiding, Jezebel and Ahab put out a contract on a man named Naboth so as to steal his family estate. "Then the word of the Lord came to Elijah the Tishbite, saying, 'Arise, go down to meet Ahab, King of Israel'" (1 Kings 21:17-18). And what is Elijah supposed to say? "I forgive you"? "I understand your human frailty"? "Those family estates are so tempting?" Even Ahab knows better than that. When Ahab sees Elijah approaching him, he says, "Have you found me, O my enemy?" "I have found you," replies Elijah, "because you have sold yourself to do what is evil in the sight of the Lord."

Cal Thomas writes in his column that "access" is what preachers want nowadays. Once a preacher gains access to the White House, as Billy Graham and Jesse Jackson have, it becomes intoxicating; preachers withhold the word of accountability in order to preserve access. Former presiding bishop Edmond Browning had a lot of problems during his tenure with the Episcopal Church, but there are two photographs of him that illustrate what we are talking about this morning. The first image shows Bishop Browning in the Oval Office schmoozing with President Bush. The second picture, taken on the eve of the Gulf War, shows him outside the White House at night, holding a candle. The candlelight vigil was sponsored by various groups who had questions about the wisdom of that war. On that very same night, at that very same moment, Billy Graham was spending the night in the White House.

I am not taking a political position today, although there are times when preachers must take such positions. I happen to be a great admirer of Billy Graham at every point except this one: As his own autobiography reveals, his great weakness is his love of access to Presidents. What is at stake in this sermon today is not any particular political position, but the whole matter of the relationship of God's judgment to God's mercy. The Bible shows us in a thousand different ways that God's judgment is an *instrument of* his mercy. Judgment does not mean everlasting condemnation, as we are conditioned to think; it means a course correction in the direction of salvation. Wise parents have always known this. Rebuking a child, correcting a child in the context of unconditional love is an action taken for the child's health. Permitting a child anything and everything is harmful to that child's development.

The book of Jeremiah gives us an intimate look at the tribulations of a prophet who spent his whole life calling the rulers and the people to account for their sinful ways. As you can imagine, Jeremiah's life under these circumstances was just plain miserable. Far from having "access," he spent much of his life ostracized and ignored. He fought night and day against the false prophets who always smoothed everything over. Because Jeremiah was faithful to his calling, he has bequeathed to us a great deal of powerful Biblical prophecy about the human being before God. The Lord accuses his people: "In spite of all [you have done], you say, 'I am innocent!' . . . Behold, I will bring you to judgment for saying 'I have not sinned.' How lightly you gad about! . . . You shall be put to shame" (2:34-36). Jeremiah continues, "Were they ashamed when they committed abomination? No, they were not at all ashamed; they did not know how to blush. Therefore . . . they shall be overthrown, says the Lord" (8:12).

David is the great example here. What did he do after Nathan pointed to him and said "Thou art the man?" Did he order Nathan thrown into prison? Did he send him to Siberia? Did he say "No more overnights in the Lincoln Bedroom for you"? Quite the opposite. Listen to what the Bible says. "When Nathan finished speaking, David said to Nathan, 'I have sinned against the Lord.' . . . and Nathan returned home to his own house; and David continued to honor the prophet Nathan" (2 Sam. 12:13, 15).

"Never explain," goes the saying attributed to the Duke of Wellington, "Never apologize." The famous first line of the novel *Love Story* goes, "Love means never having to say you're sorry." Never was there worse advice. Confession of wrongdoing lies at the very heart of Biblical faith. The man who can acknowledge his sin and repent is a man after the Lord's own heart. There is nothing the Lord loves more than a repentant sinner. A thousand years after King David, we see Jesus of Nazareth, in his parables and actions, definitively demonstrating God's special welcome for the penitent.

So this is not really a sermon about the President after all. This is a sermon about you and me. It is easy to point the finger at someone else. What really counts in the Christian life is the capacity for looking into one's own heart and discerning the sin that lies embedded there. What really matters for Biblical faith is the willingness to think to oneself, maybe *I* am the man. What really makes the difference in human relationships — especially in marriage — is a readiness to admit fault and ask forgiveness. It is not a weakness to acknowledge that one has been wrong; it is a sign of strength. From beginning to end, the Bible shows us that a free admission of guilt is the royal road to redemption and new life. True access to power does not consist in buttering up the big shots of this world. True access to power is found in coming before the throne of God without defenses, without pretensions, without posturing, in the secure knowledge that the Father kept all his promises to his deeply sinful servant, so that when the time of fulfillment had come, the Lord Jesus Christ himself was called the Son of David.

AMEN.

July 17, 1999

Hope *among the* Weeds

DUKE UNIVERSITY CHAPEL

We know that the whole creation has been groaning in travail together until now; and not only the creation, but we ourselves, who have the first fruits of the Spirit, groan inwardly as we wait for adoption as sons, the redemption of our bodies. For in this hope we were saved.

(ROM. 8:22-24)

Another parable he put before them, saying, "The kingdom of heaven may be compared to a man who sowed good seed in his field; but while men were sleeping, his enemy came and sowed weeds among the wheat, and went away. So when the plants came up and bore grain, then the weeds appeared also. And the servants of the householder came and said to him, 'Sir, did you not sow good seed in your field? How then has it weeds?' He said to them, 'An enemy has done this.' The servants said to him, 'Then do you want us to go and gather them?' But he said, 'No; lest in gathering the weeds you root up the wheat along with them. Let both grow together until the harvest; and at harvest time I will tell the reapers, Gather the weeds first and bind them in bundles to be burned, but gather the wheat into my barn.'"

(MATT. 13:24-30)

[63]

Last week, our granddaughter Dabney, nine years old, came to visit us in New York. My husband and I took her to a number of events, including a concert of spirituals and gospel songs by a wonderful African-American choir called the Great Day Singers. The director introduced each number with a little explanation, which inevitably included a good many references to the suffering of slavery. About halfway through the program Dabney turned to me and whispered, "Are white people bad?"

As soon as there was an opportunity, I attempted to explain to her that, as Christians, we do not divide the world up into good people and bad people, for we are all sinners. I suggested that it was better to think of good thoughts and actions versus bad thoughts and actions, and that most human beings were a mixture. We agreed that keeping another person as a slave was a very bad thing to do, but that slave owners might have done some good things in other areas of their lives. I probably should have let it go at that, but you know how grown-ups are, always trying to make things more complicated. I went on to say that there were a very few people who seemed to be truly evil for reasons that no one understood. Dabney nodded knowingly and said, "Like criminals." I realized I was in over my head, but tried to explain further that even a criminal might do some good things, that even they could be redeemed.

All of us have this tendency to assign moral categories to our fellow human beings. Like Santa Claus, we are forever making lists of who's naughty and who's nice. It would be funny if it weren't so pernicious. I recently spoke with a friend, someone I like very much, who had been elected as a vestry member in his church.[1] I congratulated him, and then commented that church elections could be problematic because people who weren't chosen felt rejected. "Well," he said crisply, "it's a good thing Mary Smith wasn't elected. Everybody runs away from her. Maybe losing will teach her something." The harshness of this judgment startled me, coming as it did from a very nice person.

When Jesus told the parable of the wheat and the tares, or weeds, I don't think he had vestry elections in mind. Like all of Jesus' stories, however, the meaning evolves in each generation, according to the context in which it is read. Let's take a look at it. He begins, "The kingdom of God is like . . ." So many of Jesus' stories begin that way. He doesn't describe the Kingdom of God directly. He gives homely illustrations from real life. We should remember that Jesus' original audience had had the concept of the Kingdom of God drilled into them from infancy. They would have understood that Jesus was speaking of the coming time, promised by all the Hebrew prophets, when God would take hold of his creation in a definitive and final way, reclaiming it and reshaping it permanently for his own. On that Great Day of the Lord, everything that thwarts human fulfillment would be banished forever, and only the goodness of God's purposes would prevail. "Thy Kingdom come": this is precisely what Paul is talking about in this morning's reading from Romans: "I consider that the sufferings of this present time are not worth comparing with the glory that is to be revealed to us. For the creation waits with eager longing for the revealing of the sons of God . . . because the creation itself will be set free from its bondage to decay and obtain the glorious liberty of the children of God" (Rom. 8:18-21). The two New Testament lessons are therefore closely connected in their focus on the future triumph of God's plan.

"The kingdom of heaven," Jesus begins, "may be compared to a man who sowed good seed in his field" (Matt. 13:24).[2] A few weeks later, the men who have been hired to tend the crop come to the owner with a report, a question, and a request. They report that there are poisonous weeds, called *darnel,* growing along with the wheat.[3] They inquire, "How did this bad stuff get mixed in with your good seed?" The owner says, with striking directness, "An enemy has done this," meaning Satan. The workers then ask for permission to pull up the darnel. "No," says the owner, "by now the roots of the weeds have gotten into the roots of the wheat. If you pull up the darnel, you may pull up the wheat too. Let the wheat and the weeds both grow together. When the harvest comes, I will give the order to gather the weeds and burn them, while the wheat is gathered into my barn."

Earlier generations of American Christians were very familiar with this image of the harvest as the final ingathering of God's children. They loved hymns like "Bringing in the sheaves," and, at Thanksgiving, "Come, ye thankful people come, raise the song of harvest home." Everyone understood that that didn't just mean food in the pantry; it meant that *we ourselves* were to be the fruitful ears of corn and wheat. This is what Jesus has in mind with his image. There is an extra edge in the parable, though, that isn't so folksy. Our Lord is thinking of the decidedly non-pastoral figure of John the Baptist. Earlier in the Gospel of Matthew, John declares, "He who is coming after me is mightier than I, whose sandals I am not worthy to carry. . . . His winnowing fork is in his hand, and he will clear his threshing floor and gather his wheat into the granary, but the chaff he will burn with unquenchable fire" (3:11-12). Matthew places this early in his Gospel to indicate that Jesus himself is the Lord of the final harvest, the one who will be the Judge of good and evil in the Last Day. When you realize that some of Jesus' original audience would have actually heard John's preaching, you get a better idea of the drama in Jesus' repeated claim that "The Kingdom of God is at hand," meaning that *he himself* is bringing it.[4]

By the time Matthew wrote all this down, some time had gone by. The early Christians were trying to figure out how to coexist with a world that was hostile to the gospel of the Son of God. It was becoming increasingly obvious that the new faith was going to be persecuted in very serious ways. This led to a lot of questions. If Jesus was truly the Son of God, why had not the Kingdom arrived in its plenitude? Why were there so many "bad people" around? What sort of attitude were Christians supposed to have toward evil in their midst? Why did God allow Satan to rampage around sowing weeds?

This leads us again from the parable to Paul. One of the trickiest problems in all Biblical interpretation is the relation between the teaching of Jesus and that of Paul. Many Christians are confused about this. Paul is often thought of as the spoiler who took the simple lessons of Jesus and made them intellectual, abstract, harsh, and — God forbid — theological. It comes as a shock to many to realize that there is far more teaching about judgment, condemnation, hellfire, and good versus bad people in the words of Jesus than in the letters of Paul. If all we had of Jesus were the parables dealing with judgment, we would all be turning gratefully to Paul. Indeed, if it were not for Paul, we might not have known how to place the emphasis in many of Jesus' stories. In today's parable of the wheat and the tares, for example, it certainly sounds as though the point is that there are good people and bad people and the bad ones are going to be firewood in the end. It is Paul, obliquely if not directly, who keeps reminding us that Jesus habitually kept company with tax collectors and prostitutes, and that he "came not to call the righteous, but sinners" (Matt. 9:13) — because it is Paul who explains, in chapters 2 and 3 of Romans, that "there is none righteous, no, not one . . . all human beings, both Jews and Gentiles, are under the power of sin" (3:9-10).

This is not an abstraction. The way we interpret these things will shape our attitudes and actions in very deep ways. Like my granddaughter, every one of us grows up dividing the world into good people and bad people. It's inevitable, really, human nature being what it is. All of us are bookkeepers by nature: credits here, debits there.[5] Christians seeking maturity have to spend our adult lives unlearning what we took for granted as children. Thomas Cranmer, author of the Book of Common Prayer, put it memorably; we come before God knowing that he is "not weighing our merits, but pardoning our offenses."

In Shakespeare's play *All's Well That Ends Well,* two young French lords are speaking together about the ambiguities of the other characters' actions.[6] One says to the other, "The web of our life is of a mingled yarn, good and ill together" (act IV, scene iii, line 83). Thus in the parable of Jesus, the landowner says, "Let both weeds and wheat grow together until the harvest."

Recently, a person very important to me died of multiple illnesses at the age of seventy-five. Some of you will recognize his name: J. Christiaan Beker. He was one of the premier New Testament theologians of our day. His book *Paul the Apostle* will be a classic for decades to come. His story is remarkable. He was a teenager in Holland when the Nazis came. Young, sensitive, and vulnerable, he was taken away from his family and sent on a train to a work camp near Berlin where he contracted typhus. Lying near death in an infirmary, another young patient dying beside him, the whole city of Berlin shuddering and in flames from the American bombardment, young Chris felt that he was viewing the apocalypse and committed himself to God. Thus was born a theologian in the midst of evil and death.

Professor Beker was one of my important teachers, but more still, he was for many a living illustration of "the creation groaning in travail." Never were weeds and wheat more entangled in one human life. He deeply offended me and many others on numerous occasions. Yet he was one of the most gifted and inspiring Biblical interpreters I have ever known. It was the "mingled yarn" that made him so unforgettable. He was a road map of suffering, what with manic-depressive illness, wildly impulsive behavior, and uncontrolled urges. He cut himself off from most people near the end, and the circumstances leading to his illness and death suggested failure. It was given to him to fight what seemed like a losing battle against overwhelming forces. Many of us took comfort, however, in the evidence that God was powerfully at work in him. His whole life was an apocalyptic battlefield, so scarred and damaged that the hidden presence of God there seemed all the more miraculous. His theme in spite of everything was the ultimate victory of God over every form of evil. The motif of his work was hope — hope in impossible circumstances, hope when human resources have come to an end, hope which embraces the suffering of all creation as a sign of God's coming triumph. In the spirit of the parable of Jesus, Chris Beker urged solidarity with all who are in bondage until the day of harvest, not making any premature claims for who is going to heaven and who is not, but waiting, as he wrote, "until such time [as] the power of death and its attendant sufferings, in accordance with the Biblical perspective of hope, will be lifted from all God's creatures and all humankind can rejoice together in the defeat of suffering and death in God's kingdom."[7]

"Are white people bad?" Let's return to the gospel concert. The founder and director of the Great Day Singers is a very elderly, very dignified white-haired African-American lady named Louvinia Pointer. She has won many awards and honors for her sixty years of work in music, especially with young people. The singing group was all black; the audience was almost all white. Despite the repeated references to slavery, nothing could have been more inviting than Mrs. Pointer's manner toward us. She would turn on her stool and gesture to the white folks to join the singing. She welcomed us into the universal meaning of the hymns and, at the same time, helped us to see their particular significance for the slaves. I was particularly struck by one I hadn't heard for a long time, evoking the Crucifixion of Jesus who, in the words of the chorus, "never said a mumblin' word."

> He hung down his head and died;
> And he never said a mumblin' word;
> Not a word, not a word . . .
> He never said a mumblin' word.

How moving that was, to ponder the deep sense of identification that the slaves in their powerlessness felt with the suffering Master. But the climax for me was the song called "Prayer Is De Key."[8] I didn't get all the words, but they evoked a powerful sense of longing for a key to unlock the doors of captivity. "Prayer is de key," they sang, but it was the chorus that made the most indelible impression. With a lightly syncopated melody coming in repeatedly over the verses, the singers softly and prayerfully reiterated these words:

> Open up the heaven door for me.

Mrs. Pointer told us that they had recently given a performance at Rikers Island, the infamous New York City jail. It was this song, she said, that moved the prisoners the most. Obviously moved herself, she wonderingly described how many of the men had literally gotten down on their knees as those words were sung. Hope had drawn near to them. "Open up the heaven door for me."

Criminals, slave owners, tax collectors, prostitutes, vestry members, deacons, elders, clergy, Pharisees, tobacco executives, faculty, students, adulterers, idolaters — here we all are growing along together by the grace of God. Who is to say who is good and who is bad? It is the Lord who will make the distinction. And make it he will. In the end, that is the principal thrust of the parable. There will be a separation, just as John the Baptist said, and the Son of God will make it. The enemy will be destroyed. Sin will be overcome. Evil will be rooted out for all time. I look forward to the day when the evil in my own soul will be rooted out.

John the Baptist made one mistake. He thought the Messiah was going to swing the scythe of judgment as soon as he appeared. We get the feeling that John was sort of looking forward to seeing the bad people polished off. He had expected the Coming One to execute judgment on evildoers as his first act. It had not yet been revealed to John that the judgment would be executed in a way that no one expected.[9] The last thing he could have imagined was that Jesus Christ would undergo the judgment himself.

It is Paul the Apostle who lays out before us the paradox of God's mercy revealed in his judgment, the promise of deliverance even in the midst of suffering, the hope of redemption beyond condemnation. He summons up a cosmic picture in which all humanity, believers and unbelievers alike, and the whole created order participate together both in the suffering and in the hope, as we wait for the final harvest: "The whole creation has been groaning in travail together until now; and not only the creation, but we ourselves, who have the first fruits of the Spirit, groan inwardly as we wait for adoption as sons, the redemption of our bodies. For in this hope we were saved" (Rom. 8:22-24). When Jesus the Judge comes again, that will be the Great Day when the "heaven door" will swing open, yes, not just for the pious and the polished but for "lives of mingled yarn" everywhere, yes, even for prisoners and sinners like you and me.

AMEN.

True Inclusiveness

Circumcision is nothing, and uncircumcision is nothing: but what matters is keeping the commandments of God.

(1 COR. 7:19)

Neither is circumcision anything, nor uncircumcision, but a new creation.

(GAL. 6:15)

If thou should mark iniquities, O Lord, who could stand?

(PS. 130:3)

Like most people my age, I used to be a cigarette smoker. I started when I was sixteen and I smoked for seventeen years. I remember the exact date that I kicked the habit for good — cold turkey — in 1973 in Louisville, Kentucky. That was the year of the first General Convention to deal with the ordination of women. (It was voted down that year, you may be aware, and voted in three years later in Minneapolis.) That year in Louisville, I was a thirty-three year old seminary student. I was attending the convention as what you might call a lobbyist. One evening I was invited to a dinner with a group of Virginia Seminary alumni. At the table, I was seated with the late great Albert Mollegen on my right and a rising young clergyman on my left. This man on my left, who was at the time the rector of a large Southern parish, was known to me by name, but I had never met him before and knew little about him. The main thing I noticed was that he was attractive and personable. After the meal, I took out a cigarette and turned to him for a light. Great was my mortification when, instead of reaching for a match, he drew back in his chair and said, "I can't stand women smoking!" That did it. I have never smoked a cigarette since.

That is a true story. Guess who the man was? John Shelby Spong.[1]

Like most converts, I have a tendency to feel superior to the unconverted. I regularly pass by a small group of women who smoke. Even in sub-freezing weather one finds them huddled outside their office building, furtively (or defiantly) puffing away. When I pass them I try to remember to say to myself, "There but for the grace of God go I." Is it not wonderful that God's grace to me, in my addiction and my vanity, came in the person of the now famous (some would say infamous) Bishop Spong?[2]

One of the great certainties about the human race is that we perpetually make distinctions among ourselves in order to judge ourselves or our own group more favorably than others. I have just as much trouble with this as the next person. I love to get good seats in restaurants. I love it when somebody invites me to sit in a box at the opera. I love it if I get to ride first class on the Metroliner. How quickly we come to think that we really *deserve* our privileges! I *deserve* to be in first class because I *am* first class! I *deserve* to be healthy because I quit smoking!

In the Corinthian church, as you know, this sort of pride had taken over the whole congregation. The church at Corinth was what we call today a charismatic or Spirit-filled church. The Corinthians were the Olympic athletes of spirituality. They had every endowment but one, the one without which all the rest were worthless: "If I speak in the tongues of men and of angels . . . if I have prophetic powers, and understand all mysteries and all knowledge . . . if I have all faith, so as to remove mountains, but have not love, I am nothing" (1 Cor. 13:1-2).

We know that Paul took up certain themes according to specific contexts. In 1 Corinthians, he seems to have the idea of "nothingness" on his mind. I think this is because the Corinthians thought they were *really something* and Paul seeks to deflate them. They are arguing, for instance, about whether they should eat idol meat or not. Paul says, "A thing sacrificed to idols is nothing, and an idol is nothing"; in fact, he says it twice (8:4; 10:19). He says that a person or congregation can have all the spiritual gifts in the world, but "If I have not love, I am nothing." When he is going after their pride in having been baptized by this or that spiritual hero, he says, "What then is Apollos? What is Paul? . . . Neither he who plants nor he who waters is anything, but only God who gives the growth" (3:5, 7). Paul is nothing, Apollos is nothing. And then Paul also says, "Circumcision is nothing, and uncircumcision is nothing; what matters is keeping the commandments of God" (7:19).

Now as it happens, circumcision was not a big issue for the Corinthian church. The text I just read is in the middle of a section in which Paul is expounding the relative insignificance of *every* sort of human arrangement in view of the fact that, as Paul resoundingly states in 1 Corinthians 7:31, "The form of this world is passing away." For the Galatian church, however, circumcision is a very big issue indeed; it lies at the heart of the struggle that is going on between Paul and the Jewish-Christian teachers who are threatening the church. So Paul writes to the Galatians, "Circumcision is nothing and uncircumcision is nothing, but a new creation" (Gal. 6:15).

The Corinthian situation and the Galatian situation were opposites, and Paul said somewhat different things to each. This might bother some people, but Paul was an eminently *contextual* theologian. As he says himself, "To those under the law I became as one under the law. . . . to those outside the law I became as one outside the law . . . I have become all things to all men, that I might by all means save some" (1 Cor. 9:21-22). In view of this flexibility, isn't it curious that Paul is so often accused of *rigidity* by those who do not know his letters well?

The Galatian church was being slowly strangled by the *nomos,* the Law. The Corinthian church, on the other hand, was *antinomian,* that is, without the Law altogether. That is why Paul says to the Corinthians, "Circumcision is nothing, and uncircumcision is nothing; *what matters is keeping the commandments of God*"; whereas he writes to the Galatians, "Neither is circumcision anything, nor uncircumcision, *but a new creation.*" The Corinthians, for their part, knew all about the new creation, or thought they did; they thought they and the new creation were already the same finished thing. They needed to be brought up short by Paul's chapter on love with its dialectic of *now* and *not-yet:* "Our knowledge is imperfect and our prophecy is imperfect . . . for *now* we see in a mirror, dimly, but *then* face to face; *now* I know in part; *then* I shall understand fully, even as I have been fully understood" (13:12).

Paul writes of the commandments of God to the antinomian Corinthians because he does not want them to think that when he says "circumcision is nothing" he is also saying "obedience to God is nothing." The Galatians, on the other hand, are a different breed; for them, circumcision separated the first-class Christians from the lower-class Christians. In their case Paul is ready to trust the fruits of the Spirit altogether; "Against these there is no law" (Gal. 5:23).

When I first came to Grace Church in New York in 1981, the congregation was like the Corinthians and the Galatians mixed together. The "Corinthian" members had heard the new creation message and were running off the map with it, whereas the "Galatians" were trying to reintroduce a whole lot of Law. We had all we could handle trying to keep these two elements together. One time back in the early '80s a group of "Corinthians" from Grace Church went to a beachfront retreat center for the weekend. A group of "Galatians" arrived later that evening to find a party in progress, with some of the *bons vivants* already quite tipsy. These "Corinthians" greeted the arriving "Galatians" with boozy shouts along these lines: "'Drinking is nothing and sobriety is nothing, but a new creation,' and aren't we glad we belong to 'Grace' Church!" The latecomers, the "Galatians," were deeply shocked, and the story was told afterwards to support the view that the Grace Church clergy had gone too far with this business of justification by grace through faith alone.

In preparation for this sermon, I read the first letter to the Corinthians very, very carefully this week, looking for any hints that Paul might have been pulling back from the proclamation of righteousness by grace through faith. I didn't find any. What I found was statements like these: "All things are from God" (11:12). *"All things are lawful"* (twice repeated: 6:12; 10:23). "All things belong to you, and you are Christ's, and Christ is God's" (3:22-23). "No one can lay a foundation other than . . . Jesus Christ" (3:11). You can see for yourselves that these are not legalistic ways of construing the commandments of God.

In fact, Paul, if he had remained a Pharisee, could not have uttered either one of these two things that he says in our Corinthian text. To say that *circumcision is nothing* would have been an indescribable sacrilege to any Jew. To compound it by saying that the only thing that matters is keeping the commandments was adding insult to injury, because of course, circumcision *was itself* one of the primary commandments of God, the very sign and seal of the covenant. Therefore the radicality of the statement "circumcision is nothing" is almost unthinkable; we draw as close here to the revolutionary leveling of human social organizations as anyone has ever come. Legalism and moralism are undercut at the roots. After all, it is at the climax of 1 Corinthians 15:56 that Paul says "the power of Sin is the Law."[3]

The story is told that two women attended a Christian education conference where both enrolled in a study of Galatians. After one particularly rousing session, the two of them walked out on the deck of the conference center. One of the women took a pack of cigarettes out of her purse. "You know," she said to the other woman, "This message of 'the freedom we have in Christ Jesus' [Gal. 2:4] has really reached me. I don't need to rely on these cigarettes anymore." She started to throw them over the railing of the deck. "Stop!" said the other woman. "I'm going to smoke a cigarette for the first time in my life!" *Smoking is nothing, and quitting smoking is nothing, but a new creation!*

Are we recommending cigarette smoking? "God forbid; how can we who died to sin still live in it?" (Rom. 6:2). But is it worth the risk of proclaiming radical grace to think that some may get lung cancer "because we are not under law but under grace" (v. 15)? This will always be a live issue for any congregation that has heard the gospel. How far are we prepared to go in teaching "the freedom we have in Christ Jesus"? Paul must have asked himself this a hundred times in view of the Corinthian situation, where he was faced with a whole congregation full of people who were either libertines and conceited about it, or ascetics and conceited about that.

What is at stake here? Are we who are evangelicals prepared to go so far as to say "Good theology is nothing, and bad theology is nothing"? God forbid; no one in Christian history cared more about right theology than Paul. "If anyone is preaching to you a different gospel from that which you received, let him be accursed" (Gal. 1:9). But what is the gospel? What is the heart and soul of the evangelical message? I summon as my witness no less a figure than that of F. F. Bruce, who stated in an interview shortly before his death that the irreducible core of the gospel was nothing less than "the justification of the ungodly" (Rom. 4:5; 5:6).

Dear fellow sinners! You and I are sometimes Galatians and sometimes Corinthians. Either we are looking down on others for breaking God's commands or we are looking down on others for not being as free as we are. Either way, the apostle says to us what he says to the Corinthians, "Let him who stands take heed lest he fall" (10:12), and "What do you have that you did not receive {as a gift} from God?" And if you received it as a gift, then "Why do you boast?" (4:7).

I myself stand before you today as what we used to call in the 1928 Prayer Book a "miserable offender." I miss that phrase very much. I always knew that my salvation somehow was signified in our common willingness to take that designation unto ourselves. I gladly take it to myself as a sign of the greatness of my Redeemer. I stand today in the same place as the Psalmist three thousand years ago when he wrote the words we said earlier: "If thou were to mark what is done amiss, O Lord, who should stand?" (Ps. 130:3).

Fellow evangelicals! You know, and I know, that the hallmark of the wider Episcopal Church today is "inclusiveness" — as the presiding bishop puts it, "no outsiders." You know also, and I know, that the reproach continually brought against us evangelicals is that we are "narrow," "intolerant," "rigid," and "exclusive." I believe that we must not let the idea of inclusiveness be wrested away from us. The gospel is *more inclusive* than anyone who does not know Scripture could ever imagine. Who could ever have spoken of the justification of the *un*godly and the *un*deserving except by revelation? We do not stand on our spiritual gifts, our religious habits, our extemporaneous prayers, our right doctrines, our correct interpretations. We stand on only one thing: the grace and love of God freely given to us in the Cross of the One of whom it is written that at the moment of his death the curtain was rent asunder from top to bottom. There is neither first class nor second class, black or white, slave or free, Jew or Greek, male or female, oppressed or oppressor, liberal or conservative, gay or straight, deserving or undeserving.

For circumcision is nothing, and uncircumcision is nothing. In Christ Jesus, there is a new creation.

AMEN.

Mrs. Hamer, Mrs. Durr, Brother Will, and the Word of Faith

VIRGINIA THEOLOGICAL SEMINARY
COMMENCEMENT SERMON

Being ignorant of the righteousness that comes from God, and seeking to establish their own, they did not submit to God's righteousness. For Christ is the end of the law, that every one who has faith may be justified.

. . . The word is near you, on your lips and in your heart, that is, the word of faith which we preach. . . . So faith comes from what is heard, and what is heard comes by the preaching of Christ.

(ROM. 10:3-4, 8, 17)

In the May 17 issue of *The New Yorker,* political writer Joe Klein reports on the presidential candidacy of Elizabeth Dole. He describes how she chose the New Hampshire Republican Party's Campaign 2000 kickoff dinner to make a statement in favor of modified gun control. Since the Republicans of that state are notoriously attached to their weapons, this was a courageous thing to do. There was just one problem. Mrs. Dole stated her position as she strolled around in one of her signature walkabouts, so that her words seemed to vanish into the far corners of the room. Mr. Klein concludes, "One wonders what the impact . . . would have been had [her words] been delivered *from the authority of a lectern.*"[1]

Our theme on this day of commencement is not speaking styles or church furniture, however. We have before us a class of freshly minted servants of the Word. This is a sermon about the *authority* of the gospel, *the word of faith which we preach.* In our text for this morning from Romans 10, Paul writes: "The word is near you, on your lips and in your heart, that is, *the word of faith which we preach;*" and, he continues, "if you confess with your lips that Jesus is Lord and believe in your heart that God raised him from the dead, you will be saved. . . . *For there is no distinction* between Jew and Greek; the same Lord is Lord of all and bestows his riches upon all who call upon him" (Rom. 10:6-9, 12).

I'm going to be referring to three books I've just finished reading. All three of them are related to the civil rights movement. The first is called *Outside the Magic Circle.* The author lived right here on the Holy Hill for fifteen years in the 1930s and '40s.[2] She died just a few weeks ago at the age of ninety-five. Her name was Virginia Foster Durr, and of all the natives of the American South of whom I have ever heard, I believe I admire her the most. She and her husband, Clifford Durr, became famous in 1963 when they went down to the jail in their home town of Montgomery, Alabama, to bail out Rosa Parks. But they had already lost most of Mr. Durr's law practice and many of their friends years before because they would not knuckle under to the communist-hunters who were striking fear into the hearts of so many during the '50s. Cliff and Virginia Durr were born into privilege in the Old South, but all their lives they had very little money because of the positions they took. The courage, wisdom, humor, and insight of Virginia Durr, in particular, almost defy belief, and I urgently recommend her autobiography to you.[3]

There is only one aspect of her book that is out of tune. She was theologically tone deaf. This is understandable, since her father, a Presbyterian pastor, was thrown out of his pulpit because he refused to sign a statement saying that he believed Jonah was literally eaten by a fish. His daughter Virginia never could see any point in theological hairsplitting after that. She said, "I think the teachings of religion have been nearly ruined by theology. . . . It seems to me that the essential point of every religion I've ever studied is the Golden Rule, to treat people as you want them to treat you."[4]

Virginia Durr heard Martin Luther King preach many times. She admired him greatly as a leader, but she understood him largely as a politician. She was oddly oblivious to the *theological* power of his message.[5] The opposite is true of Charles Marsh, who wrote the second book to which I refer, called *God's Long Summer: Stories of Faith and Civil Rights*. It's a theological thriller. The heroine is Fannie Lou Hamer, the semi-literate Mississippi sharecropper whose astonishing physical courage and transcendent spiritual leadership placed her in the very first rank of movement leaders. Mrs. Hamer (as she is always called) holds the key to the theological puzzle posed by Marsh.[6] He presents her not only as a Protestant saint of no small dimensions, but also as a genuine theologian "every bit the equal of our canonized masters of conceptual thought." Marsh shows how Mrs. Hamer instinctively understood — and preached — the crucial distinction that Paul makes in today's reading between "the righteousness which is based on the law" and "the righteousness based on faith" (Rom. 10:5-6).

Fannie Lou Hamer was arrested in Winona, Mississippi, for the crime of attempting to register to vote. While she was in the Winona jail, a group of male law enforcement officers orchestrated a savage beating intended not only to hurt her physically but to degrade and humiliate her spirit. She never forgot that night and until the end of her days continued to talk about it, but she never kept what Maureen Dowd calls a "*dis* list." Moving around the encampments of young civil rights workers as they prepared to go out into the Mississippi night, she was a living embodiment of Paul's apostolic preaching: "There is neither Jew nor Greek, there is neither slave nor free, there is neither male nor female [there is neither black nor white], all are one in Christ Jesus" (Gal. 3:28). She spoke to the young people about a new world in which they were not going to hate white people no matter what suffering they endured. The *word of faith which she preached* was anchored by her radical understanding of the work of Christ.

The problem with many of us — not all, but many — who run around quoting Galatians 3:28 is that, without meaning to, we are using the passage to set up a new kind of righteousness by the law. In Paul's later letters, specifically Romans, he shows that he is aware of this danger. Those who "have a zeal for God," he writes, are "not [necessarily] enlightened. For, being ignorant of the righteousness that comes from God, and seeking to establish their own, they did not submit to God's righteousness" (Rom. 10:2-4).[7] I could keep you here all day with stories about my husband and me in the '60s and '70s when we were in love with our own righteousness. We had great scorn for those who had not been converted as we had. We did not understand that Christian social action arises out of the radical breaking down of distinctions, not the introduction of new distinctions. This radical breakdown is expressed most succinctly in Paul's crucial words in Romans 5:6: "Christ died for the ungodly."

The Episcopal Church is presently in danger of a new kind of legalistic sentimentality that threatens the very causes we care about. Sentimentality says that if we just elect enough minorities to General Convention our problems will be solved. "Just look at our diversity!" we boast. Christian realism says this is just window dressing compared to the real work of love and struggle that must go on day in and day out on the local level. I'm not saying don't elect minority deputies. I'm saying let's not think that because we have done it we have thereby established our own righteousness. With all due deference to Virginia Durr, theology *is* important. Paul's proclamation, "There is no distinction between Jew and Greek," is impossible to live by unless there is righteousness by grace through faith, because unaided human nature always wants to divide Jews from Greeks, godly from ungodly, righteous from unrighteous — according to works, according to law. But "Christ is the end of the law, that every one who has faith may be justified" (Rom. 10:4).

There's always some kind of law rearing its head in the church. Today it seems as if there has to be a litmus test for everything, from inclusive language to sexuality to tithing to "personal sharing." There is this pressure to conform to one ideology or another. It can be found in Cursillo as well as urban coalitions.[8] When I was in seminary, the law divided those who boycotted Gallo wine from those who did not.[9] Today the distinction seems to be more in the realm of what we're calling "spirituality." What a change in twenty-five years! Seminarians hardly prayed at all in the early '70s; today one is suspect if one is not in spiritual direction. This presents us with a fresh problem, as people begin to feel alienated because they don't want to join prayer groups. If Paul were here today he might be saying, "Christ died for the *unspiritual*."

This theological emphasis, as of course you know, comes from Paul through Augustine to the Reformation. For reasons truly mysterious to me, the Episcopal Church doesn't want to be Protestant any more. Well, God knows Protestantism has been divisive.[10] Human behavior always threatens to undo whatever good there is. However, and this is where *the word of faith* comes in, it is the Protestant emphasis that preserves the nerve center of *true inclusiveness*. It is the Protestant emphasis that keeps reminding us, "there but for the grace of God go I."[11] Without a continuing commitment to the righteousness that is by grace through faith, we have no theological hedge against that other, most pernicious kind of righteousness — namely, self-righteousness. Listen again to the King James Version of the way Paul describes what happens to godly people when they get self-righteous: "For they being ignorant of God's righteousness, and going about to establish their own righteousness, have not submitted themselves unto the righteousness of God." Paul then concludes (RSV): "But Christ is the end of the law, that every one who has faith may be justified" (Rom. 10:3-4)

Now we are going to appear to undo everything we have said so far. Charles Marsh ends his theological thriller with a strong hint that there are certain times when distinctions *do* have to be made in the church. He cites a question posed by James Cone: "How could both black and white churches be Christian if they took opposite stands and both claimed Christ and the Bible as the basis of their views?" Tightening the screws, Marsh evokes Dietrich Bonhoeffer, who in 1934 said that German Christians who were not in the resisting Confessing Church were not Christians. A whole chapter in

God's Long Summer is given to the unexpurgated theological views of Sam Bowers, Imperial Wizard of the White Knights of the Mississippi Ku Klux Klan, who ordered the murders of the three civil rights workers during Freedom Summer. Reading Bowers's opinions and contemplating his works, most would agree that Sam Bowers is not a Christian. Well, are you and I Christian? What are the defining issues of our own time? It is difficult to say, because there are no clearly drawn lines as there were in 1934 and 1964. Perhaps the death penalty is the test case for us today. The saying I quoted earlier is attributed to a sixteenth-century Englishman, John Bradford, who, when watching some malefactors being taken off for execution, did not say, "They are getting what they deserve," but rather, "There but for the grace of God goes John Bradford."[12]

Are you and I Christians? What ground do we have to stand on? There is something out of tune when we clergy and other Christian leaders allow ourselves to be known in our communities purely for our good works, as though we ourselves were the message. David Boies, probably the most brilliant litigator in America today, was recently quoted: "I never want people to say, 'That's a great lawyer.' I want them to say, 'He has a great case.'"[13] What is our case? Is it the Golden Rule? Or is it *the word of faith which we preach?*

Anybody who has seen a Eucharist at an international Anglican gathering will agree that the sight of all races and peoples coming together to the Lord's Table is unforgettable and transforming. But "faith comes from what is *heard,* and what is *heard* comes by *the preaching of Christ*"; the Eucharist must be interpreted by the Word. If it isn't, it will deteriorate into sentimentality. How long has it been since anyone, anywhere in the Episcopal Church was refused the Eucharist? What about a man who abruptly leaves his wife for another woman in the same parish and three weeks later comes to the altar rail with the new lady friend, in full view of the congregation? (A true story.) How about Charlton Heston?[14] Just kidding . . . but what *would* be a reason strong enough to excommunicate someone, at least temporarily? Paul called for an excommunication in the Corinthian church, as you know.[15] Would we give the Eucharist to Sam Bowers? How about the unrepentant killers of Matthew

Shepard?[16] Whether we do or whether we don't, however, the point is that we have to be prepared to defend our position *theologically* in the light of the Christ who justifies the ungodly (Rom. 4:5). It is a lot more complicated than the Golden Rule. It is a lot more complicated than just saying "God loves everybody." Indeed God *does* love everybody, but that is not a sufficient account of the gospel. It turns into sentimentality in the blink of an eye. Paul's crucial words "Christ died for the ungodly" have a bite to them. The implication is that there is such a thing as ungodliness and that *all* human beings need to be saved from it, including you and me.

So that puts the preacher and the congregation on the same plane. To the Class of 1999, I offer congratulations and thanksgivings with all my heart. I am sure you are proud and grateful that you have accomplished the difficult academic challenges of the past three years. Now, however, the really hard work begins — the work of teaching and leading all kinds of folks. You will be driven to near-desperation at times because your people will not support your best ideas, your highest aspirations. You will have completely unspiritual people in your parishes. Like Virginia Durr, they respond to calls for action. They won't come to your quiet days and they won't even try to learn centering prayer. They may be in your office more often than you would like, hectoring you about some social program or other. Other people in your parishes will be breaking out into prayer at every pause in the conversation ("O Lord, I just ask you to help our rector see the light"). Still others will be badgering you to have more praise music, or to get rid of praise music. Those of us who envisioned ourselves out on the barricades leading the battle against injustice have been disillusioned to find ourselves bogged down in quicksand with the Altar Guild. What's going to hold us up? Where do we find that firm ground at the bottom of this human muck?

This brings us to book number three, by Will Campbell. No greater servant of the radical gospel lives today. He was, as he says, "in the crosshairs of the Klan" for many years, but everything Brother Will writes is constructed around the gospel message that Christ died for the ungodly.[17] His latest is *And Also With You:*

Duncan Gray and the American Dilemma.[18] Duncan Gray was a genuine hero of the Episcopal Church in Mississippi during the civil rights movement, and the book is written as a tribute to his witness. I want to give you some idea of the book's ending, but please be aware that it is far more intricate, poetic, artful, and profound than I can even begin to suggest. That said, let us follow as Brother Will describes a day with a most unlikely and unholy triumvirate. Picture Will Campbell, Sam Bowers, and civil rights activist Kenneth Dean, colleague and friend of Duncan Gray. Bowers is escorting them on foot through the "deep, foreboding" Mississippi swamps, "as remote a place as I had ever seen," where "dark rituals [had] uneased the night" at "nocturnal, clandestine gatherings" of the Ku Klux Klan.

> Beside me was Bowers, a man alleged to have been responsible for multiple murders, bombings, and mayhem. On the other side of me was [Kenneth] Dean, a man who had risked his own life trying to save the lives of black citizens. . . . It was the greatest test my tentative understanding of unconditional grace as overshadowing, overcoming, conquering humanity's inherent sinfulness I had ever known. The scandal of the gospel I had heard preachers and theologians talk about in generalities all my life assumed an even more outrageous posture. Is grace abounding here in this darkening arcane forest? Truly unconditional grace? Something as crazy as Golda Meir chasing Hitler around the pinnacles of heaven, and after a thousand years he stops and lets her pin a Star of David on his chest? Who said that? . . . I felt a strange oneness with the two men with me. And an even more unfamiliar concord with those I knew had convened on this ground to plan missions of atrocity.

What is that oneness? What is that concord? That is the theological question. Is it simply "God loves everybody?" No one who cares about God's justice can be satisfied with that. Religious reassurances of the ordinary variety do not reach the deepest pain or bridge the widest chasms. Nothing will do it but this Word: *Christ died for the ungodly* — "not weighing our merits, but pardoning our offenses." That is our oneness, that is our concord. The unconditional grace of God, the righteousness of Christ in his death, "overshadowing, overcoming, conquering humanity's inherent sinfulness"; the purpose of God at work with Resurrection power to reclaim this whole human race of "miserable offenders" for his glorious kingdom: that is *the word of faith which we preach.*

You graduates are invested with authority today, not because you have a new degree, but because you have been called to the ministry of the gospel. John Calvin wrote that "God puts his words on the lips of human beings while angels keep silence." Paul writes, "How are they to believe in him of whom they have never heard? And how are they to hear without a preacher?" (Rom. 10:14). Lectern or no lectern, high pulpit or low pulpit or no pulpit, it is not your own authority that you exercise in worship, in preaching, in the sickroom, and by the deathbed; it is the authority of the Word. Week in and week out you will wrestle with the text of Scripture as you go about your pastoral or teaching ministry. It will be confirmed for you again and again: we have a great case, the greatest that the world has ever known. The foundation of true Christian preaching, liturgy, prayer, and action is the knowledge that not one of us can claim a righteousness of our own, but instead the unconquerable righteousness of Jesus Christ, given in his death for the ungodly, the unrighteous, and the unspiritual. In every generation this revolutionary message is proclaimed afresh. The dispatch from the Commander passes now to you. There is no power in heaven or earth that can wrest the righteousness of Christ away from a sinner whom he loves. May it be said of us all, in the words of God from John Milton's *Paradise Lost:*

> Servant of God, well done! Well hast thou fought
> The better fight, who single hast maintained
> Against revolted multitudes the cause
> Of truth, in Word mightier than they in arms.

(Book VI, line 29)

AMEN.

The Last Sunday after the Epiphany,
February 26, 1995

The Faces of Love

GRACE CHURCH IN NEW YORK

Text: 1 Corinthians 13

L ast November, on "60 Minutes," I watched Mike Wallace interview the great French film star Jeanne Moreau. I sent for a transcript, because it was an astonishing exchange. When Moreau first appeared on the television screen, she looked so old and so ravaged that I was shocked. But after she had talked for a while, the sight of her famous face, untouched by plastic surgery, began to speak with greater power than a hundred face-lifts. One could tell that Mike Wallace himself was captivated. On the voice-over he said in a knowing way, "Part of what makes this woman fascinating is that she's been as passionate about her life off the screen as on." Shortly after, speaking to Moreau directly, he said with a conspiratorial air, "There's a feeling in America that passion in a woman of a certain age is unseemly." There was a long pause. Moreau said, calmly, "They're right." Mr. Wallace, dumbfounded, could not formulate a response; he repeated himself incredulously, *"Passion* is *unseemly?"* "Oh, come on," said the star. "Passion! When you get sixty, you know about *love.* Love is not passion." "But there's nothing wrong with passion," protested Wallace, his face a picture of disappointment. You could almost see him think-ing in dismay, "This is a *French* woman?" He stammered (it's all there in the transcript), "Wha — I mean, why is passion at the age of sixty . . ." Moreau replied, "I would hate — *I would hate* to be still overcome with passion." The crestfallen Mike Wallace could only respond, "I'm astonished that you said that." As though she were a wise grandmother talking to an adolescent boy, Moreau explained, "I have passion for *life,* but I know about *love.* Love and passion don't go together. Passion is destructive. Passion is demanding. Passion is jealous. Passion goes up and down. Love is constant."

Mike Wallace, stunned into semi-silence, said, "Mmm-hmm." And the great star said, "Compassion. That's what love is about. You give even more than you receive. I would hate to be still victim of passion. And I would think, 'God, I've lived all these years and I've learned nothing?'"[1]

It was almost as though Jeanne Moreau were saying to Mike Wallace,

When I was a child,
I spoke like a child,
I thought like a child,
I reasoned like a child;
when I became a woman, I gave up childish ways. . . .

Love is patient and kind;
love is not jealous;
love is not boastful or arrogant;
It is not rude nor does it insist on its own way. . . .

Little did I know when I tuned in to "60 Minutes" that night that I would be seeing a classic confrontation: *eros* versus *agape.* Mike Wallace was talking about *eros* — sexual love, the love that drives for possession of the other. The *femme fatale,* though she prob-ably did not know it, was talking about what Paul calls, in Greek, *agape.*

Love *(agape)* bears all things, believes all things,
hopes all things, endures all things.

(1 Cor. 13:7)

There is a great deal to be learned from this exchange between
a man and a woman, each "of a certain age." Mike Wallace's expec-
tations are entirely oriented toward an understanding of love as *eros,*
and he appears to be unable, at least in the two or three minutes
that we see on film, to make the mental shift necessary to understand that Jeanne Moreau is talking about something altogether
different. This is not unlike the challenge set before us today as we
listen to this celebrated passage on love. It isn't saying what we
think it says.

This passage from 1 Corinthians is one of the best known and
most loved passages from Scripture. Even people who have never
read the Bible are familiar with some of the phrases in the King
James Version. It is not poetry, but it can be arranged on the page
like poetry because, unlike most of Paul's work, it is written in a
lofty rhetorical style; "the sentences roll along like waves."[2]

If I speak in the tongues of men and of angels,
but have not love,
I am a noisy gong or a clanging cymbal.
And if I have prophetic powers,
and understand all mysteries and all knowledge,
And if I have all faith, so as to remove mountains,
but have not love,
I am nothing.
If I give away all I have,
and if I deliver my body to be burned,
but have not love,
I gain nothing.

(vv. 1-3)

The majestic cadences and emotional power of the passage are
such that it has often been called "a hymn in praise of love." It has

become associated in many minds as a passage that one can expect to hear read at weddings. There are many misapprehensions here. First of all, it is not a hymn and it is not *in praise of* love. It is *a description of* love, with actual results in mind. It is a specifically Christian exhortation to a new way of life. It is not especially appropriate for weddings unless it is carefully interpreted by a wedding sermon, because Paul here is most emphatically not describing the romantic love of two people for one another. Romantic love, *eros,* comes to an end. It crashes against the reality of the other person. It burns itself out. Jeanne Moreau knows that better than some Christians; she is nothing if not unsentimental. "Passion is demanding. Passion is jealous. Passion goes up and down. Love is constant."

It is important to note that Moreau's life does not seem to bear out her words. By her own frank admission, she has left one man after another all her life. Constancy does not seem to have been conspicuously present in her conduct. She was married only once, very briefly. But let us honor her for her truthfulness; "love does not rejoice at wrong, but rejoices in the truth" (v. 6). She has not held herself up as a model, but she has spoken the truth about love. She has remarkably avoided the fatuous self-congratulation typical of most celebrities in their interviews. This is a good lesson for the rest of us. We do not have to be perfectly behaved in order to honor the truth when we see it.

Paul tells us these truths about *agape*. It is not a feeling; it is being for others. It is not an emotion; it is service. It is not passive but active. It seeks the good of the other, forgets itself, always believes and hopes for the other, spends itself for the sake of the other. "You give even more than you receive." It does not act like this from weakness; it acts from strength. *Agape* is victorious over all the forces arrayed against it. Passion *(eros)* comes and it goes, but *"agape* never ends."

Indeed, love as it is described in 1 Corinthians 13 is not within the realm of human capability:

Love is patient and kind;
love is not jealous;

love is not boastful or arrogant;
It is not rude nor does it insist on its own way;
it is not irritable or resentful;
It does not rejoice at wrong,
But rejoices in the right.

(vv. 4-6)

People who hear those words and smile with sentimental satis-
faction are not really hearing. Human beings may act this way
briefly and on occasion, but it is not within our power to act like
this on a consistent basis. Rather than gazing benevolently on a
man and woman as these words are read at their wedding, we
should be on our knees begging the Lord to give them that which
by nature they cannot have. Paul, in this text, is drawing a distinction between human capacity and the transcendent power of the
love that God gives. We see this in the buildup of negatives in the
passage: Love is not jealous, is not boastful or arrogant, is not rude,
does not insist on its own way, is not irritable or resentful, does not
rejoice at wrong. Paul contrasts the behavior of love with the all-
too-typical behavior of human beings. In and of ourselves we do not
have the disposition to act lovingly in a constant way.

And yet Paul is quite seriously calling the Christian community to this way of life. He says so in a most striking fashion:

If I speak in the tongues of men and of angels,
but have not love,
I am a noisy gong or a clanging cymbal.
And if I have prophetic powers,
and understand all mysteries and all knowledge,
And if I have all faith, so as to remove mountains,
but have not love,
I am nothing.
If I give away all I have,
and if I deliver my body to be burned,
but have not love,
I gain nothing.

This is strong stuff. It might be easy enough for secular-minded wedding guests to nod knowingly at the suggestion that piety and good deeds aren't worth anything without "love" (conceived in a very loose and undefined way), but this wasn't written for them. It was written for the members of the Christian community, and it was especially designed for the Corinthian congregation. If Paul were writing to us here in this congregation, he might say, "If I contribute to the Capital Fund Campaign, and pray for people with AIDS, and attend a class on the Atonement, and give up a pint of my blood to the Blood Drive, but have not *agape,* I am nothing." To the preacher he might say, "If I stay up all night working on a sermon on 1 Corinthians 13, but have not *agape,* I might as well be a bag of wind." These are pretty severe strictures. They aren't so easy to listen to. If we are not shaken by this text, if we persist in hearing it as human wisdom, even wisdom of the very best sort, then we are probably keeping Paul's words away at a safe distance because they are too much for us.

Really to hear this passage is to throw oneself on the mercy of God. This is not a story about nice relationships and human successes. This is not a description of typical married life. This is not a snapshot of church life, either. We will recognize in this chapter the story of the Lord himself. It has been said that the meaning of the text will become clear if we substitute the name "Jesus" for the word "love": "*Jesus* is patient and kind, is not jealous; is not boastful or arrogant; is not rude, does not insist on his own way; is not irritable or resentful; does not rejoice at wrong, but rejoices in the truth. . . . *Jesus* bears all things, believes all things, hopes all things, endures all things."

There is therefore a secret at the heart of this passage. *Agape* would be unattainable for the human being if it were not for God's invincible activity on our behalf, through the power of his Son's sacrifice of himself. Love does not lead to God; God in Jesus Christ leads us to love. Love does not arise out of the unaided human heart; God puts it there. *Agape* is not an ideal for me to aim at; *agape* is already actively at work in me from beyond myself. As John puts it, "We love, because he first loved us" (1 John 4:19). Love is therefore

the first thing and the last thing; first, because the love of God
brought us into being, and last, because love is that which remains
when all else has passed away in the Resurrection of the dead.

In the last lines of the last canto of Dante's *Divine Comedy*, the
poet who has made his long and weary way through all the levels of
Hell, Purgatory, and Paradise is finally brought into the presence of
God and shown by revelation, in words that are generally agreed to
approach the uttermost limit of human speech, that the power that
moves the entire universe, from atoms to galaxies, is the power of
love. The love of which he speaks in these transcendent final lines is
not "love" in some vague and generic sense, but the luminous core
of love that burns and radiates within the Trinity itself: Father, Son,
and Holy Spirit. This is the love that moved God to give himself up
in the supreme act of self-sacrifice; as Paul says in another place,
"Christ, though he was in the form of God, did not think equality
with God a thing to be grasped, but taking the form of a servant,
became obedient unto death, even death on a cross" (Phil. 2:3-11).

Think along with me for a minute. Think of what it means
to be loved. Some people are very blessed, because they knew love
from childhood; others were deprived of love and are achingly
aware of their deprivation. In either case, the love that was present
and the love that was absent can be recognized by its true characteristics:

> Love is patient and kind;
> love is not jealous;
> love is not boastful or arrogant;
> It is not rude nor does it insist on its own way;
> it is not irritable or resentful;
> It does not rejoice at wrong,
> But rejoices in the right.
> Love bears all things, believes all things,
> hopes all things, endures all things.

The person who loves thinks constantly of the needs of the
other. He anticipates those needs and provides for them. Whether it

is pocket money for a child's train trip or a strong presence in the middle of the night when there is an emergency, the person who loves is always there. She thinks about what you need before you think of it yourself. If you are in difficulties, he is there, not to lecture or rebuke, but to support and to understand. When there are trials to undergo, she will be there with you to give you strength. He will hear your cries in the night and wipe away your tears and soothe your hurt places and feed you something warm when you are a child, and when you are at the end of your life's journey she will visit you, read to you, play your favorite music, help you to the bathroom and change your sheets, with infinite patience and without reproach, with care and tenderness. These actions and others like them are merely "hints and symbols" of the love of God for us, mere shadows of the glory that is to be revealed:

> For our knowledge is imperfect,
> and our prophecy is imperfect;
> But when the perfect comes,
> the imperfect will pass away. . . .
> For now we see in a mirror dimly,
> but then face to face.
> Now I know in part;
> then I shall understand fully,
> even as I have been fully understood.
>
> (vv. 9-12)

That is about the love of God. But it is clear from the context that Paul has confidence in the power of the Holy Spirit to make love happen in the Christian congregation even now. If it is not happening, all the religious activities and spiritual manifestations in the world will not amount to anything. If love is not the motive force, if the good of the other is not actively sought, then it is all just self-indulgence.

Real love, unlike passion, is so unself-conscious! People who perform genuinely loving acts do not even know that they are doing them. They arise spontaneously, without calculation; that is one of the chief features of *agape*. A few moments ago, when I was writing that description of love in action, I realized that I could not do it without thinking of particular people. I started to envision several women from my own life: two of them family members, two of them parishioners, one of them a housekeeper. All of them would be shocked to think that they were examples of love in action. Love is not calculating, does not keep score. The women I am thinking of would not recognize themselves in this sermon; they would be like the people on Jesus' right hand in the last judgment who say, "Lord, when did we see thee hungry?" I particularly think of our beloved Frances Nance, who worked for us for twenty-five years until she died this past year. Whether she *felt* love for us I do not know; she did not talk about her feelings. Sometimes I used to tell her that I loved her, but it embarrassed her and she usually changed the subject. The reason I say with confidence that she loved us is that we could see it in her actions. We did not in the least deserve her care. She gave it because she was, whether she knew it or not, an agent and instrument of God's love, the love that Paul describes in Romans 5:8: "God shows his love for us in that while we were yet sinners Christ died for us."

I recognize myself when I hear that word "sinner." I know that I have not been a conspicuously lovable person. Yet I have learned something of love. I have learned it from my mother and father. I have learned love from many of you. In this way the love of Jesus Christ has become real to me. That is what Paul means when he writes of love to the Corinthian church. Love is to become enfleshed, embodied in the Christian community, and if it does not, all our religious activity is like the empty noise of a gong that makes a loud sound and then vanishes.

Love must have a face. I could not write of love had I not been loved by human beings with faces. God's love, too, must have a face. Love that exists only as an abstraction somewhere off in the heavens does not have any meaning for us. God's love for us has a face, and it is the face of our Lord Jesus Christ.

Jeanne Moreau, with all her wisdom, did not know, or did not say, what Paul says in 1 Corinthians 13: "Love never ends." In fact, earlier in the interview when she is talking about the end of her affair with the director Louis Malle, she says, "That's what life is about. Nothing lasts." Humanly speaking, she is quite right. We cannot affirm Paul's words about love glibly or quickly. Nothing lasts. "The wind goes over it and it is no more" (Ps. 103:16). The human being does not have the capacity for undying love.

Our greatest poet, however, had this to say:

Love is not love
Which alters when it alteration finds;
O no, it is an ever-fixèd mark
That looks on tempests and is never shaken;
. . . Love's not time's fool, though rosy cheeks and lips
Within his bending sickle's compass come;
Love alters not with his brief hours and weeks,
But bears it out even to the edge of doom.
(William Shakespeare, Sonnet CXVI)

That is *agape,* and it has a face. Jesus of Nazareth sets his face toward Jerusalem. We, in our sinfulness and failure, are not deserving of his sacrifice, yet God has deemed us infinitely worthy of his love, bearing it out even to the edge of doom and beyond. For on the hill of Calvary, the Son of God in his last extremity showed how much we were worth to him. Dante only *visited* Hell; Jesus Christ entered it in all its annihilating power for our sake, and emerged victorious. "Love alone counts, love alone conquers and love alone endures."[3] Love was raised from the dead on Easter morning.

So faith, hope, love abide, these three;
but the greatest of these is love.

AMEN.

Love and Power

ST. JOHN'S, ESSEX, CONNECTICUT

{Jesus said} "I am the good shepherd. . . . I know my own and my own know me, as the Father knows me and I know the Father; and I lay down my life for the sheep."

(JOHN 10:11, 14-15)

An often-retold story in our family concerns some favorite cousins from Philadelphia, Sylvia and Frederic Nelson. We admired them for their cultivation and wit. They were attending a performance of Handel's *Messiah.* As you will recall, one of the well-known sections of the oratorio is from the prophet Isaiah: "All we like sheep have gone astray; we have turned every one to his own way" (53:6). In the fashion of Baroque vocal works, the various phrases are repeated many times. "All we like sheep have gone astray." The chorus sings, "We like sheep . . . we like sheep. We like sheep . . . we like sheep." Finally Frederic turned to Sylvia and muttered, "I like sheep too, in moderation."

When your rector and I selected this date for my next sermon at St. John's, I was thrilled because it was in Eastertide, far and away the most glorious season of the church year. I had forgotten that it was also Good Shepherd Sunday. When I looked up the lessons, I thought, oh, darn it, sheep again. I think I got too much of the Good Shepherd in Sunday school. Maybe it would have been all right in moderation, but there were just too many pictures of a soft-looking Jesus holding a fuzzy lamb. Even in my youth I thought it was sort of icky. Much as we might not want to admit it, there are similar problems with the 23rd Psalm. Sentimental overuse of that great Psalm has diluted its original power. Every clergyman will tell you that when people who haven't been to church for decades suddenly show up to bury a member of their family, ninety-nine times out of a hundred they will choose the 23rd Psalm for a reading. Why is this? Sadly, one reason is that it is the only part of the Bible they know. Another reason is all that imagery of still waters and green pastures and cups running over. If you didn't look at it too closely you might think it was an ad for an inn in Tuscany. Admittedly, however, there is another reason for its popularity that cuts much deeper and we'll get back to that shortly.

One of the hardest things about being a preacher and teacher in our time is that, except in some parts of the African-American community, Biblical memory no longer exists in the American church. It is impossible to recreate the situation of those who first heard Jesus' words *I am the good shepherd.* All the same, we have to try, because if we do, we will begin to see that it is not just a warm and fuzzy concept but also a reality of incomparable power.

One of the main differences between Jesus' audience and us today is intimate knowledge of the Hebrew Bible. Everything Jesus said in his earthly life was related to, or was inspired by, or was an exact quote from the Jewish scriptures. It is impossible to understand Jesus without some grasp of the Old Testament. When Jesus said, "I am the good shepherd," those who heard his words were immediately aware of a rich background stretching back through centuries of their own history. Americans today have such a poor knowledge of our own history that it is very difficult to think of analogies. Perhaps it will be helpful to think of how boring it is to listen to someone talking about people you have never met, compared to the way you react when the subject of conversation is people you know well. When Jesus said, "I am the good shepherd," those who heard him were on intimate terms with the image. They knew immediately that he wasn't talking about cuddling fuzzy animals.

The shepherd image was deeply embedded in the living faith of Israel. There are a number of important passages in the Old Testament that portray God as the shepherd of his people. That may sound ho-hum to you and me, but it was electrifying for those who, after the Resurrection, remembered how Jesus had spoken of himself. Listen to this crucial passage from Ezekiel, remembering that it was written when the people had been sent into miserable exile in heathen Babylon:

> For thus says the Lord God: Behold, I, I myself will search for my sheep, and will seek them out. As a shepherd seeks out his flock when some of his sheep have been scattered abroad, so will I seek out my sheep; and I will rescue them . . . I myself will be the shepherd of my sheep, and I will make them lie down, says the Lord God. I will seek the lost, and I will bring back the strayed, and I will bind up the crippled. . . . [For] you are my sheep, the sheep of my pasture, and I am your God, says the Lord God. (Ezek. 34:11-12, 15-16, 31)[1]

It is not easy for us to appropriate the impact of such a passage, and many others like it, upon the collective memory of a people who had been living for centuries under the rule of first one and then another colossal, overwhelming pagan culture. We just have to try to imagine what it meant to them to know that in spite of everything there were these promises that the Lord would bring them home again, restore their losses to them and shelter them from every evil.

With this little bit of background it is perhaps possible to glimpse the impact of the way Jesus talks about himself. In the New Testament, the motif of the shepherd — remarkably — is no longer used to refer to God the Father. The imagery has shifted entirely to Jesus. This is true in all four Gospels, but it is most obvious in John's Gospel: "I am the good shepherd; I know my own and my own know me. . . . My sheep hear my voice, and I know them, and they follow me; and I give them eternal life, and they shall never perish. . . . No one is able to snatch them out of the Father's hand. I and my Father are one" (John 10:14-15, 27-30).

[99]

So you see, these are not just sweet sayings about what a kind and loving person Jesus is. These are not just assurances that Jesus is going to stroke us a lot, as though he were some sort of New Age massage therapist. Everybody who knew the Jewish Scriptures knew that only God was able to fulfill the promises made through the prophet Ezekiel; therefore this utterance, "I am the good shepherd,"[2] makes Jesus equal to God, and the final clincher just nails that into place: "I and my Father are one."

What does this mean?

It means that ultimate power and ultimate love are united in one person. Let's think about that. Power and love are the two things people can't do without. Everybody knows about the data that has come in about children in orphanages in Romania and other places where they are not touched or held or talked to. The human being cannot thrive without love. We know that. What is less generally acknowledged is that powerlessness is very bad for human beings. Powerlessness produces anger, which produces paralyzing depression at one end of the spectrum and at the other, murderous violence. We are much less likely to admit the ill effects of powerlessness than of lovelessness. After all, giving love doesn't sound threatening. Granting power is another matter. All around the world, Christians on the top of the socioeconomic heap have talked endlessly about love while preventing people of a lower bracket from having any power. Power to the powerless is an infinitely threatening idea because it might mean that you and I have to give up some of it.

In the Good Shepherd, power and love meet. If the shepherd loves the sheep but cannot protect them, the image becomes merely sentimental. Any parent will understand this, because every parent must inevitably learn what it is like to be unable to protect your child from illness, or accident, or false choices. Faith cannot protect us or our children from the sorrows of life; but there is a reason for the fact that study after study shows that people of faith cope better in times of trouble. The reason is that a decision to trust Jesus is a form of re-empowerment.

There is a church group meeting over at the conference center

where I am staying. I had to go into the common
book, and I saw all the materials they had laid c
dles and images. There were mandalas and labyrint....
structions and all the other paraphernalia of '90s "spiritualit,
not see a Bible anywhere. It made me very sad. Why are ....
churches turning to these other avenues, looking for enlightenment
and wholeness and whatever, when the Good Shepherd is right at
hand, present with us in his own living Word?

My husband and I both have deceased fathers and elderly
mothers. We are aware for the first time that the death of the second parent, however much expected, will mark a watershed our
lives. Whether we human beings know it or not, we are all conclusively shaped by our childhood influences. The perpetual
strength of childhood memories, which get stronger as we grow
older, arise from the determinative experience of how we were
cared for, or not cared for. Here is the deep-down reason, under all
the sentimentality, for the perpetual popularity of the shepherd
image. In the inmost recesses of our being we are molded
throughout our lives by the universal human need for a mother or
father, and later a husband or wife or friend, who will live for us,
die for us, who will think of us and our welfare first, last and always, who will guarantee our security and never leave us or abandon us, never, never. And there is no such person, as I realize upon
contemplating the losses that lie ahead; my mother is going to
die, and everybody my age is going to die, and our children have
their own lives, and there is no person who can guarantee that I
will always be safe and never in want and never left alone, not
anyone, not anywhere.

"I am the good shepherd. . . . My sheep hear my voice, and I
know them, and they follow me; and I give them eternal life, and
they shall never perish, and no one shall snatch them out of my
hand" (John 10:14, 27-28). And Jesus continues, in words that
have no parallel in religious literature: "The good shepherd lays
down his life for the sheep. . . . For this reason the Father loves me,
because I lay down my life, that I may take it again. No one takes it
from me, but I lay it down of my own accord. I have power to lay it

down, and I have power to take it again; this charge I have received from my Father" (vv. 14, 17-18).

Here is the power, and here is the love. Do you see how the love between God the Father and God the Son issues forth in love so great that it gives itself up for the sheep? Life for the sheep comes through the death of the Shepherd. But that is not the end. Good Friday is not the end. "I have power to lay it down, and I have power to take it again; this charge I have received from my Father." The dominion of Death is blown to bits on Easter Day. The Good Shepherd is not dead. He is alive and speaking tenderly to you this very morning. "I know my own, and my own know me."

And so the little child enters upon life with the prayer,

Jesus, tender shepherd, hear me,
Bless thy little lamb tonight. . . .[3]

And the Christian at the end of life is committed to the care of that same tender and powerful shepherd in the great prayer of commendation:

Into thy hands, O merciful Savior, we commend thy servant, now departed. Acknowledge, we beseech thee, a sheep of thine own fold, a lamb of thine own flock, a sinner of thine own redeeming. Receive him [receive her] into the arms of thy mercy, into the blessed rest of everlasting peace, and into the glorious company of the saints in light.[4]

Jesus, the Good Shepherd: he alone is the loving and powerful One who is able to secure the safety and the fulfillment and the eternal destiny of his beloved children forever and ever, our Father and our Mother, the Resurrection and the Life, our Lord and our God.

AMEN.

Rewriting the Book of Love

CHRIST CHURCH, SHEFFIELD, MASSACHUSETTS

(This sermon was written for a congregation that included children and youth.)

> *Have this mind among yourselves, which is yours in Christ Je-*
> *sus, who, though he was in the form of God, did not count*
> *equality with God a thing to be grasped, but emptied himself,*
> *taking the form of a servant, being born in the likeness of men.*
> *And being found in human form he humbled himself and became*
> *obedient unto death, even death on a cross.*

(PHIL. 2:5-8)

The performance artist Laurie Anderson, whose new show is opening at the Brooklyn Academy of Music next week, is a reader of the Bible and the literary classics. According to *The New York Times* article about her, she deals in "big ideas" about history, philosophy, science and religion. Well, I don't know. She is very bright, very committed, and very well read, but not many people's ideas are as big as the Bible's ideas. She wrote a song called "Kerjillions of Stars" in which she sings "If I were queen for a day/ I'd give the ugly people all the money/I'd rewrite the book of love/ I'd make it funny." That sounds quite appealing, although I don't think we could call it a Big Idea. A lot of people have enjoyed imagining what they would do if they ran the world; her idea is more endearing than most. It wouldn't work, though. We know that. It's just an attractive fantasy.

In the beginning of our passage, Paul says he hopes that all the people in the Philippian church complete his joy "by being of the same mind, having the same love, being in full accord" (Phil. 2:2). Do you think that's possible? Have you ever seen a church where everybody was of the same mind and loved everybody the same and were in full accord? Isn't that just Paul imagining he's king for a day? I don't think it would work, do you? People just don't have the same mind and the same love. In the many churches I've belonged to over the years, there has always been a lot of fighting. People have disagreed about the music and the Sunday school and the color of the carpet in the church. I'm not kidding. I remember to this day when a committee of ladies in one church put a blue carpet in the chancel where it used to be red. A great uproar occurred. So it's hard for me to imagine everybody in the church being of one accord. Do you think the Christians of Paul's time maybe had less to fight about? After all, they didn't even have churches then, much less carpets. But let's not kid ourselves. There was plenty to fight about back in those days. If you read Paul's letters you'll see that Christians were fighting with each other, way back then, about what kind of food to eat and what kinds of prayers to say and whether Jesus really was raised from the dead or not. Paul even got into a huge public fight with Peter, if you can imagine that, about who was sitting with whom at the church supper (see Gal. 2:11-14). So how can Paul ask everybody to be of one mind? Is it just a fantasyland?

Paul goes on: "Do nothing from selfishness or conceit, but in humility count others better than yourselves. Let each of you look not only to his own interests, but also to the interests of others" (vv. 3-4). Is that just fantasy too? Who acts that way? Who "does nothing from selfishness"? The older I get the more I discover selfishness in myself. Even the good things I do, I do for selfish reasons, like wanting to feel good about myself. There was a news story two weeks ago about people who give their kidneys to strangers, even though the operation is painful and they are left with only one kidney. The article said that whereas this was certainly a noble thing to do, it might proceed out of a need to be regarded as heroic. I recognize that. So how can Paul expect the Philippian Christians or the Sheffield Christians or anybody else to be so unselfish?

Let's look back at Laurie Anderson. She sings, "I'd rewrite the book of love." That's the most interesting part of her song. Would you call that a Big Idea? Maybe so, maybe not. We can be sure of one thing, though; not in a million years could any human being come up with the Big Idea that we have in this passage from Philippians today, no matter how brilliant, well-read, or "spiritual" they are. I don't think a lot of Christian people realize this. We are so used to this Big Idea that we don't react to it. For a lot of us, coming to church is sort of routine. It even becomes predictable. We do more or less the same things every Sunday morning and go about our business during the week. We forget that we are here because of a staggeringly new thing that happened two thousand years ago. No scientist or philosopher or religious thinker who ever lived could ever have imagined One God in Three Persons with a Second Person, a Son, who would come into the world *to be crucified*.

Here's what Paul says. Verse 6: "Christ Jesus . . . was in the form of God [yet] did not count equality with God a thing to be grasped, but emptied himself, taking the form of a servant, being born in the likeness of men. And being found in human form he humbled himself and became obedient unto death, even death on a cross." Christ was in the form *(morphē)* of God . . . he took the form *(morphē)* of a slave *(doulos)*.[1] We all know about God becoming a human being because we hear about it so much at Christmas. God became a human baby and was born in the same messy way that all human babies are born. That in itself is mind-boggling if we really grasp it. But that's only the beginning. God did not become the Bill Gates or the Donald Trump of his time. He was not rich, not a celebrity, not elected to anything, not commander of anything. He became like a slave, one who belonged completely to others. Instead of being the boss of us, the Son of God let us be the boss of him. And what happened? We put him to death. Because he let us be the boss, he died the death of a slave. That's what happens when you and I get to be king or queen for a day.

Christ Jesus was in the form of God. He was at home in the

realm of pure love, pure light, pure power — the kind of power that God has, the power that works only for good, the power that makes everything beautiful and right. He left it all. "He emptied himself." He was in the *form of God;* he took the *form of a slave.* The King James Version says, "He made himself of no reputation." Can you imagine that? Most of us are forever trying to inflate our reputations. Most of us are jealous of others who are more successful, more accomplished, better looking, better athletes, taller, richer, whatever. The Son of God made himself of no reputation at all. He was born into a poor family of no social standing. He had to walk everywhere because he had no money to pay for an animal to ride on. He never had a house of his own. But what happened to him in the end was much worse than that. Paul says, "he humbled himself and became obedient unto death, even death on a cross." A lot of people today don't realize what that meant, because we have never seen a crucifixion. Everybody in Paul's time had seen one. People were put on crosses by the side of the road; you couldn't miss them. It was a horrible way to die, more horrible than you and I can begin to imagine, but that isn't the worst of it. The worst of it is that it was a form of execution by the state that declared a person to be totally outcast, not fit to have a decent death. It was a method specifically designed to be as degrading and dehumanizing as possible. Rich powerful people were never put to death that way; it was known as a death for slaves. So when Paul says that the Son of God "took the form of a slave" and became "obedient unto the death of a cross," he means something a lot more serious than you or I would normally realize.

What was the purpose of this? Why did the Son of God choose to give up all his privileges and come to die like that? Paul says that "he humbled himself and became obedient." This means that he became obedient to God the Father. Let's see if we can grasp this next idea because it is part of the truly Big Idea. Jesus rewrote the book of love. He wrote it in his own life. It had to be written over again because you and I and Laurie Anderson and everybody else messed it up. The way to be perfectly loving is to be perfectly obedient to our heavenly Father, and we aren't and we can't and we don't. That's why we have war and crime and violence. That's why even the most loving families have problems that stretch down the generations. That's why we have shootings in schools. Don't you believe that the parents of Eric and Dylan, the Columbine High School killers, loved their sons? Of course they did. Human love is not good enough. We have strayed too far from the center of God's will. The book of love had to be rewritten *from that center* — not from *our* wills, but from *God's* will. The Son of God is the only one who could do that, and the Son of God is the one who did do it. He stepped into our place and lived out the story the way it was supposed to be lived, without a single break between the will of the Father and his own will. And in doing that, he gave himself up to us, loving us without reservation, without qualification, without conditions. He let us be the boss so that we could see just how much we really were set against God. If there had been any doubt about it before, there couldn't be any doubt about it now. God came among us making blind people see, lame people walk, poor people joyful, mentally ill people sane, dead people alive again, offering us all the bottomless resources of his love, and what did we do? All the religious people and all the political people got together and put him on a cross. So the Cross reveals to us just how godless we really were. Jesus took all of that onto himself when he died a godless death.

He rewrote the book of love. He is the only one who could do it, and he is the only rewriter we will ever need. He rewrote it in his life and in his death, by being perfectly at one with God's will all his life, and by giving himself up to the worst we could do in his death, so as to pour his divine life into our sinful human life. That's what love really is. The will of the Father and the Son together was that Jesus would relive our human life for us in the right way so that we would be saved from our disobedient, selfish, messed-up wills. By rewriting the story of love in his own life, by taking the form of a slave to show that he belonged to others — to us — and not to himself, by pouring out the last drop of his blood and the last breath of his body, by holding back absolutely nothing of himself whatsoever, he has brought us into the safety of his realm of perfect love forever. This love now is given to you and to me; we receive it into our hearts when we hear this Word, into our hands when we come to Communion.

So the ugly people are going to get the money after all. You and I are the "ugly people," every one of us, and the "money" is the everlasting love of God in Jesus Christ. The ugly people put Jesus on the Cross, but he never stopped loving us and he is going make us beautiful. He is going to give us all his riches. Paul said exactly the same thing in a different way in another letter: "For you know the grace of our Lord Jesus Christ, that though he was rich, yet for your sake he became poor, so that by his poverty you might become rich" (2 Cor. 8:9). This is the Biggest Idea of all time. The new life in Christ is no fantasy. It is real because God is real. Yes, there will be church fights. Yes, we will have disagreements. Yes, there will continue to be sin until Jesus comes back the second time to make everything right forever. But what Paul wants us to remember is that even now we can "have this mind among ourselves that we have in Christ Jesus." Because he has rewritten the story, we do not have to be prisoners of our worst selves anymore. That's why Paul is so confident. We can actively move toward "being of the same mind, having the same love," because we know that God has moved toward us. We know that at any moment of our lives, God may break through with yet another miracle of rewriting.

What is bothering you right now? What is hindering love and unity here at Christ Church? What steps can you take to rewrite your own story? You can be sure that the Lord is already at work to break down those barriers and create in you the mind of Christ. You never know at what moment that might be. This very day he might be calling you to perform a miracle of love and humility that you never thought you were capable of. And you know what? It will make you laugh. It will be both fun and funny. "Rejoice in the Lord always; again I will say, Rejoice" (Phil. 4:4).

AMEN.

THE GOSPEL AND RELIGION

No Religion Here Today

RENSSELAERVILLE, NEW YORK

God has consigned all human beings to disobedience — in order that he may have mercy upon all.

(ROM. 11:32)

Summer preaching programs like the one you have here in your lovely setting are typically made up of an eclectic variety of voices. This can be interesting, but it can also be disconcerting. One week there is a trendy cleric bent on overturning all the received wisdom of the church, and the next week you get a Bible-thumping evangelical. What's a summer churchgoer to do? The time-honored, if not indeed downright fashionable stance is that it is all rather like a panel discussion or colloquium that one goes to at one's college ten or twenty years after graduation; hearing all those different viewpoints is challenging and educational and one comes away feeling intellectually improved while at the same time rather relieved that there has been no necessity for committing oneself one way or the other. You may feel at the end of this service that the preacher has not quite played fair with this expectation today, but then, a gospel sermon is always subversive in some way. In just what way, only the Holy Spirit fully knows . . . so let us stop talking about it and get right down to it.

Here goes with an opening question. What is religion, and

what is its purpose? Is it of any real use, or is it just a question of "whatever works for you"? The dictionary gives a number of definitions of religion, all of them originating as human activities: worship, belief, ritual. "Religion" is what we make it. It moves from the human being to God; the arrow points from earth to heaven. The key ingredient in religion is the spiritual capacity and development of the religious person. This is such a familiar idea to all of us, whether we are believers or not, that it comes as quite a shock to discover from the Scriptures of the Old and New Testaments that *God is not interested in religion.*

We have heard a reading from the apostle Paul's letter to the Romans. In the fourth and fifth chapters of that crucial document, we come across a word and a phrase, repeated twice, that undercut the notion of religion altogether, exposing its weakness and making it obsolete. Paul says in Romans 4 that Father Abraham trusted in the God "who justifies the *ungodly,*" and in Romans 5 he writes these key words: "While we were still helpless, Christ died for the ungodly." Here is the irreducible core, the nerve center, the heart and soul of the Christian faith. Notice that it is the exact opposite of the good old American gospel, "God helps those who help themselves." Contrary to public opinion, this bromide is not now and never has been in the Bible. Instead, we read, "While we were still *helpless* Christ died for the ungodly."

People prefer the good old American version of this proclamation because the Biblical version is so radical. If God has made the ungodly and the irreligious the object of his special concern, what is the purpose of religion? It is fascinating to observe how often this phrase of Paul's is glossed over or ignored altogether. I remember once being asked to write something for an important church publication. I sent it off to the person in charge, who, as it happened, was a prominent evangelical bishop. When it was published, the reference that I had made to the text about the justification of the ungodly had been excised. It had simply disappeared.

Paul has always made people nervous, and this is the reason. He seems to be knocking the props out from under everything religious and controllable. Religion, being a human construct, allows people to create a God after their own image instead of the other way round. Religion makes God more manageable by setting up conditions that God will be bound by. At the risk of sounding crass, we can put it this way: religion is a human means of putting God in our debt, as though God owed us something for our faith.

Christians are just like everybody else in that we are constantly slipping back into religion. When we get mad at God because he didn't answer our prayers the way we wanted; when we adjust the Scriptures or the Creeds to suit the latest trends; when we think that in some way or other we have figured out how to make Christian faith *work for us,* then we have fallen away from the gospel and back into religion.

In religion, there are always *distinctions.* When we say "God helps those who help themselves," we are neatly making a distinction between ourselves — the religious, the moral, and the worthy — and others who do not help themselves and are therefore among the ungodly. These distinctions that we make run all through religion: some people are more spiritual than others; God listens to certain people's prayers in a special way; a few people are so godly that they become saints; certain types of good works qualify a person more than other people. As soon as we start thinking like that, we are becoming "religious," and that means that we are moving away from the unique truth of Christianity, back into the world of "God helps those who help themselves."

Christianity in its true sense is not a religion because religion depends for its validity upon human spiritual endeavor, whereas Scripture sweeps all that away. Isaiah says that even "our righteous deeds are like filthy rags" (64:6) compared to the righteousness of God; Paul, again in Romans, declares, "There is no distinction" (3:22), and, "a blessing [is pronounced] upon the person whom God reckons righteousness *apart from works*" (4:6). Thus the entire foundation of religion, namely human spiritual attitudes, achievements, and accomplishments, is removed. What religion would say that its adherents needed to become irreligious? It would be putting itself out of business! Yet that is exactly what Paul is saying. God does not sit at the summit of human religious achievement, waiting for us to make it to the top; God is down in the valleys where sinful human beings are struggling with their daily lives.

When religion is put out of business, there is a radical leveling. This is part of what scares people so much about Paul's letters. The idea that no one has any spiritual advantage over anyone else terrifies us. The whole purpose of religion is to show that God is on our side, whereas the first two and a half chapters of Romans are written precisely to show that God is not on anyone's "side." Paul brings that section of the letter to a ringing conclusion with "there is none righteous, no, not one," and "there is no distinction, since all have sinned; they are justified by his grace *as a gift*" (Rom. 3:10, 22-23).

Religion is a way of getting God on our side so he can't say "no" to us. We perform our religious and moral duties as we conceive of them, and we expect God to live up to his side of the bargain. This kind of thinking is perpetuated by snappy book titles like *Why Bad Things Happen to Good People.* From the standpoint of mature Christian faith this way of formulating the problem is fundamentally mistaken, because we cannot bargain with God not to let bad things happen to us, and none of us is "good" enough anyway. It has been suggested, only partly in jest, that a title more in the spirit of radical Christianity would be *Why Do Good Things Happen to Bad People?*

Yet we spend our energies, day and night, on strategies to convince ourselves and others that we are "good." As T. S. Eliot wrote in his play *The Cocktail Party,* we are "absorbed in the endless struggle to think well of [our]selves." There are many strategies for doing this. Many religious people become convinced, perhaps even from reading the Old Testament itself, that God is indeed not interested in piety ("Take away from me the noise of your songs; I hate, I despise your feast days" — Amos 5:21-23). This enables them to substitute instead what is called "good works," which then become subtly transmuted into another kind of religion where some do good works by the ton and others fail to measure up.

There are many different kinds of religion. When Helen Gurley Brown published her book about women over fifty, there was a very funny review of it in *The New York Times Book Review* by Judith Viorst. It seems that Ms. Brown has a religion of her very own. She forbids guilt concerning sex — the more of that commodity the better, with or without love — but she definitely believes in sin. According to Ms. Viorst, Ms. Brown uses the word "sin" repeatedly to describe eating too much. She is equally hard on women who don't exercise according to her standards, and woe betide the poor soul who falls ill, because she must have brought it on herself with unhealthy attitudes. I can definitely relate to that last one, because I pride myself on never getting sick. I was badly wounded in my vanity when I got the flu last winter. Sickness, like the gospel, is a great leveler.

Jesus of Nazareth treated people with sovereign freedom. In his approach to them, he gave no advantage to the religious. For instance, in the fourth chapter of John's Gospel, we are told that he makes a special point of addressing an ungodly person — a Samaritan, and a woman at that — causing her to become an agent and messenger of his good news. The story is a breakout moment in the Gospel of John; it represents the movement of the good news of Jesus from the religious to the unreligious, the righteous to the unrighteous, the correct to the incorrect. But note this: Jesus does not say *yes* to a person without saying *no* also. His address to the Samaritan woman includes an unmasking of her sin, for she has gone through five husbands and now has a live-in boyfriend. Helen Gurley Brown would approve; Jesus does not. Yet he says no to the sin (by bringing it into the light) with the express purpose of saying yes to the sinner. The Samaritan woman becomes a new person because of the word Jesus has spoken to her. It is the same with the woman taken in adultery; Jesus' words to her, "Go and sin no more," are preceded and made operative by "Neither do I condemn thee" (John 8:11).

The basis of liberal religion, or so its proponents in the mainline denominations say, is the desire to be "inclusive." But the supposed inclusivity of religion always fails at the sticking point, because, eventually, somebody has got to say no somewhere to somebody. We can't just be endlessly permissive. The difference between religion and the gospel is that God has said no to *everybody,* so that no one can boast before God. As Paul puts it in the climactic eleventh chapter of Romans, "God has consigned all men to disobedience" (11:32).

That is a startling text if you have never heard it before. Chapters 9-11 of Romans have often been suppressed in the church because they are so radical. "God has consigned all human beings to disobedience." This means that there really is no one who can claim to be righteous, and that there are indeed therefore no distinctions among us. Our common denominator is our human frailty. This realization of our solidarity is the foundation of the Christian community when it is working the way it is supposed to. Romans 11:32 has for some years been one of the defining texts for my own congregation of Grace Church in New York. It comes at the end of a section in Romans in which Paul has declared the freedom of God from all religious criteria whatever, at which point the apostle breaks out into a paean of ecstatic praise. Listen now to the rest of this astonishing verse: God has consigned all human beings to disobedience — "in order that he may have mercy upon all." All! Not just the righteous, not just the slender, the toned, the healthy, not just the politically correct or the socially correct or the top income earners or the members of the right clubs but *all* are to be recipients of the mercy of God.

You see, we are all Samaritan women. Helen Gurley Brown is one too, though perhaps she does not know it. Along with "the fat, the flabby and the flu-ridden" (Ms. Viorst's words), she too is a Samaritan woman; she is not excluded. I, too, I am a Samaritan woman — one of the ungodly — and so I have no advantage over her and she has no advantage over me. "There is no distinction"; she and I and you, *all* of us are in need of the living water that Jesus gives.

There is a line in *Much Ado About Nothing* that (and this is so typical of Shakespeare) precisely illustrates our text. Dogberry, the comical constable who always gets his ideas mixed up, says to one of the malefactors in his custody, "O villain! Thou wilt be condemned into everlasting redemption." Think of it! You and I, too, are "condemned into everlasting redemption." There is nothing in "religion" equal to this message. There is nothing else like this declaration of freedom from sin, freedom from guilt, freedom from failure, freedom from condemnation, not on account of our deserving but on account of God's mercy.

So there is good news today. The arrow doesn't point from us to God. It points from God to us. He has arrived with salvation for all. There is good news for Samaritans, good news for the irreligious, good news for the ungodly. There is good news for sinners of all sorts, and good news also for those who do not even know that they are sinners. This is the only true "inclusivity."

Jesus said to the Samaritan woman, "If you knew who it is that is saying to you, 'Give me a drink,' you would have asked him and he would have given you living water."

The woman said to him, "I know that the Messiah is coming, he who is called Christ; when he comes, he will show us all things."

"Jesus said to her, 'I who speak to you am he'" (John 4:10, 25-26).

Jesus speaks to you today. He addresses you in the midst of your struggles to make something of your life. He offers you living water. He does not offer you "religion"; what sort of good news would that be? He offers you himself. He goes to his death in order to take our condemnation away. *His* condemnation becomes *our* everlasting redemption. Let us ask him to give us that living water, for the pinnacle of spiritual achievement is no achievement at all, but the stretching out of empty hands to Jesus, with the prayer, "Lord, have mercy on me, a sinner," and the certainty that the answer will be *yes*.

AMEN.

The Once and Future Doctrine

ST. JOHN'S CHURCH, ESSEX, CONNECTICUT

Text: The Epistle to the Galatians

(N.B.: The translation used herein is J. Louis Martyn's,
in his Anchor Bible commentary on Galatians)

D id you see the front page of the Friday *New York Times*? Here it is. Right here along with Clinton's visit to China we see this headline: "Vatican Settles a Historic Issue With Lutherans." Gustav Niebuhr, the *Times* religion reporter, writes that a new declaration soon to be signed by both churches is "intended to resolve an issue that split the Western Christian world nearly 500 years ago." Do you know what that issue is? I could hardly believe my eyes when I read the article. This is potentially the most important development in Christian faith and life in 1,600 years, and I'm not exaggerating.[1] The document is called "A Joint Declaration on the Doctrine of Justification."

The doctrine of justification lies at the very heart of the faith, yet most Episcopalians have no idea how foundational it is. If you wanted to find the most concentrated teaching on justification in the Bible, where would you look? You would look in the Epistle to the Galatians, the most radical piece of writing in human history, and there is not likely to be any competition for the title until Judgment Day.[2]

I think the people who put together the Sunday readings for the church must have been afraid of Galatians. Very little of it is in the lectionary. It only comes around once every three years, for a mere four Sundays. Some of the most important parts of Galatians never get read in church at all, unless a preacher decides to jump the fence, which is what I am going to do this morning.

The first thing you need to know about this letter from Paul to the congregation in Galatia is that it's a dispatch from the field of battle. Paul understands himself to have been directly commissioned by Jesus to be the commander of the gospel forces.[3] "Onward, Christian soldiers" is his motto. There is a war on and Paul sees that the enemy has seized an advantage. Paul sends a set of marching orders. There's no time to be bothered with the usual formalities. He leaves out most of the customary greetings that people of his time used at the beginning of letters and he says, abruptly, "You are rapidly defecting from the God who called you in his grace, and are turning your allegiance to a different gospel" (1:6). In other words, the Galatian Christians are on the verge of going over to the enemy. Who is the enemy? Well, they are Christian teachers who came into Galatia after Paul left. Here's what Paul says about them: "They wish to change the gospel of Christ into its opposite." Two teachings: one is the gospel, and the other is the opposite of the gospel. Paul says, "If someone is preaching to you a gospel contrary to the one you originally received, let him stand under God's curse" (1:9). It isn't polite, but this is a theological emergency.

Paul uses opposites constantly in his preaching and teaching. In the Epistle to the Galatians, the principal opposites are slavery versus freedom, and flesh versus Spirit. Paul says that the teachers "came in stealthily in order to spy out our freedom that we have in Christ Jesus, their purpose being to enslave us" (2:4).

Everybody in America loves the idea of freedom. It's our thing. Christian freedom, however, is very different from American-style freedom. In America, we have built an altar to the idea of freedom of choice. "Free will," we call it. For Paul, as well as for Sigmund

Freud in our own time, there is no such thing as "free will." Our human wills are bound over to error and impulse.[4] For Paul, true freedom is freedom *from* self-will. In the realm of the Holy Spirit, our wills become identical to God's will.

Let me try to illustrate this. A lot of us are really trying not to be prejudiced or racist. Yet our subconscious keeps sending signals to our conscious mind that we don't intend. We catch ourselves looking down on others because of their appearance or their clothes or their behavior, even though we don't mean to be doing it. We are not as much in control of our thoughts and actions as we think we are. Knowing that racism is against the will of God doesn't stop those impulses from reaching our brain.

I mentioned Judgment Day. You may think you don't believe in Judgment Day, but you do. Everybody does. If we don't believe in it for ourselves, we believe in it for somebody else. Albert Camus, the French writer, created a powerful, worldly character for his novel *The Fall (La Chute)*. Here is what the character says:[5]

> People hasten to judge in order not to be judged themselves. . . . Each of us insists on being innocent at all costs, even if he has to accuse the whole human race and heaven itself . . . the essential thing is that [we] should be innocent. . . . As I told you, it's a matter of dodging judgment. . . . I'll tell you a big secret, *mon cher*. Don't wait for the Last Judgment. It takes place every day.

An article in *The New York Times* described the lives of the men who were held hostage by rebels for 126 days in Lima, Peru, last year. During their long incarceration, they had no idea if they would ever get out alive. Many of them, wrote the reporter, began to think of dodging judgment. They drew up "the balance sheets of their lives." Some of them, the article continued, "turned to religion."[6]

Well, it all depends on what kind of religion. The message of the Bible is that the gospel of Jesus Christ is not religion at all. If you look up the word "religion" in the dictionary, you will see that religion is something that *human beings* do. (Paul calls it the Law.)

Religion is defined as belief, ritual, reverence, morality, spirituality. The Christian gospel is not any of that at all. The gospel is from beginning to end something that *God* does, not something that *we* do. That's why Galatians is so radical. If you really understand Galatians you come to see that the gospel of Jesus Christ means the end of religion.

Religion is what people do to escape judgment. Religion is what human beings use to make the balance sheet of their lives come out right. We go through certain motions in order to convince ourselves and others that we are on the right side of God, whoever God might be. We go to church some of the time, we pray some of the time, we give a little bit of our money occasionally, we do a good deed here and there, and we figure that's enough, or we hope that's enough — or maybe we worry that it's not enough. Well, you know what? The message of the Bible from end to end is this: *it's not enough.* It's not enough, writes Paul, because "by works of the law shall no one be justified" [or *rectified*] (Gal. 2:16). Whatever it is that you are counting on to clear you in the Day of Judgment, it's not enough. Why? It's not enough, because try as we might, we live under the power of sin and death. The whole Bible is about that. When we say we have "free will," we mean that we can make decisions about this or that. We can "just say no" if we want to. But can we? The "just say no" campaign against drug use has been widely ridiculed because people came to see that it's not so simple. Some people can't say no. Other people are not even tempted to take drugs. For instance, I never wanted to take drugs in my life. Does that mean I get a star in my crown? Does that mean I can look down my nose at someone who is vulnerable to that temptation in a way that I am not? Does that mean I can stand at the pearly gates and demand to get in because I "just said no" when somebody offered me a joint? Of course not. I can't take any credit for not taking drugs since I never wanted to take them in the first place. That was never something that I decided for myself. It was God's gift to me, not my own merit. Free will, in that case, meant freedom from having to make a decision to use drugs or not to use them. I knew I wasn't going to do it, and that was that. In that case,

God's will for me and my own will coincided — according to his mercy.

But here is another angle on the matter. Procrastination is one of my besetting sins. It gets me into all kinds of trouble. I confessed this once to a Bible study group. A couple of weeks later a well-meaning person sent me a cassette tape. The name of the tape was "Twelve Easy Steps to Avoid Procrastination." I must admit I burst out laughing. That well-intentioned soul has not yet grasped the idea of the bound will. If I could avoid procrastination by taking twelve "easy" steps, my problem would have been solved long ago. And if there are any members of AA present, you know very well that if anybody tells you the Twelve Steps are "easy," they are sadly deceived.

The grace of God. That's what the gospel is about. It isn't about religious attitudes or beliefs or choices or works or spiritual exercises or anything else that human beings can dream up to do. It's about what *God* has done, what *God* is doing, what *God* will do. Paul hurls his missile at the Galatians because he sees the false teachers trying to drag them back into the realm of slavery where God's grace is dependent on our works. Here's the issue that the Catholic-Lutheran declaration addresses. Paul writes, "A person is not rectified [the balance sheet isn't made right] by works of the Law, but by the faith of Christ Jesus . . . not a single person will be rectified by works of the Law" (2:16-17).[7] This throws religion out of the window.

When we shoot down the Law like this, it seems as if all the underpinnings of everything are coming loose. Are we recommending immorality? Are we supporting vice? Paul dealt with versions of that question a thousand times. "Shall we sin that grace may abound?" . . . His answer was, "You were called to freedom, brothers and sisters; only do not allow freedom to be turned into a military base of operations for the flesh . . ." (5:13).[8] In today's reading Paul says: "Lead your daily life guided by the [Holy] Spirit, and you will not end up carrying out the impulsive desires of the flesh. . . . In the daily life of your community you are being consistently led by the Spirit, [so] you are not under the authority of the Law" (5:16, 18). In other words, the person who is being set right by the faith granted in Jesus will be led by the Holy Spirit to do those things that are right. If *The New York Times* is correct, that's exactly what the new declaration says, and the Catholics have moved toward the Protestants.[9]

How far are we prepared to go in teaching "the freedom we have in Christ Jesus"? The proclamation that we are now free from religion is the unique idea that sets Christianity apart from other faiths.[10] The Pharisees sensed this when they saw Jesus eating his meals with every sort of improper and godless person. We should remember that Jesus' ministry was implacably opposed by the religious leaders. This was not a coincidence. Those leaders sensed that they were going to lose control if the people started living according to the Spirit instead of the Law.

There's a war on, Paul explains: "The Flesh [sinful human nature] is actively inclined against the [Holy] Spirit, and the Spirit against the Flesh. Indeed, these two powers constitute a pair of opposites at war with one another" (5:17). The Galatian teachers said that the thing to do in this war is to get your will under control and do the right thing. They were trying to persuade the church that behaving in the right way is the primary message of religion. Paul mounted his counteroffensive as an apostle of the Lord. The balance sheets of our lives are never going to come out right, Paul is saying, because our human wills are bound over to sin. Behaving in the proper way never can and never will deliver us from judgment. The good news (the gospel) from God is that *God himself has acted* to create a completely new situation.

No matter what you may hear, Jesus was not a teacher of religion. He was, he is, and he will be the power and the agent of God's salvation. He is himself our deliverance from the judgment.[11] This was the great issue of the Protestant Reformation, and it remains a great issue of religion today, for it means the end of religion.[12] There is no freedom like Christian freedom. There is no merely "religious" message that can touch this for the liberation of the human spirit. That's why Paul ends his letter as we can end our lives, in total confidence that the balance sheet is made right in Christ: His final words to the Galatians are, "Let no one make trouble for me any more. For I bear in my body scars that are the marks of Jesus" (6:17). According to the limitless grace of God, may it be the same for us.[13]

AMEN.

SIN, EVIL, AND SUFFERING

God-damned Christians

ST. PAUL'S CHURCH IN RICHMOND, VIRGINIA

The five sermons this week have had one verse as their foundation, a verse written by Paul the Apostle to the Romans: "I am not ashamed of the gospel" (1:16).

Why, we might ask, should Paul be ashamed? What is there about the gospel to be ashamed of? Various cultural settings might call forth various answers to this question. For instance, we have been exploring the cultural embarrassment that Christians often feel today in conversations with sophisticated unbelievers. On the most fundamental level, however, the answer is more direct and specific. In Paul's time, it was the Cross of Christ that was shameful. Crucifixion was shameful. Crucifixion was deliberately designed to be the most degrading method of execution. We are not saying most painful or most prolonged. We were saying most degrading, most dehumanizing. The purpose of crucifixion was to display the person in a subhuman way. Historians of the Roman era have taught us that it was an obscene and revolting method and was designed to evoke disgust.[1]

What is the meaning of this? Why did the Son of God submit to this particular mode of execution? This is a very important question. The early Christians had quite a job on their hands, explaining why their Messiah had suffered a God-forsaken death. Here are four brief but crucial Biblical passages on the subject:

Sending his own Son in the likeness of sinful flesh and for sin,
[God] condemned sin in the flesh. (Rom. 8:3)

For our sake he [God the Father] made him [God the Son] to be
sin who knew no sin, so that in him [Christ] we might become
the righteousness of God. (2 Cor. 5:21)

Christ redeemed us from the curse of the law, having become a
curse for us — for it is written, "Cursed be every one who hangs
on a tree" [Deut. 21:21]. (Gal. 3:13)

He himself bore our sins in his body on the tree, that we might
die to sin and live to righteousness. (1 Pet. 2:24)

There is a common insight running through each of these passages. In various ways the New Testament is saying that human sin
entered into Jesus on the Cross. Sin is condemned *in the flesh* of Jesus. God made him *to be sin*. Jesus *became accursed* for us. He himself
bore our sins in his body on the tree. From here, it doesn't require too
much of a leap of the imagination to see that there must be some
connection between the hideousness of crucifixion and the ugliness
of sin.

Some of you are probably thinking at this point that you don't
want to hear any more about sin this noontime. There are many
people who would agree with you. I particularly remember a
woman I knew quite well in my former congregation. She told me
about a funeral she attended at a Roman Catholic church. The service was for a teenage girl who had been killed in an accident. As
my parishioner told me of the burial service, her voice trembled
with outrage. "They prayed for her sins to be forgiven!" she said in
passionate outrage. "Her *sins!* A fourteen year old *child!*" I have remembered this episode for a long time because it so clearly illustrates the confusion we are in. We think of sin as a series of misdeeds, but in Biblical theology it is a condition. As one of Flannery
O'Connor's characters says, sin is not something we *commit*, it's
something we *are in*.[2] Sin is "a powerful force that grips us beyond

the sovereignty of our wills." Sin cannot be fully explained "in terms of concrete actions wilfully committed, but as compulsions from which [we] cannot extricate [our]selves."[3]

The reaction of the parishioner to the prayer at the girl's funeral tells us something about ourselves. We are sentimental by nature. Flannery O'Connor defined sentimentality as an insistence on innocence. We want to believe in innocence. Childhood is supposed to be the essence of this quality. How young does a child have to be to serve as an example of innocence?[4] Here is a sample of childhood behavior. I read about this in *The Virginia Episcopalian,* as I am sure many of you did also. The story is taken from the memoirs of a heroic young man, Harry Merica, who has struggled all his life to overcome muscular dystrophy. His mother carried him in her arms to the school bus stop each day because he could not walk that far. His family was so poor that the only new things his family could afford each school year were paper and pencils. On the first day of school, he recalled, "One of the boys took one of my new pencils and broke it in half. That made me cry. Every person on the bus started to call me a crybaby. This, I think as I look back, was the cruelest thing that ever happened to me."[5]

A few years ago, pop singer Madonna said to an interviewer, "I was raised in a traditional Catholic environment. Shame and sin and guilt were a big part of how I was raised. I guess I'm trying to cast off those feelings through my work." This is a familiar refrain of our time, but it is based on a purely individualistic understanding of sin. If Madonna does not feel the weight of sin herself personally, she might reflect upon the condition of the human race at large. There are evils done to individuals by individuals, and there is evil done both to individuals and to groups by social or corporate structures. The breaking of Harry Merica's pencil would be an example of the former, and the massacres in Kosovo would be an example of the latter, but in both cases there are multiple forces at work. The child who broke the pencil was acting with confidence because he was pretty sure that his "society" (the other children on the bus) would support him and join in. Similarly, the rebel soldier in Sierra Leone who chops off the hands of a former friend and neighbor, for no reason except terror, has been conditioned to do this deed by his comrades-in-arms who aid and abet the atrocity.[6] It is impossible to unravel the interconnections between the individual and the corporate. That is why Ash Wednesday is a day set apart especially for corporate repentance; on that day, the church goes to its knees as representative of all humankind.

Am I talking too much about sin? I am talking about it for two reasons: (1) the Bible talks about it, and (2) it is a daily reality in my life. Three days ago I was driving from St. Paul's to Westhampton. I was in a hurry. I took several wrong turns and ended up on the south side of the James. It took me half an hour to get back into town and then I made yet another mistake as I tried to get onto Interstate 195 going west. I was frustrated and angry. Then I saw a sign, 195, and an opportunity. The only problem was that there was another sign, with an arrow going left and a line drawn through it. That meant that the turn I wanted to make was forbidden. I glanced around, looking for police, and decided to ignore the sign. I sped up and started to pull into the left lane to make the forbidden left turn. It is not an exaggeration to say that I missed a broadside collision and probable death by a fraction of an inch as a car I had not seen zoomed by me on the left. By a miracle of God's undeserved grace I swerved at the last second. The driver of a car coming up behind me blared his horn at me for a very long time as if to say, "I saw what you just did, you (expletive deleted)."

Sometimes when I tell a story like this people will say, "That's not sin!" They will say, well, you were tired, or you made a mistake, or you did a dumb thing, but it wasn't a *sin*. People say those things partly because they are trying to make me feel better but also because they don't understand what sin is. In this episode on the highway, we see how deeply ingrained certain attitudes are within the human being. In making that forbidden left turn, I had acted on the assumption that the rules did not apply to me. I did not take proper precautions. I put other lives in danger. I did not think of what it might mean to my family if I were killed. I put my own wishes ahead of the common good. Perhaps worst of all, I presumed upon God's mercy.[7] These traits are so tenaciously imbedded in human personality that we scarcely think about them. The Christian tradition has taught us to call them sin, but the Christian tradition is weakened and diluted nowadays and we think that we will be better off if we don't talk about sin any more in this enlightened age. If we can just get our consciousness right — so the thinking goes — we can eliminate these problems.

What have we seen in the past year in America? We have seen a young man crucified on a fence simply because he was homosexual. We have seen a man dragged to death simply because he was black. In the news this week is a story about a young man tormented for hours and then set on fire simply because he was retarded. These stories grip us because we are able to identify with the victims in a new way that enlarges our consciousness. What we are less likely to understand or identify with is the sickness in the souls of the perpetrators.

This morning, it is impossible not to be moved by the front-page pictures of the black and white sheriffs embracing in Jasper, Texas. If we are going to have the death penalty at all, John William King, who dragged James Byrd to death, is the one to have it for. But reflect a moment on the spectators in Jasper who watched King being led away. They jeered, "Bye, bye, King!" and "Rot in hell!" Executing a person like King perpetuates the delusion that if we can just get rid of evil people we can solve our own problems. It allows us to feel superior without going through the process of examining our own souls. Projecting our own fears and hatreds onto a person like King is easy. It is far more difficult to confess our own sin and seek transformation. Jesus died not only for the victims *but also for the perpetrators.* "He was numbered among the transgressors" as Isaiah said. He was crucified between two malefactors (*male-factor,* one who does evil). If we are not willing to acknowledge Jesus' death for the perpetrators as well as the victims, then, whether we realize it or not, we are rejecting what he has done for us, ourselves.

Will Campbell of Tennessee and Mississippi is one of the truly radical Christians of our time. He risked his life for civil rights repeatedly during the '60s, yet he never cut his connections to members of the Ku Klux Klan. He has been for many years a living parable of Jesus' death for victims and victimizers alike. Just a few months ago, Will, now approaching his eighties, was in the news again. I ask you to excuse the language in the story I am going to tell, because Will is quite a character and without the salty language it won't be an authentic Will Campbell story. For several days last year the Mississippi trial of Sam Bowers for the murder of Vernon Dahmer was on the front page of *The New York Times*. Sam Bowers, the Grand Imperial Wizard of the Klan, is believed to have ordered the deaths of several people, but Vernon Dahmer was the best-known. A courageous local leader in the voter registration drive, Dahmer was burned to death by the Klan, defending to the end his blazing home as his wife and children fled out the back door.

Sam Bowers was tried and acquitted twice in Mississippi. The third time, in 1998, it was a foregone conclusion that this time he would be convicted. Will Campbell attended the trial every day. He mostly sat with the Dahmer family, but from time to time he would go over and sit with Sam Bowers, whom he has known for forty years. The Dahmer family today is large and loving; Sam Bowers is almost alone in the world. Will Campbell went back and forth. After the trial was over, a mystified reporter asked him, "Mr. Campbell, why do you seem to be on both sides?" Will answered, "Because I'm a God-damned Christian."

Yes. We are all God-damned Christians — literally. As Paul wrote in Galatians 3:13, we are under God's curse on account of sin. Here are Paul's exact words: "Christ redeemed us from the curse of the law, having become a curse for us." This helps us to understand the hideous shamefulness of crucifixion. "God made him to be sin who knew no sin." Human sin entered into Jesus on the Cross. He had never experienced sin before; until that moment, *he knew no sin*. No wonder he said, "My God, My God, why hast thou forsaken me?" In the Cross of Jesus, we see the God-forsakenness of sin. The Son of God was broken for Harry Merica's broken pencil, for James Byrd's broken body, for John William King's broken soul, for my broken self and your broken self.

And in the same moment we see the victory of God over sin.

As the first epistle of Peter says, "He himself bore our sins in his body on the tree, that we might die to sin and live to righteousness" (2:24). All week we have been reading from the first part of Paul's letter to the Corinthians, where Paul sets the Cross at the very center of the Christian message. Here from the fifteenth chapter of that very letter is his conclusion, and mine:

> If Christ has not been raised, your faith is futile and you are still in your sins. . . . But in fact Christ has been raised from the dead, the first fruits of those who have fallen asleep. For as by a man came death, by a man has come also the resurrection of the dead. For as in Adam all die, so also in Christ shall all be made alive. (1 Cor. 15:17-22)

AMEN.

Common Sense,
or Christ Crucified?

CHRIST CHURCH, GREENWICH, CONNECTICUT

I decided to know nothing among you except Jesus Christ and him crucified.

(1 COR. 2:2)

A few years ago I had a good-natured dispute with a friend of mine. He was an admirer of a certain well-known celebrity preacher. I said I thought this preacher was shallow. My friend, a businessman, said, as though to clinch the argument, "He's not shallow! He preaches good common sense!"

I thought about that last month when I read the coverage about Pope John Paul's visit to St. Louis. As you know, a front-page news event took place there. The pope made a direct personal appeal to the governor of Missouri for the life of a prisoner on Death Row. The governor, to the amazement of many — perhaps most of all himself — actually responded to the pope's appeal and commuted the sentence to life in prison without parole. In the wake of this surprising event, many newspapers conducted interviews with Catholics and other Americans. One woman said that, as a Catholic, she was "totally against" abortion, but not capital punishment. She said, "I feel, God forgive me for saying this, that it may be common sense to have the death penalty."[1]

Last week and this week, we have been reading Paul's first letter to the Corinthian church. In our lesson for today, he writes as follows:

> When I came to you, brethren, I did not come proclaiming to you the testimony of God in lofty words of wisdom. For I decided to know nothing among you except Jesus Christ and him crucified. And I was with you in weakness and in much fear and trembling; and my speech and my message were not in plausible words of wisdom, but in demonstration of the Spirit and of power, that your faith might not rest in the wisdom of men but in the power of God. (1 Cor. 2:1-5)

Last week's reading and this one lie at the nerve center of Paul's teaching and therefore at the very heart of the Christian gospel. Paul's message, for which he lived and for which he died, was the exact opposite of common sense. That's the whole point of the passage for today. I did not speak in plausible words, the apostle insists. I did not come to tell you something that you could have figured out for yourselves. I did not come to Corinth with new packaging for generally accessible religious truth. I did not come, he declares, with popular wisdom or, indeed, with any kind of human wisdom at all. Going back to last week's lesson, this is what Paul says he came with:

> For Christ did not send me to . . . preach the gospel . . . with eloquent wisdom, lest the cross of Christ be emptied of its power. For the word of the cross is folly to those who are perishing, but to us who are being saved it is the power of God. For it is written, "I will destroy the wisdom of the wise, and the cleverness of the clever I will thwart." Where is the wise man? Where is the scribe? Where is the debater of this age? Has not God made foolish the wisdom of the world? (1 Cor. 1:17-20)

So you can see that Paul insists in the strongest possible terms that the Christian gospel is precisely *not* common sense. Paul does not set the gospel alongside common sense as though they can be friends. He sets it *over against* common sense and conventional wisdom and, for that matter, even the Olympian wisdom of the Greeks, so widely revered throughout the educated world. Why does the apostle do this? What is it about the Christian faith that makes it so intractably, so perversely, even so outrageously *opposite?* It is not wisdom, it is not cleverness, it is not plausibility, it is not common sense. What is it then? Paul has one word for what it is. It is Power. "For the word of the cross is folly to those who are perishing, but to us who are being saved it is the power of God."

When we consider this word "power," everything depends on the context. The message of the New Testament is power, all right, but be assured, it is a strange kind of power. One time when Paul had prayed earnestly for deliverance from his "thorn in the flesh" (whatever it was), God's answer came to him. The "thorn" would not be removed, said the Lord, "for my power is made perfect in weakness" (2 Cor. 12:9).

Next Sunday will be the last Sunday of the Epiphany season. Already we are turning our eyes toward Ash Wednesday. Much as we might like to think of our religious faith as positive thinking, as spiritual uplift, as a program for personal improvement, Lent will not allow it. The approach of Lent means that you and I, the people of God, are going to be turning our attention to what Paul calls "the word of the cross."

I just saw a full-page ad in *The New York Times* for a new book by John Gray called *How to Get What You Want and Want What You Get.* I have not read this book and for all I know it may have some good stuff in it. But listen to this ad copy:

John Gray offers the ultimate guide to personal success. Combining insights from Western psychology and Eastern meditation, he presents a brilliantly innovative program that points the way to joy, confidence and contentment in just four easy-to-

follow steps. You'll release your emotional blocks and realize your
soul's desire. . . .

Do you find that funny? It seems to me that anyone who is any
kind of Christian would find it preposterous and even hilarious.
What does a full-page ad in the *Times* cost? Five thousand? Ten
thousand? Obviously the publisher thinks this book is going to sell
a zillion copies. I guess there are a lot of people who really do believe that somewhere, somehow, there are four easy steps. But the
word from the Scripture today is that if the steps to "joy, confidence, and contentment" are "easy," then they are bogus and the
promises they hold out are false from beginning to end. *There are no
easy steps,* not even to a flat stomach. Compare these four steps,
whatever they are, with the twelve steps of AA. As every member of
AA knows, nobody says they are going to be easy. In fact, they are so
hard that you have to be part of a community of support in order to
make any progress at all.

Well, the Corinthian church was sold on easy answers too.
They thought they had discovered the true spirituality and it was
going to be clear sailing.[2] Paul writes to explain that they have it all
wrong:

> For since, in the wisdom of God, the world did not know God
> through wisdom, it pleased God through the folly of what we
> preach to save those who believe. For Jews demand signs and
> Greeks seek wisdom, but we preach Christ crucified, a stumbling
> block to Jews and folly to Gentiles, but to those who are called,
> both Jews and Greeks, Christ the power of God and the wisdom
> of God. For the foolishness of God is wiser than men, and the
> weakness of God is stronger than men. (1 Cor. 1:21-25)

We preach Christ crucified. You and I are so accustomed to looking at crosses around people's necks and on top of steeples that we
are immune to the shock of it. It is hard for us to understand what
an affront to common sense it was to preach a crucified Messiah.
The Messiah wasn't supposed to be pinned up alongside the dregs of

society to die a torturous death. The Messiah was supposed to offer "the ultimate guide to personal [and national] success." He was supposed to restore Israel's lost glory. It was supposed to be "morning in America," or morning in Israel, or morning in whatever country was in need of a Messiah. It was not supposed to be darkness at noon. Common sense had nothing to do with this event on Calvary.

Darrell J. Mease, the man whose sentence was commuted because of the pope's appeal, is certainly one of the least sympathetic killers one could imagine. His crime was a premeditated triple murder and one of the victims was a paraplegic. Even Mease's own defense attorney said, "Quite frankly, this case was probably one of the weaker clemency cases."[3] No common sense was involved here.

What *was* involved, then? What was involved when Jesus, the man who was without sin, was sentenced to the death penalty? Why was the Son of God executed, and in such a particularly horrible way?

"The word of the cross" was not easy to proclaim in Paul's time and it is not easy in ours. It is still a stumbling block to Jews (religious people) and foolishness to Greeks (secular people). Like the Corinthians, we would rather hear something more inspirational, more uplifting. Why was God's Messiah subjected to "cruel and inhuman punishment"? There is a great mystery about this. Have you thought about it? Perhaps every Sunday you say these words: "I believe in Jesus Christ our Lord, born of the Virgin Mary, suffered under Pontius Pilate, crucified, dead and buried." Notice how the creed skips from the birth to the crucifixion as though there was nothing in between. It is the Cross that sums up the life. Do you know why?

Mease's younger brother made a suggestive statement. He had always been an advocate of the death penalty. However, when his brother committed the triple murder and was sentenced to death, he became less certain. Before, he said, "I was looking at the victim's side. It's different when you're on the other side."

Let's see if we can get our minds around this. Jesus was put to death by the legitimate government of his time. He was publicly denounced by the Roman governor, flogged, and along with other criminals was taken outside the walls of the city, meaning that he was cast out of decent society. He was condemned to die by all the best people of church and state, condemned for crimes against religion and government. In other words, the Son of God voluntarily went over to "the other side," the side of the perpetrators. It is common to think of Jesus as a victim in solidarity with other victims, but that is not the most startling aspect of the Crucifixion. What should really rock us back on our heels is that he became "numbered with the transgressors" (Isa. 53:12). He became one with the malefactors. As Paul writes to the Corinthians a few chapters later, "[God] made him [Jesus] to be sin, who knew no sin" (2 Cor. 5:21).

So you see, Jesus is on both sides. He is on the side of the victims, and he is also on the side of the perpetrators. That is why the Christian gospel is so radical. It is radically inclusive in ways that the politically correct crowd doesn't dream of. The gospel refuses to divide the world up into the correct and the incorrect, the righteous and the unrighteous, the innocent and the guilty. Jesus takes all that into himself.

Not everyone will see this. Not everyone will have the eyes of their hearts opened. It is not by worldly wisdom. It is by revelation and faith. As Paul says, "We have received not the spirit of the world, but the Spirit which is from God, that we might understand the gifts bestowed on us by God. And we impart this in words not taught by human wisdom but taught by the Spirit" (1 Cor. 2:12-13). Up here in this pulpit there is a little plaque. It is a quotation from the Gospel of John. It says, "We would see Jesus." Every time I am in this pulpit I pray for the Holy Spirit to be with me so that you and I can see Jesus together. I pray for the Spirit to be with many of you so that "to us who are being saved [the word of the cross] is the power of God."

What is this foolishness, this *scandal* of the Cross? Who is it hanging there beaten, brutalized, bleeding? The Holy Spirit speaks to you now through the word of the Cross. This is no common sense. It is the power of God at work. Paul writes, "What no eye has seen, nor ear heard, nor the heart of man conceived, what God has prepared for those who love him, God has revealed to us through the Spirit" (1 Cor. 2:9-10). And what the Spirit reveals is the most unexpected, most outrageous, most scandalous thing in the history of religion: God has suffered cruel and inhuman punishment. This is what the Spirit reveals at the Cross: the One who hangs there is the Son of God, who suffered the death penalty instead of us. You and I were condemned to death because of sin. That is what we acknowledge on Ash Wednesday. Our situation could not be more serious. But something has happened to change that situation. Against all common sense, the power of God has intervened on our side through the sacrifice of the only Son for our sin. Who is Jesus? "For our sake [God] made him to be sin who knew no sin, *so that in him we might become the righteousness of God*" (2 Cor. 5:21). You, me, thieves, murderers, perjurers, frauds, failures, victims *and perpetrators* of all sorts, to us and for us the word of the Cross is the power of God for a transformed life. That is why the preacher today, a sinner like you, is "determined to know nothing among you except Jesus Christ and him crucified."[4]

AMEN.

Steering Toward the Pain

ST. PAUL'S CHURCH IN RICHMOND, VIRGINIA

I am not ashamed of the gospel.

(ROM. 1:16)

Why did Paul write to the Roman church, "I am not ashamed of the gospel"? Yesterday I suggested that it is tempting to back off from the Christian message if we are seeking to be accepted in sophisticated circles. Today and tomorrow we are going to be more specific. The aspect of the gospel that was particularly shameful for Paul was the Crucifixion of Jesus.

When Paul wrote to the Christians in Corinth, he admitted forthrightly that the Cross is an offense. The Greek word is *skandalon;* the Cross is *scandalous,* a *stumbling block.* He writes, "Jews demand signs and Greeks seek wisdom, but we preach Christ crucified, a stumbling block to Jews and folly to Gentiles, but to those who are called, both Jews and Greeks, Christ the power of God and the wisdom of God" (1 Cor. 1:22-24). "Jews demand signs." *Jews* here doesn't mean Jews. It means religious people. *Greeks* can be construed to mean secular people. In that sense, nothing has changed. The religious people want to see signs and wonders, they want auras and angelic sightings and spiritual ecstasy. The secular people, on the other hand, want data, surveys, protocols, science, technology. Nobody — *nobody* — wants a crucifixion. A crucifixion was the most ungodly thing in the world. People in polite Roman society did not mention the subject of crucifixion; it was considered disgusting, revolting, beneath contempt. The Cross of Christ is therefore a stumbling block to religious people and foolishness to secular people. "But to those who are called, both Jews and Greeks, [it is] the power of God and the wisdom of God."

When I recently visited my sister in South Carolina, we attended Sunday services in a prominent African-American Baptist church there. I was struck by the number of references in the songs to the cleansing blood of Jesus, and the unabashed way that the preacher referred to sin. Once, when I was younger, I was the Good Friday preacher in a fancy Episcopal church (it will remain nameless). The rector was a great friend and booster, but he took me aside a few hours before the service and said, "I hope you're not going to say anything about the *blood.*" Being a young and inexperienced preacher at the time, I was intimidated by this. Now, years later, I am not ashamed of the gospel. The blood of Christ for our salvation is mentioned more than thirty times in the New Testament. There was certainly no squeamishness about the blood that Sunday morning in the black Baptist church. They sang a round of choruses, "There to my heart was the blood applied/Glory to his Name." It was wonderful. It was an experience of intense rejoicing that God in Christ is cleansing us, sanctifying us, counting us as righteous even in the midst of our sin (1 Cor. 6:11). I would have thought that the black church would be spending its time pointing to the white church, accusing us of sin. Not at all. I read once that white mystification about the reelection of Marion Barry as mayor of Washington even after all his misdeeds was easily understood in the context of the black community where the reconciliation of sinners is a central theme. Consider the reaction of the mother of the African-American security guard who was shot over in Bon Air last week. She told a reporter that she held no malice in her heart for the man accused of killing her son. She said, "I'm praying that he will find peace within himself. God will be the judge."[1]

At the same time, people who have lived all their lives under the shadow of prejudice are more attuned to the injustices of life than privileged people like many of us here today. You will remember that the master tennis player Arthur Ashe, a Richmond native, said that being black was a greater handicap than having AIDS. Our older daughter has been involved all year in a program called Leadership Atlanta which brings blacks and whites together to try to work things out. She has been staggered to hear personal testimony about the amount of pain and anger that African Americans have to deal with all day, every day. Those of us who are white have to work overtime to achieve any understanding of this. Many of us are, as we say today, "in denial" about it. People who are in denial are unable or unwilling to admit that something is wrong. In order to understand the Crucifixion, we need to admit that something is indeed very wrong and needs to be put right. I remember a few years ago in Teaneck, New Jersey, when a young, unarmed black boy, Philip Pannell, was shot by white police officers when his hands were raised in surrender. His anguished father cried, "Somebody has got to pay!"

Susan Cohen is a woman who lost her only child on Pan Am Flight 103 over Lockerbie. Almost a decade later, her grief and rage have scarcely abated. "The pain will not go away," she said. "It will never go away. My daughter's murderers are still out there. No one has been punished."[2] What we notice here is the overpowering sense of injustice and wrong. It isn't just a sense of grief and loss that she feels, though that is bad enough; she must struggle against her utter impotence in the face of unnamed and unrepentant terrorists who are still at large. Her pain has not been addressed. The Christian message of forgiveness is pallid and insufficient if it does not take account of the agony of those who suffer injustice.

One of the things that clergy learn about pastoral care is that you never try to move the hurting person away from the pain. You don't change the subject. You don't try to solve the problem. You don't suggest looking on the bright side. You yourself must enter the pain in order to help. I will never forget a workshop I went to on suicide prevention. The leader said, "Steer toward the pain." This is the most deeply Christian thing that we can do for another human being. It reflects the love of the Crucified One. In the Cross, we see that God has not only steered toward the pain, but has done more; he has taken the pain upon himself.

But — and this is where we move into the truly radical heart of the Christian faith — what of those who are not the victims, but the victimizers? What of those who inflict pain on others, either directly or by lack of caring? If Christ is the helper of the helpless, what of those who live comfortable lives while others struggle and die in anonymous misery? It is a fact of life in our cities that poor minority people must live with a fear of the police that you and I cannot even imagine. Affluent white parents do not have to live in mortal dread every hour of the day that their children are going to be caught in a drive-by shooting. This causes pain to the heart of God. What about the famous phenomenon called white flight? Are you at ease in your mind about this? My guess is that you are not, any more than I am. There is something awry. What galvanizes privileged white people? I can't speak for you, but I can tell you what galvanizes my suburban community in New York. Here are the things that bring the gentry out in force: increased airport noise just north of us; the plan to build a fire station near our street; the possibility of a group home for retarded citizens moving into the neighborhood. Nothing is too important to prevent the good neighbors of Rye Brook — and I include myself — to assemble on a rainy night to protest a plan to build five houses on a parcel of land zoned for three houses. These are the great and mighty issues that motivate us. What will it take to bring us out to protest the inadequate schooling and substandard health care endured by millions of Americans while you and I worry about the bacteria level in our swimming pools? What will motivate us to steer toward the pain of our brothers and sisters who live in circumstances so different from ours that we have great difficulty understanding their struggles? If Jesus is for the victims, what will happen to the victimizers?

Are you ready for a change of pace? Some of you probably know the song by Mary Chapin Carpenter called "Sometimes You're the Windshield, Sometimes You're the Bug." This puts it all together. Human beings spend our lives fluctuating between being the victim and being the victimizer. The boy who is bullied on the playground (he's the bug) comes home and torments the cat (he becomes the windshield). The woman who was ridiculed and tyrannized as a child by her mother (bug) is malicious and domineering at her club (windshield). The tribe that loses half its members in a massacre is still exacting revenge generations later. Bugs today are windshields tomorrow.

All this week I have been suggesting that it is relatively easy to see how Jesus, in giving himself up, became the victim on behalf of all victims. The death of Jesus has always exerted a strong emotional pull on the disenfranchised and oppressed of the earth. What is more challenging and more radical is the fact that Jesus is also paying the price for the sins of the *victimizers,* and make no mistake, that includes you and me. The indifference of the affluent classes of the earth to the sufferings of the poor and invisible members of society makes all of us victimizers. You and I contribute to the victimization of others without even thinking about it. What responsibility do I have for people who have lost their welfare benefits? Surely those nice people at my bank have nothing to do with poverty in Asia. If people choose to smoke, that's their problem, not the manufacturer's. It's not the gun, it's the gun owner. There are a thousand ways that you and I separate ourselves off from those who make bad choices. We are the righteous, they are the unrighteous. Yet Jesus said, "I did not come to call the righteous, but sinners" (Matt. 9:13 and parallels).

Paul's congregation in Corinth thought they were past being sinners. They wanted spiritual excitement, not the hard work of steering toward the pain. They didn't like the Cross, because they sensed it would interfere with their happy spirituality. Paul wrote to remind them, "We preach Christ crucified, a stumbling block to Jews and folly to Gentiles, but to those who are called, both Jews and Greeks, Christ the power of God and the wisdom of God" (1 Cor. 1:22-24). A man who understood these things was Bishop Oscar Romero of El Salvador, murdered as he said Mass because he was the champion of the poor. In one of his sermons he said, "The person that is converted to Christ is the new human being that society needs to organize a world according to God's heart."[3] Where do we see God's heart? We see it in Jesus during his Passion. "Somebody has got to pay!" cried Philip Pannell's anguished father. In Jesus, God paid. In Jesus, Mr. Pannell's pain and Susan Cohen's pain and the security guard's mother's pain are taken up by God himself.

As the affluent endowed parishes of America go through Lent, may we be so struck to the heart by the price Jesus paid for us all, by his entering our pain and bearing it on our behalf, by his undergoing the judgment of God on sin in our place, that we will become new human beings, full of the power of the Holy Spirit to "organize a world according to God's heart." But listen, brothers and sisters, do not go away today feeling that a burden has been laid upon you. Remember the joy! "There to my heart was the blood applied/Glory to his Name!" The message is one of liberation and freedom. Let us not be intimidated by the hugeness of the task. Paul did not call the Corinthian church to tackle the entire Roman Empire right at the first. Tackling the Roman Empire came soon enough. The call to the Corinthian church was the call to love the fellow human being right there in the next pew, and to love him with all the love of God. For the love of God is the love of Christ, and the love of Christ is for victims and victimizers alike. Here is the word from the sixth chapter of 1 Corinthians:

> Do you not know that the unrighteous will not inherit the kingdom of God? Do not be deceived; neither the immoral, nor idolaters, nor adulterers, nor sexual perverts, nor thieves, nor the greedy, nor drunkards, nor revilers, nor robbers will inherit the kingdom of God [everybody I know is on that list!]. . . . But you were washed, you were sanctified, you were justified in the name of the Lord Jesus Christ and in the Spirit of our God. (1 Cor. 6:9-11)

Glory to his Name!

AMEN.

King, and God, and Sacrifice[1]

ALL SAINTS CHURCH, PRINCETON, NEW JERSEY

Behold the Lamb of God who takes away the sin of the world.

(JOHN 1:29)

When do you take down your Christmas decorations? We could probably find out a lot about each other if we asked that question and listened for the nuances in the replies. In my family, we were liturgically correct to a fare-thee-well. My mother did not believe in putting up the tree until Christmas Eve and we took it down on Twelfth Night. My favorite story about this concerns an Episcopal priest friend of ours, Jeffrey. He had a friend, also a priest, who used to scold his parishioners if they put up their trees too early in Advent. Jeffrey decided that instead of taking this negative approach he would accentuate the positive by encouraging his own flock to leave their decorations up until Epiphany. One day, on Christmas afternoon at twilight, after his family had opened all their presents and were taking naps, he took the dog out for a walk. What was his dismay to discover his neighbor's Christmas tree out in the gutter. Jeffrey couldn't help himself; he went up to the house, knocked on the door, and when his neighbor opened it, he said, "Bob! What is your tree doing out on the curb on Christmas Day? You should know better; you're a *Catholic!*" To which Bob responded sheepishly, "Yeah, I know, but my wife's a Presbyterian."

Last Sunday, after the 11:15 service was over, I watched the altar guild as they did exactly what they are supposed to do: they removed the poinsettias and the crèche. I didn't have any problem with that. I knew it was time. But when the Epiphany star came down too, I felt a real stab of loss. I knew that Christmas was really over. I went home and tried to extend the season a few more days, but it was not a success. The time had come. Back into the packing boxes went the Christmas china and the strings of lights. In just a few more weeks, it will be Lent.

I don't like Lent. I don't like bare altars and fasting. I like flowers and feasting. There will be no fasting in the Kingdom of heaven. It will be Christmas and Easter all the time. But we don't live in the Kingdom of God now. Here and now, there is a worm eating away at the core of things. The seasonal changes in the church's ancient calendar incorporate not only the joy of life in Christ but also the heartbreak of life in this world, not only the blessings of salvation but also the challenges of discipleship, not only the star at the beginning of the life of our Lord but also and uniquely the Cross as the culmination of that life.

So there comes a time, early in the season of Epiphany, when the hints of "gathering gloom" begin to overshadow the fading light of Christmas and we know that the feasting is over. Indeed, those hints are present even at the heart of the Christmas story, for Herod seeks to murder Jesus from the very beginning. During the season of Epiphany, the hints become explicit and unmistakable. For instance, take another look at the hymns we are singing this morning. Most of them are centered on Christ's baptism, because that event is recapitulated in today's Gospel reading. Every one of them indicates the turn toward the Cross. The first hymn, ("O love, how deep, how broad, how high") begins with the baptism and then moves directly to the passion:

> For us to wicked hands betrayed,
> Scourged, mocked, in purple robe arrayed,
> He bore the shameful cross and death,
> For us gave up his dying breath.

The second hymn is a morning hymn, so it is theoretically bright and cheerful ("Christ, whose glory fills the skies, Christ the true, the only light, Sun of righteousness, arise!). But we soon are reminded that "the gloom of sin and grief" separates us from the light of Christ unless he is pleased to pierce that gloom. You get the idea. It's a long way from "Have yourself a merry little Christmas, make the Yuletide bright; from now on our troubles will be out of sight."

The third and fourth hymns are both about the baptism of Jesus, but they waste no time turning us toward the bitterness of our Lord's struggle. The first of the two has these lines,

> Straight to the wilderness he goes
> To wrestle with his people's foes.

And the second,

> Straightway and steadfast until death,
> [He] then obeyed [God's] call,
> Freely as Son of Man to serve
> And give [his] life for all.

Our final hymn is great fun to sing because of its archetypically Welsh tune *Bryn Calfaria* (which means "mount of Calvary"), but in terms of its words it is most striking of all, because it brings us to the sermon text for today:

> Paschal Lamb, thine offering finished once for all
>   when thou wast slain
> In its fullness undiminished shall for evermore remain.

And so we come to our Gospel reading for today. For the second Sunday in a row we have an account of the baptism of Jesus in the Jordan River. Like so much of the Gospel of John, it is very different from the versions in Matthew, Mark, and Luke. If you weren't clued in, you wouldn't know that it was a description of the baptism at all. It is not a direct depiction, but, strikingly, is a third-person account by the one who did the baptizing, John the Baptist himself:

> And John bore witness, "I saw the Spirit descend as a dove from heaven, and it remained on him. I myself did not know him; but he who sent me to baptize with water said to me, 'He on whom you see the Spirit descend and remain, this is he who baptizes with the Holy Spirit.' And I have seen and have borne witness that this is the Son of God." (John 1:32-34)

"I did not know him," John says, but now, following the baptism, he knows him. The identity of Jesus has been revealed to him by God.[2] This is a true epiphany. The meaning of the Greek word *epiphany* is manifestation, or showing forth. A good way to understand the meaning of the season of Epiphany is to think of the familiar Christmas carol, "What child is this?" The answer comes, "This, this is Christ the King, whom shepherds guard and angels sing." But this answer was by no means self-evident. Many people, looking at the manger scene, see only a baby. "What child is this?" That is the question that the Epiphany season is designed to reveal. John himself did not know the answer until it was told him by God the Father. "I have seen and have borne witness that this is the Son of God."

Something far more is revealed to John. There was a lot of talk in the ancient Hellenistic world about sons of God. There were gods and goddesses, sons of gods and daughters of gods all over the place. That in itself was not so remarkable. John, however, is not speaking of the generic gods of Hellenistic religion; he speaks of the unique Son of the God of Abraham, Isaac, and Jacob, the God of Moses and Elijah, the God who made Israel a people and sent the prophets to prepare the way for the Messiah. There is more: today's reading contains the most singular of all John's utterances: "The next day, [John] saw Jesus coming toward him, and he said, 'Behold, the Lamb of God, who takes away the sin of the world!'" (John 1:29).

My husband has been a committed Episcopalian all his life; he

never misses a Sunday service. I asked him if he knew what "the
Lamb of God" meant. He had absolutely no idea. I was really
shocked. We have a job to do, in the church; we need more crash
courses in Biblical teaching. Let's go back to the book of Exodus,
chapter 12. It is the night of departure from Egypt. The Israelites
are packing up to leave.

> The Lord said to Moses and Aaron in the land of Egypt, "This
> month shall be for you the beginning of months; it shall be the
> first month of the year for you. Tell all the congregation of Israel
> that on the tenth day of this month they shall take every man a
> lamb, one lamb for a household. . . . Your lamb shall be without
> blemish, a male a year old; you shall take it . . . and you shall keep
> it until the fourteenth day of this month, when the whole assem-
> bly of the congregation of Israel shall kill their lambs in the eve-
> ning. Then they shall take some of the blood, and put it on the
> two doorposts and the lintel of the houses in which they eat
> them. They shall eat the flesh that night, roasted; with unleav-
> ened bread and bitter herbs they shall eat it. . . . It is the Lord's
> passover. . . . And [in time to come] when your children say to
> you, 'What do you mean by this service?' you shall say, 'It is the
> *sacrifice* of the Lord's passover, for he passed over the houses of the
> people of Israel in Egypt, when he slew the Egyptians but spared
> our houses.'" And the people bowed their heads and worshipped.

So you see that the blood of the sacrificed Passover lamb is the
powerful sign of the Lord's deliverance of the children of Israel from
their slavery, from the house of bondage. This has been the language
of deliverance ever since. In a few minutes we are going to say,
"Christ our Passover has been sacrificed for us; therefore let us keep
the feast." These are the famous words of Paul in the First Letter to
the Corinthians, and we say them in every service of Holy Eucharist. It really would be better if we said, "Christ our Passover *lamb*
has been sacrificed," because that is what Paul really means. We
don't always realize when we say these mighty words that they are a
shout of victory. We are praising the triumphant Christ who

through his sacrifice releases his people from every bond of every kind; whether it is the bondage of apartheid or the bondage of addiction. Christ our Paschal Lamb is the one who gave himself up for slaughter that we might be free.[3]

But there is more. The title "Lamb of God" encompasses another Old Testament concept. John the Baptist's image combines the Passover lamb with a different lamb. In the book of Leviticus, the sin offering is described. The sinner brings an animal — a goat or lamb — to the priest to be ritually slaughtered. The blood of the animal is sprinkled on the mercy seat and in this way, by means of this sacrifice, atonement for sin is made and the sinner goes away forgiven.[4] So, in a manner that takes the breath away when you understand it, the saying of John the Baptist combines the Passover lamb with the sin offering of Leviticus, and Jesus becomes not only the Paschal lamb but also "the Lamb of God who takes away the sin of the world."

Yesterday's *New York Times* reports that former Prime Minister de Klerk of South Africa has written a book revealing that he can't abide Nelson Mandela. One of his principal grievances is that the great Mandela exhibited pettiness toward Mrs. de Klerk when she wanted to refurbish their government-issued living quarters.[5] These are the two men who won the Nobel Peace Prize together! Such is human foolishness and perversity. The Christmas decorations have come down in South Africa, for sure.

Two days before Christmas, an article in the *Times* revisited the scene of the massacre of 45 women and children in Chiapas, Mexico, exactly one year before, on December 23, as they worshiped in their church.[6] The headline of the article is, "Where Killings Defiled a Church, No Forgiveness." A Jesuit priest who serves the community said, "The situation here is exactly the same as it was a year ago, maybe worse."[7] I can't speak for you, but as far as I am concerned all this talk of the millennium is a big bore because there is no reason to think that the new millennium is going to be any different from the old one — same old "gloom of sin and grief," same old violence, hatred, oppression, apathy, stupidity, and death. Forgiveness is not enough. We need deliverance. We need a power from outside this realm, a power to set things right.

And so the saying of John the Baptist points us to a greater reality which opens up a new horizon. He does not say "Behold the Lamb of God who *forgives* the sin of the world." He says, "Behold the Lamb of God who *takes away* the sin of the world."

There is a great mystery and a great truth here. I do not really understand, nor can I express to you, the layers upon layers of meaning in the image of the Lamb of God. I can only say that it is clear to me that the human race — and I include myself — is in deep trouble and that the only solution ever put forward that has meant anything to me is the Cross of Christ, and that is why we take our decorations down and prepare for the season of Lent. It is a way of acknowledging our willingness to enter into judgment upon ourselves, not the sort of judgment that crushes, but the judgment that cleanses — judgment voluntarily assumed for bringing the Lord to his sacrificial death in our place.

Taking down the decorations symbolizes, for me, the conscious and intentional taking up of the Cross. We don't like it, we don't want it, we would rather not, but somehow the figure of the Lord draws us toward his path of suffering for others — for us. Listen to the next verses: "The next day John was standing with two of his disciples; and he looked at Jesus as he walked, and said [again], 'Behold, the Lamb of God!' The two disciples heard him say this, and they followed Jesus" (John 1:35-37). They had been following John, but when John revealed the true nature of Christ to them, when he pointed away from himself to Jesus, they turned and followed the Master.

John the Baptist is the model for every preacher. A good preacher points away from herself to our Lord Jesus Christ, the Lamb of God. "This is my story, this is my song."[8] I see no message in religion or history that can compare with this. When I look back upon the twentieth century, often called the most violent and murderous century in human history, I see nothing that would cause me to believe in a merciful God. Nothing, that is, except the Crucified Son. Somehow, in the unique event on Calvary, God's heart is revealed; his heart for those who suffer. Who can see this? Can the poor people in that Mexican village see it? One way they will see it is through the faithful ministry of that priest. Just think: some of the people in your life will come to know the love of God through *your* ministry. That is what it means to take up the Cross. Our troubles will not be "out of sight"; rather, in many respects they will be intensified as we determine to face the truth about ourselves, as we are moved to come alongside those who suffer, as we confront the dark places in our society and take up arms against them in the name of Jesus. But that is not all. Beyond the Cross there lies the empty tomb.

Who can see Easter beyond the massacres? Who can see the sin of the world *taken away* in the self-offering of the Son of God? Who can believe in the everlasting feast in the Kingdom of God? To those who suffer for Christ's sake, it is revealed. To those in the shadows longing to hear the news of salvation, the message comes. To those whose hearts bend this morning toward the outstretched arms of our Lord, the promise is given. As God the Father spoke to John the Baptist, so he speaks to us, to you, to me, here, today, at this moment, through his living Word. It should have been me, up there; it should have been you; but it was not. It was him. The great High Priest has become the sacrifice. "Behold, the Lamb of God who takes away the sins of the world."

AMEN.

FAITH AND WORKS

The Resurrection Reach-Out

ALL SAINTS CHURCH, PRINCETON, NEW JERSEY

*Thanks be to God, who gives us the victory through our Lord Je-
sus Christ. . . . Therefore, my beloved brethren, be steadfast, im-
movable, always abounding in the work of the Lord, knowing
that in the Lord your labor is not in vain. Now concerning the
contribution for the saints . . .*

(1 COR. 15:57–16:1)

This Sunday at All Saints is called Outreach Sunday, or Mission
Sunday. The word "outreach" is a rather trendy recent addition
to the Christian vocabulary. We always used to call it "mission." A
Christian leader earlier in this century said, "The church exists by
mission as fire exists by burning."[1] The word *mission* comes from a
Latin root meaning *to send.* Christian mission is a sending out from
the center to the borders and beyond, as in the famous words of Jesus from the book of Acts: "You shall receive power when the Holy
Spirit has come upon you; and you shall be my witnesses in Jerusalem and in all Judea and Samaria and to the end of the earth" (Acts
1:8). Here at All Saints you have committed yourselves to various
ministries that represent needs close by (Judea) and farther away
(Samaria) and overseas (the end of the earth). This is a splendid concept that carries forward the confidence of this congregation in the
gospel of Jesus Christ. The reason that the term *mission* fell into dis-

favor is that it became associated in some people's minds with cultural imperialism. As the mainline churches have grown less confident about Christian faith and less committed to evangelism, so they have replaced "missions" with "outreach." *Mission,* however, is an apostolic concept and *ministry* comes from the word *diakonia* in the New Testament, so they are the more deeply rooted words.

Having said all that, though, let's return to the idea of outreach, or "reaching out," because reaching out is one of the most fundamental characteristics of the God of the Bible. Everything God does is a form of reaching out. The creation itself was God reaching out to make something *other than* himself with which (and with *whom*) he could be in relationship.[2] The most dramatic example in those early chapters of Genesis is what happens right after the original act of disobedience in the Garden of Eden. Adam, attempting to hide, hears the voice of God saying, "Adam, where are you?" This is one of the most soul-searing utterances in the entire Scripture. Every cry of every anguished parent across the history of the centuries is summed up here. This is God seeking after his lost son and lost daughter. It is God seeking after you and me: "Adam, where are you?" — God reaching out.

The entire Old Testament is a story of God reaching out. Remember, we were all justly condemned to death after the fall of Adam. There was no recourse for us, no appeal; our collective goose was cooked. But God,[3] not wasting a moment, reached out for Abraham and inaugurated the story of salvation, right then and there. That was only the beginning. When Abraham's descendants wound up as slaves, God reached out for Moses in Egypt. This history undergirds our Old Testament lesson today from the book of Deuteronomy: "You shall say to your son, 'We were Pharaoh's slaves in Egypt; and the Lord brought us out of Egypt with a mighty hand'" (Deut. 6:21). That's why we just sang the hymn "Through the Red Sea." This is the fundamental story that belongs to Jews and Christians alike. "It was because the Lord loved you and kept the oath which he swore to your forefathers that he brought you out with a mighty hand and redeemed you from the house of bondage" (Deut. 7:8). But let's not stop there. On this "Outreach Sunday" we look ahead in the book of Deuteronomy to see how the story of God's reaching out is linked with our doing the same. In chapter 24, it is made explicit in several verses: "You shall not pervert the justice due to the sojourner or to the fatherless, or take a widow's garment in pledge; but *you shall remember that you were a slave in Egypt and the Lord your God redeemed you from there*" (Deut. 24:17-18). This is the foundation of Judeo-Christian social ethics: "When you gather the grapes of your vineyard, you shall not [go back and take the second harvest] afterward; it shall be for the stranger, the fatherless, and the widow. *You shall remember that you were a slave in the land of Egypt;* therefore I command you to do this" (24:21, 22). Acts of kindness are not performed to gain credit or accumulate merit. Rather, they are living embodiments of the story of our own redemption. By reaching out to others, we recapitulate the prior outreach of God to us — and the wonder of it is that God's power is present in our small actions just as he was present in his own mighty action at the Red Sea.

All of us, I think, can look back on our lives and identify certain turning points. In the early 1960s, when I was a young married woman of leisure in Richmond, Virginia, I spent a lot of time in the gallery of the Virginia Legislature. I was brought up in a household where politics was always discussed with enthusiasm, and Virginia politics in particular. Some of you may have heard of the Byrd Machine. Senator Harry Flood Byrd ran the state in those days. My much beloved, much admired father and most of his friends were part of the Byrd Machine. I had grown up regarding the Byrd Machine as sacred. You know how we Virginians are; we always think we are enshrined in a special place, so obviously the Virginia Legislature was more honest, more upright, more virtuous than any other political body. So I was told and so I believed. Well, there arose in those days some Young Turks (as they were called) in the Legislature, regarded with great suspicion by my father and his friends. The Young Turks were pieces of grit in the smoothly oiled Byrd Machine.[4] So I went down to the Legislature to see what all the fuss was about and I had a great time hanging over the balcony railing listening to all the courtly debates (and they were indeed courtly, on the surface).

One day, I remember with great vividness, the debate was about the budget. Actually, the debate was almost always about the budget; what made it interesting was the specific budget items. The hallmark of the Byrd Machine was fiscal conservatism. "Pay as you go" was the slogan. So it was very difficult to wrest any money out of the Legislature. The discussion on the day in question was about the state institutions for the mentally retarded and emotionally disturbed. The Young Turks were trying to get some more money for these services. One of my father's friends got up to speak against the increase. He was elaborately deferential to the gentleman from Fairfax who had argued in favor, but at the same time you could tell he was ever so slightly dismissive. He referred to the residents of the hospitals as "these unfortunates." He wouldn't want anyone to think that he was not concerned about "these unfortunates," no sir, but he was not about to consider allocating any more money for them. I know now, looking back, that it was his use of that term that registered in my still-unformed soul. You could tell that nobody in *his* family was retarded or disturbed. You could tell that he looked upon "these unfortunates" from a great distance. He was untouched and untroubled by their needs. I never really trusted the Byrd Machine after that, and a year or two later when the Byrd Machine started telling us that Martin Luther King was a Communist, I knew it wasn't true.

What is the Christian gospel? You know what it is. *We were all unfortunate. Without the mercy of God, every one of us is terminally unfortunate.* The most holy God, looking down upon us and seeing what a mess we have made of his creation, might have remained untouched and untroubled, abandoning us to our self-chosen fate. Instead, God did something so staggering and so unthinkable that it still to this day remains — to my way of thinking — the *only* convincing reason to believe what the Christian faith teaches; I just don't think anyone could have made it up. God, sending his Son "in the likeness of sinful flesh" (Rom. 8:3), made himself one with all of us "unfortunates." Jesus took upon himself the condemnation unto death that we had incurred, and in doing so made himself not only "unfortunate," but a human outcast, thrown onto the dustbin of the

Roman Empire, publicly executed in the most degrading possible way, designated as a menace to the machinery of church and state. Everything we believe about Christian action in the world flows from this central affirmation: the Son of God entered into solidarity with the wretched of the earth, and that means you and me. "You shall remember that you were a slave in Egypt and the Lord your God redeemed you from there."

You can tell from the hymns we are singing today that this is still the Easter season. We are in the midst of the Great Fifty Days that bring the church year to its incandescent climax. It is the Easter season, and this is an Easter sermon. The principal text this morning is the passage that spans the conclusion of Paul's Resurrection chapter in 1 Corinthians 15 and the beginning of chapter 16. Today on Outreach Sunday, you will see how the Resurrection is intimately woven together with Christian mission. Paul's great sustained proclamation of the Resurrection goes on for fifty verses and then comes to his ringing peroration:

> The trumpet shall sound, and the dead shall be raised incorruptible, and we shall be changed. . . . Then shall come to pass the saying that is written: "Death is swallowed up in victory." Thanks be to God, who gives us the victory through our Lord Jesus Christ.
>
> Therefore, my beloved brethren, be steadfast, immovable, always abounding in the work of the Lord, knowing that in the Lord your labor is not in vain.
>
> Now concerning the contribution for the saints: . . . On the first day of every week, each of you is to put something aside . . . as he may prosper.

We hardly ever hear those verses read together as they were written. You can see right away how Paul moves seamlessly from proclamation to exhortation. The two themes flow as a single stream, the headwaters being the Resurrection. *Because* God has given us the victory in Christ, *therefore* we know *our labor will not be in vain,* and Paul can move straight into a discussion of money without the slightest hesitation. He is taking up a collection for the "poor saints in Jerusalem." His boldness is arresting, isn't it? Most of us are timid about asking for money. Not Paul. He is filled with all the confidence of one who knows that a new world has come into being with the Resurrection, the only world that counts. The signs of that new world are already appearing in this present evil world, markers of God's reaching out to rescue and restore. God's power is in these signs. Christianity is not Christianity at all unless there is this reaching out.

All of us are aware of the national discussion that is going on about the killings at Columbine High School in Colorado. We have all heard about the division that exists in American high schools between the popular young people, the jocks and preps, on the one hand, and on the other hand the kids who are variously termed nerds, geeks, and dweebs — who are derided as weirdos and freaks. This is human nature. Every one of us does this. We distance ourselves from others. We learn to despise them as did a little refugee boy that I read about in a superb *New York Times* story by a reporter named Barry Bearak. He writes, "Much is said about the ancient hatreds of the Balkans . . . but hatred is learned. It needs renewal, generation to generation." He then goes on to tell of a father and son that he met in a Macedonian camp.

"Are Serbs good people?" the father asked his five-year-old son.

The boy was confused. "Yes," he said.

"Who stole our money, burned our house and took our car?" the father asked impatiently.

This time, the boy was in tune. "The filthy Serbs," he said.

"And what should you do if you meet a Serb?"

"I will kill him," the little boy said.[5]

The Christian gospel is that this cycle has been broken. Not *can be* broken; it *has been* broken. We unfortunates have no power in and of ourselves to break the cycle. We seem to be unable to think of anything better to do than bomb and bomb and bomb some more. "The fathers eat sour grapes and the children's teeth are set on edge"; that is the way of the world.[6] But the way of the world has been "turned upside down," as we read in today's lesson from Acts (17:6). Those who are accustomed to being first will be last, as Jesus said, "and the last first" (Matt. 19:30 and parallels).

So being a Christian congregation means entering into a whole new way of thinking. On Friday, the op-ed page of the *Times* had an article by Orlando Patterson about the Columbine massacre, a professor of sociology from Harvard who happens to be black. It was called "When 'They' Become 'Us,'" which reflects today's theme very well.[7] He's talking about the shock felt by white people who have been forced to see that black teenagers are not the only problem. "What is at issue here," he writes,

[is our concept of] those from whom we cannot be separated without losing our identity, so that their achievements become our own and their pathologies our pathologies. We should speak not simply of black poverty but of the nation's poverty; not the Italian-American Mafia problem but the nation's crime problem; not the pathologies of privileged white teen-age boys but . . . of all our unloved alienated young men.

And, we might add, we should speak not simply of lost American lives but of lost human lives. The professor may or may not be a confessing Christian, but he speaks out of deep Biblical roots whether he knows it or not. In Christ, all of the "theys" have become "us" because Jesus became "us."

Christian mission, Christian ministry usually starts small. I have a little grandson who is blond and handsome and very athletic. God being our helper, we will do what we can to teach him to be kind to boys who are not athletic, to look for the talents that they have and to respect them equally. And yesterday, we made a donation to Doctors Without Borders, for Kosovo. These are such tiny things, aren't they? — hardly worth mentioning. Certainly such minuscule gestures as these are not going to make any difference to the unspeakable inhumanity that we see all around the world.

But you see, that is not the way to look at it. Every dollar, every action, every single example of one human being reaching out to another is part of the mighty cosmic drama initiated by God when Jesus exploded from the grave. This Resurrection power is now given to the Christian community. *Our labor is not in vain.* We will shortly sing one of the very finest Easter hymns, with words by Christopher Wordsworth:

> Christ is risen, we are risen! shed upon us heavenly grace . . .
> That with hearts in heaven dwelling, *we on earth may fruitful be.* . . .

Never underestimate the power of the heavenly grace of God "to make us fruitful." This congregation has a ministry to the homeless people on Route One. You have recognized that they are not just "those unfortunates." "They" are "us." God willing, leadership may arise out of this congregation to make this ministry still more effective, tackling not just the symptoms but also the roots of deprivation.

"Christ is risen, we are risen!" Resurrection power! This is more power than any bomb. This is the power that turns the world upside down. This is power arising out of the grave itself. This power to reach out in Christ is the door to heavenly life. This is power to move out from ourselves to join our Lord as he takes the part of the unfortunate, beginning with you and me — power to see that reaching out in the name of Christ is the door to heavenly life. And just in case there were to be any doubt about it, we have in today's Gospel lesson the promise of our risen Lord himself:

> Truly, truly, I say to you, he who believes in me will also do the works that I do; and greater works than these will he do, because I go to the Father. (John 14:12)

AMEN.

Money in Trust

ST. MARY'S, SCARBOROUGH, NEW YORK

*The master said to him, "Well done, good and faithful servant;
you have been faithful over a little, I will set you over much; enter into the joy of your master."*

(MATT. 25:21)

My husband and I have a friend whose father recently died after
a long illness. The father had at one time been in possession,
through inheritance, of a substantial amount of money. At his death
it was almost all gone. The father had not invested it, had not seen
to its growth. It simply sat in the bank. In the father's last years, it
drained away. Our friend was torn between grief and anger: grief
because he loved his father, and anger at the waste of the inheritance.

This is a subject for the end of the Christian year. After All
Saints Day, the church shifts into high gear. The "long green season" is finally coming to its conclusion. You can always tell, because
the Scripture readings begin to communicate a sense of urgency. All
three lessons today and the Psalm speak of the end-time. We can
think of this as our own personal end, or we can think of it as the
Last Judgment of the whole world, or both, for the Bible speaks of
both. The year's end puts us in mind of that future time when
Christ "will come again in glory to judge the living and the dead."

Whether he comes tomorrow or a hundred millennia from now is not the important thing; being prepared is what counts. As Paul writes in today's Epistle, "You are not in darkness, brothers and sisters, for that day to surprise you like a thief. For you are all children of light, children of the day. . . . So then let us not sleep, as others do, but let us keep awake. . . . since we belong to the day, let us . . . put on the breastplate of faith and love, and for a helmet the hope of salvation" (1 Thess. 5:4-8).

The 25th chapter of Matthew is divided into three parts, one for each of three Sundays at the end of the church year. Last Sunday, we had the parable of the ten virgins, or bridesmaids. Five of them were locked out of the marriage feast because they ran out of oil. This Sunday is the parable of the talents. Next Sunday is the Feast of Christ the King, the last day of the church year; the reading is the parable of the Last Judgment. These demanding parables are the last ones that Jesus told; it takes a certain amount of intestinal fortitude to face up to them. Preacher and congregation alike are challenged to the utmost.

The idea of Jesus as the cosmic Judge is disturbing to most American Christians. We have not grown up with those Greek Orthodox mosaics of the Lord's head looming over us in the domes of our churches. Those images show Christ as Pantocrator, Judge of the universe. Our sentimental American version of the faith is more likely to show Jesus hugging a lamb. We have managed to domesticate our Lord's parables as well. We tend to think of them as suitable for the children's story hour. The question thus becomes, how can a sweet storyteller be also the present and future Arbitrator of the cosmos? This is an important question. Here's what one New Testament scholar has to say:

> Jesus used parables, and Jesus was put to death. The two facts are related. . . . Why was this man crucified? . . . The parables must be understood as part of the drama. No one would crucify a teacher who simply told pleasant stories to enforce prudential morality . . . The parables are not harmless tales, but weapons of warfare.[1]

The weapon of warfare that we have before us today is the so-called parable of the talents. We can interpret this story in two different ways. Most of us who grew up with it thought it meant that people should use their gifts and talents for the good of others. According to this version, God gives different abilities to each of us, and he expects us to use them wisely and generously.

This, however, is not what the story means. No one would be crucified for telling a story as inoffensive as that. When Jesus originally told this parable, and when the church retold it later, it had a shocking impact. The three parables of Matthew 25 are all parables of judgment. That's why we read them at this time of year. If you were listening carefully I'm sure you noticed that this isn't just a nice little story. It packs quite a wallop. This isn't the easy-going nonjudgmental Jesus that our culture prefers.

I'm going to be reading from the J. B. Phillips translation. First we need to get the context in our minds. For seven weeks, we have been reading through the section of the Gospel of Matthew that describes Jesus' last days. He has been engaged in a three-day battle to the death (literally) with the religious leaders in the temple; now he has withdrawn with his disciples to the Mount of Olives. They ask him a question that seems very strange to us, but in Jesus' time it was very much on people's minds because of prophecies like that of Zephaniah in this morning's reading. They ask, "What will be the signal for . . . the end of the world?" Jesus tells them that they must pay no attention to the predictions of people who think they can name the date. The important thing, he tells them, is to be vigilant and faithful. "About that actual day and time, no one knows . . . only the Father. . . . You must be alert, then, for you do not know when your Master is coming" (Matt. 24:3, 36, 42). Then Jesus begins to tell the three parables of chapter 25, to show them what he means by being alert. That is the context of the parable of the talents.

"It is like a man going abroad who called his household servants together before he went and handed his property over to them to manage. He gave one $200,000, another $100,000, and another $20,000 — according to their respective abilities. Then he went away."[2] As you can see, the master does not give out what we call "talents." He gives out *money*. This parable has nothing whatever to do with talents. It is unfortunate that the English word "talent," meaning natural ability, is the same as the word for the gold coin in the original parable. As soon as we start talking about "talents," we're going to lose sight of the point altogether. There's this little slogan that Episcopalians use during stewardship season; I'm sure you've heard it — "time, talents, and treasure." My impression is that it does more harm than good. It distracts our attention from the real issue, which is *money*. Having those three t's sounds catchy, but it also sounds quaint and irrelevant, because it isn't the way we really talk; we don't use the word "treasure" when we talk about money. The slogan makes it too easy for us to avoid the issue of money. It's ineffective because it lets people off the hook. If we can divert attention to time and talents, which aren't very threatening, we don't have to think about what *really* makes us nervous, namely, giving up some of our money. Over the years, various new titles for the parable have been proposed to correct the misunderstanding about "talents." The best one is "The Parable of the Money in Trust."[3] That we can understand.

In the parable, Jesus assumes that his listeners know something about good business practice. The whole point of the master's apportionment of the money was that it be used to make more money. The expectation of the landowner was that profit would be made for him to collect when he got back. In other words, he is hiring money managers. Jesus takes for granted that his hearers are going to understand this. Money is not just to sit there. It is meant to go to work. The landowner has given the servants quite a lot of money, showing that he trusted them with a significant responsibility.

Some years later, Jesus continues, "the master of these servants arrived and went into the accounts with them." The one who had the $200,000 came in with double that amount — not much by today's standards, but we are meant to understand that he did a good job. The master is delighted: "Well done! You're a sound, reliable servant. You've been trustworthy with a few things, now I'm going to put you in charge of much more. Come in and share your master's rejoicing." The second servant did equally well with his $100,000; and received just as much praise and the same invitation: "Come in and share your master's pleasure." These two servants were eager to advance their master's cause. The note of joy and enthusiasm is pronounced; servants and master alike are thrilled with the results and look forward to celebrating. Now here comes the third servant. This is the one who was given $20,000. "Sir, I always knew you were a hard man, reaping where you never sowed and collecting where you never laid out, so I was scared and I went and buried the $20,000 in the ground. Here is your money, intact."

What a craven statement this is! Instead of acknowledging the trust his master placed in him, he seeks to transfer the blame; "you are so demanding, you are so intimidating, you make me feel so inadequate." He is like the child who says, "Look what you made me do!" We have all seen adults like this. They seek pity instead of shouldering responsibility. The landowner is disgusted: "You're a wicked, lazy servant! . . . Take his $20,000 away and give it to the one who has the $400,000. . . . Throw this useless servant out into the darkness outside, where he can weep and wail over his stupidity!"

Now this really is very interesting. We have gotten so tender-minded in the church that we get all worried about this poor servant and his fate. That's not what our response is supposed to be. Remember, this parable depends on our understanding financial practices. We're supposed to be thinking of a stock portfolio that we've turned over to an investment banker. Can you imagine how we'd react if he gave it back to us a few years later having made not one cent? Wouldn't you fire him on the spot, with perhaps a few choice words to go along with it? That's the appropriate reaction to the parable. Like our friend who was angry with his father even though he loved him, we are supposed to understand that the third servant blew it. The shock of the story is not related to the fate of the third servant, because Jesus expects the disciples to agree with the judgment on him. If an endowment does not grow, its caretakers are considered to have failed. That's just common knowledge.

The challenge in understanding the parable does not lie here. The offense lies somewhere else.

Remember, this parable was told just a few days before Jesus' arrest and crucifixion. In order to figure out why this parable, among others, would make people want to seek Jesus' death, we need to look deeper. We need to figure out who the parable was directed against. Who, in the world of Jesus and his disciples, was like the third servant? The answer may come as a surprise. Jesus told this parable against the powerful religious aristocracy of his day. All four Gospels tell us that this group found his teachings intolerable. Its members were chiefly concerned to maintain their own position. Very early in Jesus' ministry they began to see that many of his parables were directed against them. That was the reason that they began to plot his death.

It is still like that for us today. Affluent churches are particularly likely to be uneasy about Jesus' message. Instead of recognizing it as our charter of freedom, we feel it as a threat. So we cling to what we have and we don't risk anything. The more comfortable we get in our churches, the more likely we are to hang on to our money, so that it just goes round and round in a tight little circle. Jesus, however, is looking for a breakout. God gives riches, but not to hoard and hide. He means for them to be put into action. A wise Christian once said to me, "The best thing to do with God's money is to keep it moving." God asks for servants who are ready to extend themselves, to venture and to risk. God's gifts are never to be passively possessed, let alone greedily clutched. They are to be put to work, spread around, made to increase and multiply. Jesus lets us know that the third servant's timidity and lack of imagination are unacceptable. The master is totally frustrated with him, saying, "You should have at least put it in the bank so it would have drawn some interest!"

What's going to happen to the third servant? He's going to miss all the fun, all the excitement. Listen again to the landowner as he praises the first two servants: "Great job! You've done so well with what I gave you, I'm going to put you in charge of a lot more. Come into my house and celebrate with me!" That, believe it or not, is classic end-of-the-world imagery. When the Bible starts talking about a celebration or a marriage feast, that means the Kingdom of God is near. God loves a party; the theme of God's great everlasting banquet runs all through the Bible. This third servant is going to miss the party because he was afraid to trust the master's commission.

I was involved in a discussion last month with a bank executive. He was raging and storming against the politicians who want to keep taxing the rich at high rates. He says the government is punishing the people who want to save and invest, rather than consume. I've been thinking about that for weeks since. It seems to me that there is a third alternative here. Saving and investing on the one hand and consuming on the other are not the only options. There is another option: *giving*. For one thing, giving money away is a great way to get a tax break, but somehow I don't think that's what the Lord had in mind. What the Lord had in mind was the joy of giving. As Paul wrote, "The Lord loves a cheerful giver" (2 Cor. 9:7).

Last week, you may have seen the front-page article in *The New York Times* about the African men who deliver groceries in Manhattan. They are new immigrants, raised to have gentle manners, and they are hurt by the way they are treated in New York. They work twelve hours a day, six days a week, and they make less than $2.50 an hour. Needless to say, they receive no benefits. The supermarket chains contract out the service to delivery companies so they can distance themselves from these unfair and probably illegal practices. The supermarkets charge their customers $2.25 for the delivery. The men often have to deliver many heavy bags of groceries up five flights of steps and receive a dollar or less as a tip. If they deliver to a doorman building, they get no tip at all. The *Times* reporter walked along with one of these deliverymen as he carried four shopping bags to the handsome Upper East Side building of Mrs. Lillian Winston. The reporter asked Mrs. Winston if she knew about the men's low pay. "That's unacceptable!" she said, "My father always told me to fight for the little guy." When the reporter asked if she might offer the man more than her usual one dollar tip, she sighed. "I'm already paying $2.25 for this," she said; "Why should I pay more?"[4]

Why should she pay more? Here's why: for the joy of giving. For the joy of being generous. For the joy of giving a helping hand to someone that Jesus loves just as much as he loves you and me. I remember about eight years ago I was having lunch in the city with your rector. It was a plain kind of restaurant with overworked waiters. At the end of the meal, he left a huge tip on the table. He could see that I was watching admiringly. He said, without ostentation or pretense, "It's really important, don't you think? People are hurting." As you see, I remember that to this day. The joy of generosity. The joy of helping. The joy of keeping the money moving. Won't it be wonderful when the last day comes and Jesus says to us, "Well done, thou good and faithful servant; thou hast been trustworthy in a few things, I will make thee ruler over many things; come thou and enter into the joy of thy Lord" (Matt. 25:21).

AMEN.

CONTEMPORARY ATTITUDES
TOWARD THE GOSPEL

Can These Bones Live?

ST. JOHN'S, ESSEX, CONNECTICUT

*The hand of the Lord was upon me, and he brought me out by
the Spirit of the Lord, and set me down in the midst of the valley; it was full of bones. And he led me round among them; and
behold, there were very many upon the valley; and lo, they were
very dry. And he said to me, "Son of man, can these bones live?"
And I answered, "O Lord God, thou knowest."*

(EZEK. 37:1-3)

*{Jesus} cried with a loud voice, "Lazarus, come forth." The
dead man came out, his hands and feet bound with bandages,
and his face wrapped with a cloth. Jesus said to them, "Unbind
him, and let him go."*

(JOHN 11:43-44)

L ast month, a certain highbrow critic wrote in a certain highbrow journal that the "central myth" of Christianity is "now being discarded." The writer in question (Rosemary Dinnage) refers
to herself as an "ex-Christian."[1] So you know what that means, don't
you? All the truly intelligent, urbane, sophisticated people are
somewhere else this morning while you and I, along with the
Southern Baptists, Pentecostals, abortion-clinic bombers, Falwell-

followers, snake-handlers, and Bible-thumpers, poor benighted souls that we are, are still pathetically clinging to our "central myth." Or are we? Even more seductive than the siren call of *The New York Review of Books* is the idea presently popular — even within the church — that you can soak up the *rituals* of the church without actually *believing* in anything. That way, you demonstrate your intellectual superiority and still get to participate in the attenuated comforts of the modernized Anglican tradition, its celebrated tolerance and latitude overlaid with just a touch of mystery, a hint of transcendence, without any of the embarrassment of having to really *commit* oneself to such outmoded notions.

We are preparing, today, to enter Holy Week. The lessons appointed for this fourth Sunday in Lent put the life-and-death themes of our faith before us in the most uncompromising fashion. This is the "central myth" raised to the nth power. Dry bones reconnected! Lazarus popping up out of his tomb! Who believes this stuff? Certainly, this calls for unblinking scrutiny.

I'm sure some of you read Jay McInerney's memoir of his mother in *The New Yorker* a few weeks ago.[2] This writer, though no longer quite the pied piper that he once was, is still close to the epicenter of cultural cool. He lets us know in no uncertain terms that he discarded the "central myth" of his mother's church a long time ago. Nevertheless, he is sensitive in the telling of her cruel death of cancer at the age of forty-nine. She was beloved in her community for her good works, but she hated it when people referred to her as "saintly." She confessed to her son that years before, she had had an extramarital affair with a married man, a close family friend. As she lay dying, she disclosed that she was afraid. Jay tried to be encouraging. "You have less reason to be afraid than anyone I know," he said. "Don't say that," she snapped. "I'm so tired of everyone telling me how I don't deserve this. Especially your father. It makes it so much harder. I've done a terrible thing." Her son wrote, angrily, "It seemed like poor economy to have to deal with the b—s— of religion most of your life and then be unable to collect some righteous peace of mind at the end."[3]

The story is well told and very moving on a number of levels.

What interests me today is its connection to the "central myth" and the message of Ezekiel. The Biblical story has two aspects. First of all, it is about Christ crucified, risen, and coming again, or, as we say in the Eucharistic prayer, "Christ has died, Christ is risen, Christ will come again." But the second and even more urgent aspect of the message can be formulated as a question: Who will receive this salvation in Christ? Jay McInerney's mother was terrified that her eternal destiny hung in the balance because of her betrayal of her husband. Contrast this with certain famous people who have engaged in an affair, or multiple affairs, with confidence that it would not jeopardize their salvation at all, because after all, God is in the forgiving business.⁴ Ezekiel leaves us in no doubt about the inevitability and the severity of God's judgment. Paul puts it in his own way in today's second lesson: "The wages of sin is death." Poet Rita Dove has paraphrased this wittily in her line, "The wages of living are sin."⁵ In other words, we are all in this together. "The righteousness of the righteous man shall not deliver him when he transgresses," writes Ezekiel: "The righteous [woman] shall not be able to live by [her] righteousness when [she] sins" (33:12). So Jay McInerney's mother, saintly woman as she was, was in one sense right to be afraid. She knew she did not "deserve" a free pass into eternal bliss.

With all due respect, the church failed Mrs. McInerney somewhere along the way. She had not heard, or had not understood, the gospel. What is the gospel? On most days of the year, if you asked me that question, I would not think of Ezekiel. This week, though, because of today's readings, I have been on a trip with this unique prophet, and what a ride it has been!⁶ This is one of the truly great books of the Bible. I warn you that you shouldn't necessarily rush right home and read it. If you do, be sure to give free rein to your poetic imagination. Ezekiel, like Revelation, requires that you not be literal-minded. We need to try to be like the black slaves who understood it best when they sang "Ezekiel saw the wheel, way up in the middle of the air" and, "Ezekiel connected them dry bones."

I'm going to read you a gospel verse from Ezekiel. It is not a warm fuzzy version of the gospel; it certainly won't be seen on any bumper stickers. But it is the gospel nonetheless: "Thus says the Lord God: It is not for your sake, O house of Israel, that I am about to act, but for the sake of my holy name" (36:22).

That's the gospel? you may well ask. What is good news about that? To which we reply: the good news is that God's ultimate purpose of mercy for humanity is not *for our sake* — it is not because we earned his mercy or because we deserve it; rather, it is *for the sake of his holy name* — that is, because of God's essential nature going out toward us in love and mercy.

We will never understand the depth of this unless something causes us to look unflinchingly at sin. Mrs. McInerney was right in knowing she was not clean before God. She was also right to be irritated at those who minimized her concerns by telling her what a saint she was.[7] Holding back on the bad news about our sinful condition is a sure way to rob the good news of its dazzlement. A great nineteenth-century preacher, Alexander Maclaren, said that "The Bible can venture to give full weight to the gravity of sickness because it knows the remedy." All the Hebrew prophets depict humanity afflicted with the sickness unto death, a sickness from which there is no deliverance except by a miracle of God's in-breaking power.

And so we come to the one passage in Ezekiel that almost everyone has heard about, the Valley of the Dry Bones. "The hand of the Lord was upon me, and he brought me out by the Spirit of the Lord, and set me down in the midst of the valley; it was full of bones. And he led me round among them; and behold, there were very many upon the valley; and lo, they were very dry. And he said to me, 'Mortal, can these bones live?' And I answered, 'O Lord God, thou knowest'" (37:1-3).

The bones were very many, and they were very dry. This reflects a saying of the Hebrews in their Babylonian exile: "Our bones are dried up, and our hope is lost; we are clean cut off" (Ezek. 37:11). The valley of bones represents the whole nation of Israel, the covenant community, gone hopelessly astray because of persistent idolatry. "The righteousness of the righteous man shall not deliver him when he transgresses." What hope is there then? "Can these bones live?" And the prophet answers, "O Lord God, thou knowest" — or "Lord, only you know." If the prophet had said "Yes," that would have been outrageous presumption; if he had said "No," that would have been craven unbelief; but he said, "O Lord God, thou knowest" — a "noble utterance of faith and submission."[8]

"[And the Lord said to Ezekiel,] 'Prophesy to these bones, and say to them, O dry bones, hear the word of the Lord.' . . . So I prophesied as I was commanded; and as I prophesied, there was a noise, and behold, a rattling; and the bones came together, bone to its bone." It gives you goose bumps, doesn't it? You can be sure it did in the slave communities that sang "The foot bone connected to the leg bone, now hear the Word of the Lord!" Yet, as Ezekiel looked, the bodies were reconstituted, but they were not alive; there was no breath in them.

[So the Lord said to Ezekiel,] "Prophesy to the breath, prophesy, son of man [mortal], and say to the breath, Thus says the Lord God: Come from the four winds, O breath, and breathe upon these slain, that they may live." So [Ezekiel] prophesied as [he had been] commanded, and the breath came into them, and they lived, and stood upon their feet, an exceedingly great host. And the Lord said to Ezekiel, "Son of man, these bones are the whole house of Israel. Behold, they say, 'Our bones are dried up, and our hope is lost; we are clean cut off.' Therefore prophesy, and say to them, Thus says the Lord God: Behold, I will open your graves, and raise you from your graves, O my people. . . . And I will put my Spirit within you, and you shall live, and I will place you in your own land; then you shall know that I, the Lord, have spoken, and I have done it, says the Lord."

You know that the Old Testament lessons during Lent are chosen because they are mountaintop passages. This is indeed one of them. It is part of the "central myth." What does it mean?

Life is given by the Holy Spirit of God, which, Genesis tells us, "moved upon the face of the waters" at the beginning of creation. Eternal life is not intrinsic to the human being. It cannot be assumed. Even after the dry bones were reassembled and overlaid with flesh, they remained dead. "Can these bones live?" Life is given only by the Spirit of God; "Lord, only thou knowest." The prophet does as he is commanded and calls upon the living Holy Spirit; only then do the corpses breathe. This Spirit, this breath that raised the dead in the vision of Ezekiel, is the very same Holy Spirit given by the Lord Jesus on Easter Day when, according to the Gospel of John, he appears to his astonished disciples in the Upper Room, breathes on them, and says, "Receive the Holy Spirit" (John 20:22).

Jay McInerney writes resolutely that he does not believe a word of any of this. The "central myth" is to him a joy-killing, punitive taskmaster that hounded his mother in the hour of her death. And yet . . . and yet. Perhaps, in some way that you and I cannot foresee, there will be still something more revealed by the Lord of life and death to this no longer young man who in his heyday, by his own admission, spent tens of thousands of dollars on cocaine. He relates something about his mother that points us in a further direction. Personally, I have never been very interested in deathbed scenes or near-death experiences. I am skeptical about them because I think that the gullible human being is apt to believe almost any sentimental thing that comes along. However, in the context of the lessons for today I must say that the second time I read the *New Yorker* story I saw something there that I had not seen at first.

> My mother looked calm. She drifted away again; her eyes clouded over and her face looked serene. After some time, she squeezed my hand. "I was in a wonderful place," she said. . . . "My father was there, and someone else. . . . The light seemed to be coming from him." She drifted off, then said, "They're waiting for me."

She died a few hours later.

Jesus said, "I go to prepare a place for you" (John 14:3). This is part of our "central myth." A strong case can be made that this is nothing but wishful thinking, and God knows, that particular text has been trivialized to a fare-thee-well by overexposure. But there is a difference. Jesus himself cannot be explained away, no matter how hard the Jesus Seminar tries. In particular, his death cannot be explained away. Wishful thinking never created a crucified savior.

And what's more, no "central myth" of any "religion" has ever evoked what St. Paul calls the salvation of *the ungodly* (Rom. 4:5; 5:6). This is what makes Christianity different. Jay McInerney's mother cannot have found what he calls "righteous peace of mind at the end," because there is no such thing as pure human righteousness; what happens to us in spite of ourselves when we put our trust in the Lord Jesus is that *his* righteousness reaches out and snatches us from the very jaws of death and brings us, undeserving as we are, into his eternal presence. "Thus says the Lord God: It is not for your sake, O house of Israel, that I am about to act, but for the sake of my holy name." Our ultimate destiny is not dependent upon our godliness. It is dependent upon God's own nature. The nation of Israel had failed its ever-faithful God utterly, but he did not forsake his people. To us he communicates *his own* godliness.

All of us at one time or another will wonder if there is any truth to the Biblical promises. The power and majesty of the stories we have read today is a sign that God is greater than our doubts, greater than our fears, certainly greater than the scoffings of the cultural elite. His determined purpose to raise the dead is a constituent part of who he is; as we put our trust in his overriding resolve, our lives begin to be transformed in the present. Whatever tomb you feel may be closing in upon you, whatever unholy fear or doubt may cloud your mind, whatever spiritual dryness or physical death may threaten you, it is no match for the Holy Spirit of God. Submit to him this day, with joy, and know in your heart that the words will sound for you as they did for that other sinner of Bethany so long ago:

"Lazarus, come forth."

AMEN.

Nothing Virtual Tonight

GRACE CHURCH, COLORADO SPRINGS

The Lord Jesus, on the night when he was betrayed, took bread, and when he had given thanks, he broke it, and said, "This is my body which is for you. Do this in remembrance of me." In the same way also the cup, after supper, saying, "This cup is the new covenant in my blood. Do this, as often as you drink it, in remembrance of me."

(1 COR. 11:23-25)

When I was a young Christian before the age of mass media, it was regularly taught that God arranged for his Son, Jesus, to come at the time and in the place he did because the *pax romana* (the enforced peace of the Roman Empire) with its extensive system of roads, common Greek language, and relative political stability made it possible for the message to travel rapidly. Nowadays, this question immediately suggests another: Why didn't God arrange for Jesus to come in the age of the Internet?

Well, maybe there's a reason for that too. Maybe God didn't want Jesus to have a home page. Maybe God didn't want his Messiah to be on "Larry King Live." Maybe God didn't intend to have a virtual Son. Maybe it really was God's plan that Jesus would be forever alive to us as he is proclaimed in Holy Scripture, and nowhere else.[1]

However that may be, according to a recent article in *The Wall Street Journal* God has gone online. If you key in the word "God" on a Netscape search, you will be able to access more than 600,000 sites. Many people now think cyberspace is the place to go to have an experience of Jesus. A decade ago when movies were still high-tech, I ran into a woman who had dropped out of a church Bible study group that I led. She had just been to see the movie *The Last Temptation of Christ.* She couldn't say enough about how wonderful the movie was and how important it was for me to see it. I tried to say as graciously as possible that I would go to the movie if she would come back to the Bible study group. That wasn't really fair, of course, since it wouldn't be an equal exchange. The Bible summons us to a lifetime of study and application within a worshiping community, rather than two hours of entertainment in a movie house full of strangers whom one will never see again. The Internet offers the same advantages — or disadvantages, depending on how you think about it; you don't have to be with people you don't like and you won't be asked to put any money in the plate.

According to the same *Wall Street Journal* article, a woman in Coldwater, Ontario, is able to log into a website at a monastery in Massachusetts and meditate while she gazes at the virtual communion wafer. She says, "I believe [it] is the true presence of Jesus. That's what makes it so special." I am not trying to make fun of this. I am just raising some questions.

Over and over on television this week, we have been watching pictures of refugees. I saw a brief interview with a young Kosovar man who spoke pretty good English. He explained that he had been walking for six hours straight, carrying his grandmother. As he spoke, we saw his face, but we did not see the grandmother. As he finished speaking, the camera panned down to his feet where the old lady had collapsed in a heap on the ground. He indicated that he could have walked faster if he had been unencumbered, but, as he said simply, he couldn't leave her: "She is my grandmother." I don't know what was more affecting, the pathetic condition of the exhausted, heartbroken old lady or the devotion of her grandson. I thought of my own mother and my husband's mother and what it would be like for them to be homeless refugees. And yet, I think we all know that seeing it on television is *nothing like* seeing it in person. If you and I were actually there, we would be seeing *thousands* of suffering grandmothers and *thousands* of traumatized children and we would be sharing the same space with them. We would be drawn into their plight. We would not be able to push the button on the remote control to shut them off.

You know, Jesus did not just come among us as an observer. He wasn't like a fatigue-wearing correspondent who interviews people and collects data and then goes safely home. Rather, he came among us as one who was a refugee himself. His parents had to flee from their home so their baby would not be killed by the Slobodan Milosevic of their day, King Herod. In Hector Berlioz's French oratorio *L'Enfance du Christ* (The Childhood of Christ) there is a wrenching moment when the Holy Family goes from house to house seeking shelter and has every door slammed in their faces. Their donkey has died of exhaustion and they have no more food. Mary, frantically hoping someone will take pity on them, keeps pleading, *Nous arrivons à pieds* (we have come all this way *on foot*), with a kind of desperate shriek. As Jesus himself will say when he is grown up, "the Son of Man has nowhere to lay his head" (Matt. 8:20).

These are some thoughts that occur to me as I contemplate the events of Maundy Thursday. This is not virtual reality tonight. This is the real thing. You made a very important commitment when you decided to come in person to church tonight. You and I are not sharing virtual space. We are sharing the same space, the same pews. Shortly we will be sharing the same bread, the same wine. This is a unique moment in the church year, the evening when we remember how the Lord instituted the Eucharist. Listen again to the words of Paul from the First Letter to the Corinthians: "The Lord Jesus on the night when he was betrayed took bread, and when he had given thanks, he broke it, and said, "This is my body which is given for you. Do this in remembrance of me." In the same way also the cup, after supper, saying, "This cup is the new covenant in my blood. Do this, as often as you drink it, in remembrance of me."

When I was a teenager I went to a small two-day retreat. At the end of the two days we sat around a table, and our retreat leader, a priest, presided over the Lord's Supper. This sort of thing is common today, but in the 1950s it was unusual and none of us had ever done it before. We passed the bread and the cup around the table more or less as Jesus and his disciples had done. Afterward, the retreat leader asked the usual question, "How did you feel?" Usually this kind of question evokes platitudes, but one young girl said something so memorable that I still remember it after all these years. She said, "I am closer to all of you now." She didn't say "I *feel* closer;" she said, "I *am* closer." She recognized that the Lord's Supper was and is an objective event that causes new relationships to come into being. Around the table that night, Jesus spoke these words to his disciples: "This is my commandment, that you love one another as I have loved you" (John 15:12).

This is family night in the church. The closing Collect says it for us: "Almighty God, we pray thee graciously to behold *this thy family. . . .*" More than any other service in the entire Christian year, this one focuses directly on the new relationships that God brings into being through the blood of Jesus. We are family tonight. Everybody is my grandmother. We are not here to wall ourselves off in a private religious experience or to gain righteousness for ourselves. All of our ways of understanding human relationships are reordered tonight. It is described by the Lord very specifically in the Gospel reading that you just heard. Kings and others in authority, he says, "exercise lordship." Powerful men act in ways that the world recognizes and rewards. "But it is not so among you," says the Lord, "rather, let the greatest among you become as the [least], and the leader [become] as one who serves. For which is the greater, one who sits at table, or one who serves? Is it not the one who sits at table? But I am among you as one who serves" (Luke 22:25-27). And to make the point, John the Evangelist tells us, Jesus gets down on his knees on the floor and washes the disciples' feet.

We cannot understand what is going on here unless we understand something of what the Bible teaches. We learn from the narratives of the Old Testament that there is a very thin veneer separating us from barbarism. After the disobedience of Adam and Eve, the human race rapidly deteriorates. One brother kills another and we go downhill from there. In the story from Exodus that was read tonight, God's people are slaves, unable to free themselves. This great narrative has always been read during Holy Week and Easter. It tells our story: the whole race of humankind is held hostage to sin and death. Morehead (Mike) Kennedy, the foreign service officer who was held hostage in Iran for more than a year, was asked to give many speeches after he got home. He always began the same way: "Fellow hostages . . ." We are all hostages to sin and death, powerless to free ourselves. We need deliverance. Think of hostages on an airplane, who can only be liberated if some sort of SWAT team comes in. In the Exodus, God works mighty signs and wonders; the miracle of the Exodus occurs over the heads of the Israelites, so to speak. But in the death of Jesus, *God is personally involved.* He is not sending the SWAT team. He has come himself.

President Clinton was talking, today, to the military families in Norfolk, Virginia. People in power almost always talk in a certain way. I listened to him. He was talking as if America was always right, always had been right, always would be right. He was talking as if there were no articles in the paper today suggesting that the Western alliance might have made a mistake, that they had had signals months ago that Milosevic might not be deterred by bombing. I am no expert on these matters. I am only disturbed, as all Christians should be, by the whipping up of patriotism as though "American lives" were the only lives that count. Fifty years ago, the Serbs were our allies. They fought with great determination against Germany. In the world we live in, today's friends are tomorrow's enemies. Many Serbs despise Milosevic and demonstrated against him in 1996, but they have all rallied around him now. That is what bombs always do, they unify a population. But after the bombing is over, then what? What is it going to take to bring Serbs and (Albanian) Kosovars back together after the barbarity has stopped?[2] What weapons are there that can bring people together across national, racial, ethnic lines? Forty-one bullets fired in New York City have brought many people out to support the minority groups of

the city, but there are equally determined groups tl
police, right or wrong.³ Who and what is going to
elements together?

I am not taking a position on the NATO action
pit tonight. I am doing something different. I am ι ‾‾‾ₓ some
connections that are theologically and ethically suggestive for this
Holy Week. The President told Dan Rather yesterday that he was-
n't going to commit any ground troops to Kosovo. Yet a ranking
NATO officer in Brussels said this, just yesterday: "The allies chose
bombing because none of them were willing to take the risk of
sending in the [ground] troops that . . . it would take to keep
[Milosevic] from having his way with the 1.8 million ethnic Albanians." What does that suggest to you? I am not bringing up the
simplistic adage left over from the Vietnam War that if you are going to wage a war you have to wage it all the way. I am hoping that
the Holy Spirit is working in some way tonight through these images and thoughts to help us to understand the magnitude of the
sacrifice of our Lord. Jesus put himself into the battle on the front
line where a horrible godforsaken death was the only possible outcome.

Imagine, if you will, a huge military force, as in the Nor-
mandy Invasion, preparing to assault the vast territory occupied by
the enemy. Billions of dollars have been spent on tanks and planes.
The troops are hardened and ready after months of training. Suddenly there comes pushing through to the front of the forces the
commander himself, not the regimental commander or the division
commander or even the corps commander, but the five-star general
of the army and indeed of all the armies, and he says he is going
alone. Can you conceive of this? "Then [in the garden of Gethsema-
ne] Jesus said . . . 'Put your sword back into its place. . . . Do you
think that I cannot appeal to my Father, and he will at once send me
more than twelve legions of angels? But how then should the scriptures be fulfilled, that it must be so?'" (Matt. 26:52-54)

As Paul writes, Jesus was "in the form of God" (Phil. 2:6). He
could have just stayed where he was, at the right hand of power. He
could have pushed the "delete" button on all of us. Instead, he came

‗o share our space and, ultimately, to take our condition upon himself. There is nothing virtual about it. God did not send the search and rescue team. In Jesus, God sent himself.

He goes alone. He goes alone, and of course, of course, he is crushed by the steamrolling powers of darkness, malice, evil, violence, sin, death, and the devil. And that would have been the last that we ever heard of such an insane deed, had the commander not been the Son of God and the captain of the heavenly host. Only such a power as that which rolled back the Red Sea can overcome death and make enemies into friends. Because, you see, *we were all Jesus' enemies.* All of us shouted "Crucify him" on Palm Sunday. But he will not let us be his enemies. Here he is tonight, asking nothing of you at all except that you come and join him at his table as he gives you himself. "You are my friends," he says to every one of you. Jesus our Lord and Master: "Take, eat, this is my body, given for you."

AMEN.

Mine Eyes Have Seen the Glory

ST. PAUL'S CHURCH, RICHMOND, VIRGINIA

The Lord reigns; let the peoples tremble! He sits enthroned upon the cherubim; let the earth quake! . . . Let {the peoples} praise thy great and terrible name! . . . He spoke to them in the pillar of cloud. . . . Extol the Lord our God, and worship at his holy mountain; for the Lord our God is holy!

(Ps. 99)

Moses went up on the mountain, and the cloud covered the mountain. . . . Now the appearance of the glory of the Lord was like a devouring fire on the top of the mountain in the sight of the people of Israel.

(EXOD. 24:15, 17)

Lo, a bright cloud overshadowed them, and a voice from the cloud said, "This is my beloved Son, with whom I am well pleased; listen to him." When the disciples heard this, they fell on their faces, and were filled with awe. But Jesus came and touched them, saying, "Rise and have no fear."

(MATT. 17:5-7)

Whatever gain I had, I counted as loss for the sake of Christ. . . . For his sake I have suffered the loss of all things, and count them as refuse, in order that I may gain Christ and be found in him, not having a righteousness of my own, based on law, but that which is through faith in Christ, the righteousness from God that depends on faith; that I may know him and the power of his resurrection, and may share his sufferings, becoming like him in his death, that if possible I may attain the resurrection from the dead.

(PHIL. 3:7-11)

A good friend of mine is rector of a church in the Massachusetts Berkshires. She tells a story about her husband and his Sunday school class. Her husband is a physics professor at Williams College. He was teaching a class on the Transfiguration to some twelve-to thirteen-year-olds. As he related the story of how Jesus' clothing turned brilliant white, Moses and Elijah appeared, and so forth, one of the boys said, "Mr. Crampton, I don't believe that story, and *neither do you.*"

I guess that is the challenge I want to put to us today. Every Christian who is serious about the faith is going to meet this kind of reaction more often than not. I happen to know that my friend's husband the physics professor does believe the story, but he would agree that there are plenty of times when it is tempting to back off from the Bible stories, to be "ashamed of the gospel" (Rom. 1:16). I was recently acquainted with a young woman who is in the doctoral program in the divinity school of an Ivy League university. I went to hear her deliver a sermon to a group of graduate students. I found her sermon very disappointing. I knew this young woman was a committed Christian, but her presentation was unsure, hesitant. Afterwards I commented, "You seemed very tentative." She said, "I don't feel that I can really state my faith in front of that group." I knew what she meant. It's a good example of how we are tempted to be ashamed of the gospel. In many circles today, it takes courage to be forthright about Christian faith. I have been many years coming to this point, but I believe that Christian discipleship requires that we let people know that we *do* believe the story, not in a woodenly literal sense, but in a very deep and fundamental sense, and that we are willing to say so even if it is embarrassing to us.

You may think it is no big deal for a member of the clergy to say she believes in something from the Bible. But let me tell you, anybody seeking to be considered intellectually respectable is going to be tempted to deny the Transfiguration and the Incarnation and the Resurrection and pretty much anything else about Jesus that would suggest he was divine. This pressure to conform to a worldly standard is especially noticeable in the Northeast, where I have spent most of my ministry. I still remember having lunch with a well-known New York writer and intellectual. I was in considerable awe of this person. He cocked his head to one side, looked at me quizzically, and said in a conspiratorial way as though he thought he and I might share a secret, "You don't really believe in God, do you?"

Two weeks ago, on the last Sunday before Lent, the lectionary set before us, as usual, several readings from the Bible. On this particular Sunday I was struck by the force of the challenge they brought. To put it bluntly, these texts say to us: Do you see the very glory of God in the face of Jesus of Nazareth, or not?

Let us turn to the Biblical passages for the Sunday of the Transfiguration. Three of the four contain the same motif; the Psalm, the Old Testament lesson, and the Gospel all speak of a cloud. Psalm 99 is a hymn to the glory of God: "The Lord reigns; let the peoples tremble! He sits enthroned upon the cherubim; let the earth quake! . . . Let [the peoples] praise [his] great and terrible name! . . . He spoke to them in the pillar of cloud. . . . Extol the Lord our God, and worship at his holy mountain; for the Lord our God is holy!" I think most of us who read the Psalms on Sunday morning are, unfortunately, doing it in a somewhat mechanical way. I doubt if most of us think of what we are saying as we read. Over the ages, however, the Psalms have always been at the center of the church's worship. There is no theme in the Psalms more prominent than the praise of the Lord's holiness and might, his overwhelming greatness and majesty. His name is called "great and terrible" (the Prayer Book translation says "awesome," which softens it somewhat). The cloud is a manifestation of God's transcendent power, but the cloud also hides him from human sight. The Old Testament reading, from Exodus, also contains this idea of revealing while concealing: "Moses went up on the mountain, and the cloud covered the mountain. . . . The glory of the Lord settled on Mount Sinai, and on the seventh day [God] called Moses out of the midst of the cloud. Now the appearance of the glory of the Lord was like a devouring fire on the top of the mountain in the sight of the people of Israel" (Exod. 24:15-17).

The images are a little confusing, aren't they? First there's a cloud, then there's a fire. These are ways of saying that God's presence is both visible and hidden. Since the glory of the Lord is like a devouring fire in the sight of human eyes, he conceals himself — so to speak — inside the cloud so that the people will not be blinded.[1] He is present, yet he hides himself. This happens all through the story of the Hebrew people. God works mighty acts on their behalf, then appears to withdraw. There are many times in human life when God seems hidden and we question his goodness, his compassion, even his existence. One thinks particularly of the torments inflicted upon young children by adults. There was a story in the paper just yesterday about a group of volunteer anthropologists who investigate massacres. They have uncovered overwhelming evidence of more than three hundred villagers, mostly women and children, who were butchered in Guatemala by government troops in 1981 — only one of many such massacres. The leader of the scientific group showed evidence to a reporter, paused, and said, "Poor little kids."[2] Where was God when that was happening? This agonizing problem of the absence of God is explicitly and repeatedly acknowledged in the Bible; the Psalms speak of it when they ask such questions as, "How long will you hide yourself, O Lord? Will you hide yourself forever?" (89:46). Frankly, the scorn of intellectuals doesn't bother me half as much as the apparent inaction of God in so much of daily life. The doubts and difficulties that I have are concerned with the discrepancy between the Biblical promises and the actual events that go on around us. It seems that God is inside a cloud most of the time.

Of all the Biblical images of God, the most difficult for contemporary Americans to grasp is the depiction of him as fearful and terrible. Earlier generations spoke much more freely of "the fear of the Lord" than we do. They understood in a way that is almost inaccessible for us that the Lord is compassionate *and* frightening, threatening *and* gracious at the same time. The Bible stories make it clear that the mercy both precedes and follows the terror, otherwise we could not bear it; but if we insist on removing the passages about the "fear of the Lord" we will have a wishy-washy god of our own construction who will not, in the end, be the real God at all. Only a God of fearful power is strong enough to overcome evil. It is such a God that the Bible proclaims to us. In the Old Testament, appearances of God *always* cause fear. That's why angels are always saying, "Fear not."

The third reading two Sundays ago was the New Testament story of the Transfiguration. Matthew tells us that Jesus, the human being, was revealed to his disciples on the mountain as the divine Son of God. We read that, as his garments became white with an unearthly brilliance and his face shone with the blinding brightness of the sun, a cloud came between him and them, and the voice of God came from within the cloud: "This is my beloved Son, in whom I am well pleased; hear ye him." Now notice what happens as a result of this voice: "And when the disciples heard it, they fell on their face, and were sore afraid. And Jesus came and touched them, and said, 'Arise, and be not afraid'" (17:1-7).

I find myself going back to the King James Version occasionally because it is more vivid. The disciples were "sore afraid." Only the word and the touch of Jesus was able to restore them. "Arise, be not afraid." If we are going to construct a god for ourselves who does not cause us any fear, then, obviously, we don't need Jesus. If these stories about the fire and the cloud don't refer to anything real, then, certainly, we can turn our backs on the Bible as an embarrassing primitive document that doesn't speak to our advanced scientific age.

"Mrs. Rutledge, I don't believe that story, and neither do you." What have I to say to that? Do I believe that a cloud came down with a voice in it? Do I believe that Jesus' clothes and face turned so bright as to burn the human cornea?

Two things, I am convinced, happened in the sight of the disciples. A curtain was drawn back; and then it was drawn closed again. The voice spoke, and Jesus' identity was revealed — the divine, only-begotten Son of God — and then it was hidden again. That is what the story means. The divinity was there from the beginning ("the Word was made flesh and dwelt among us," John 1:14) but it was concealed under the human flesh. The disciples were shown this. The God who had appeared on Mount Sinai as a blazing fire, the God who "sits enthroned upon the cherubim" (Ps. 99:1), the God who causes the earth to tremble has committed himself to a course of suffering, humiliation, agony, and death. For you see, the lectionary is designed so that the Transfiguration is the climactic event of revelation before the Passion of Jesus begins.

The fourth reading two Sundays ago was the New Testament letter to the Philippians. These are the personal words of a man in prison, knowing that he is to die for Christ. This man, according to his own testimony, has suffered the loss of everything — possessions, reputation, status, security, liberty, life itself — counting them as worthless as "dung" [King James Version] "in order that I may gain Christ" (Phil. 3:8). The Apostle Paul continues, "I share his sufferings, that I may know him and the power of his resurrection" (v. 10).

I have been living with the words of Paul and the other New Testament apostles and evangelists all my life. I have tested their writings in the struggles and doubts of my own days and nights. I have learned that their testimony stands up against every assault. I trust them. I do not believe they made these things up. I once served a church in Connecticut where the twelve apostles were depicted in the windows around the church. I never went into that pulpit without thinking of how those apostles gave up everything they had in order to pass the news of the living Christ along to you and to me. They died for that gospel. Under, beneath, inside, beyond the human flesh of Jesus they were enabled to see something that had changed their lives utterly and for which they were more than willing to risk everything.

On the night before he was killed, Martin Luther King preached a sermon that, people said later, seemed to transfigure him. He slumped back after he finished, completely overcome by the power of the words he had been given to say. "I've been to the mountaintop," he cried. "I've seen the promised land. I may not get there with you. But I want you to know tonight that we, as a people, will get to the promised land. So I'm happy tonight; I'm not worried about anything; I'm not fearing any man. Mine eyes have seen the glory of the coming of the Lord." It was said afterward that never did a man seem less happy. It had been years since the "I have a dream" speech. Since that climactic day on the mountaintop, Dr. King had been walking in the flames. He was under attack from all sides. It was not human happiness that he felt. It was not human hope that he held. It was not human promises that he trusted. It was God that he trusted, the God who makes a way out of no way.[3] He trusted in spite of everything that God's glory would be shown forth in his weakness as he "shared the sufferings of Christ and became like Christ in his death."

The glory of God is hidden in the sufferings of Jesus. The Resurrection is known to us now only by faith. What is the source of faith? The source of faith is God himself. It is in the event of the Word made flesh *through his servants who suffer for his sake* that we know his glory. Any preacher who does not suffer in bringing you the gospel is no Christian messenger. "How long will you hide yourself, O Lord? Will you hide yourself forever?" That is the preacher's perpetual question. Yet even as the preacher stands before you bent and crippled by sin like all the rest of humanity, the message is that the light of redemption has dawned upon us all in the journey of the Son of God through death into life. It is true on the brilliant days but even more true on the cloudy ones when faith is tested and hope is nearly dead: the very glory of God shines in the face of Jesus of Nazareth.

He dies and he shines *for you*.

AMEN.

Death Shall Have No Dominion

GRACE CHURCH AND ST. STEPHEN'S,
COLORADO SPRINGS

There is no greater privilege, no more awesome responsibility in all the world than preaching on Good Friday and Easter. As I told the congregation on Good Friday, I am among you as one who, in the words of St. Paul, is "determined to know nothing among you except Jesus Christ and him crucified" (1 Cor. 2:2). That was Friday. This morning, I am here as nothing more and nothing less than a witness to the Resurrection of that crucified Lord from the dead. This is the day of incomparable gladness, the "royal feast of feasts" as we shall soon sing. I look forward to this day more keenly each year as I get older, because, with more experience of life and its disappointments, I become less and less confident about things naturally working themselves out for the best.

This morning, I am especially interested in those of you who do not always attend Sunday services. Let me make it clear how glad we are to see you. A full church is a great sight and we should be very sorry indeed not to have one this morning. But what has brought you here? Let me guess. Some of you have been coaxed or intimidated into coming by family members. Some are here out of a sense of obligation to a spouse or parent. Some of you probably respect the importance of ritual, whether you are Christian believers or not. Some of you are here out of habit or a sense of duty. Many of you have probably brought children because you do not want them to be without the fun of dressing up and hunting for eggs. Some of you have doubtless come as a sort of last-ditch effort to believe in something. One of my many unbelieving friends in New York, who was brought up as a Christian in Holland many years ago, says that the only day of the year that he goes to church is Easter Day, because, as he says, "I don't want to be a complete pagan." He wants me to know, however, that he does not believe in the Resurrection. (I suggested that he ought to go on Good Friday instead, but that is another story.)

So why are you here? Is this really a day of incomparable gladness for you? Or is it basically just a good excuse to celebrate spring and the return of vitality to the earth? Is it really a "royal feast of feasts," or is it just one more of our three-day American holiday weekends, giving us a break in our routine and a chance for a family gathering?

Some of you may be here this morning because you would like to have a religious experience. I think it's a safe bet that many people who go out to the Garden of the Gods at sunrise are there for that reason. Spectacular scenery helps to get us in the mood. Or does it? The glory of nature can actually interfere with our understanding. After all, the sun comes up over the mountains every day, whereas the Resurrection of our Lord is a radically discontinuous event having nothing to do with nature. In this respect I hope you will forgive me a small dissent from the hymn, "Now the green blade riseth." Don't get me wrong; I decorate our house at Easter with flowers, eggs, and even (horrors!) bunnies. These things are fine as long as we don't get them confused with the real thing. But the words "Forth he came at Easter like the risen grain . . ." are a little bit deceptive, because they suggest that the Resurrection was a natural, predictable event, when in fact it was *anti*-natural and uniquely *un*predictable.

The Resurrection has been an embarrassment to many modern, sophisticated church people. Just this week, the Jesus Seminar released its latest findings to the press. This group of seventy-odd New Testament scholars, with exquisite timing, gladdens the hearts of Christians at major festivals each year by announcing yet one more "discovery" that the Bible cannot be believed. There was no Resurrection, they declare; Jesus was not buried in a tomb and his body was probably disposed of by the Roman authorities, perhaps even thrown out to be eaten by scavenging animals. This ineffable band of spoilers delights in scandalizing the faithful. I know, because I used to be like that myself when I was first in seminary. I wanted very much to be part of the cutting edge. I wanted to be recognized as a Christian intellectual, not as one of the unthinking simpleminded. This attitude has penetrated deeply into the church. Parishes like this one have not been as weakened by these cultural assaults as some others, but speaking generally, it is hard in mainline churches nowadays to find robust belief in the Resurrection.

I keep a file of newspaper clippings about Easter preaching; even *The New York Times* occasionally does a pretty good job of canvassing the city churches for sermon quotations. I went through several dozen of these excerpts last night, and I am about to give my Easter file a new name: "One Hundred Ways to Avoid Saying That Jesus Christ Is Risen from the Dead." Over and over in these sermons and messages, the same words appear, year after year: *renewal, revival, rebirth*. These words are used far more than the word *resurrection*. We hear of a new season, new growth, new life. We hear of sap rising in the trees, the singing of birds, the warmth of the lengthening days. We hear of "a new season in the earth and in the heart of humanity." We hear that "the early Christians came to understand that love is stronger than death."

Seriously, now: does this turn you on? Is it possible that ideas like this would have taken hold of a tiny band of utterly demoralized, beleaguered, disgraced, scattered disciples and transformed them into a mighty power that within a few years was shaking the foundation of the Roman Empire? One journalist who wrote a story about Easter recently described it as a spring festival celebrating "the ancient myths of the Mediterranean imagination." Is that what turned the disciples around?

Put yourself in the place of the women who went to the tomb that Easter morning to anoint the body of Jesus. Do you think they were expecting anything? Maybe the flowers were blooming and the birds singing as they walked along. Do you think they took comfort from that? Is it likely that they looked out over the fields and said to each other, "Maybe the Master is going to come again like wheat that springeth green"? Not on your life. If you go to take flowers to a cemetery, do you expect to see an empty grave? If you did see one, would it occur to you to think that the body was risen from the dead? Of course not. You would think immediately of vandals and grave robbers. Luke's Easter story goes on for two more verses after the part we heard just now; the evangelist goes on to tell us that "Mary Magdalene and Joanna and Mary the mother of James . . . told . . . the apostles [of the empty tomb], but their words seemed to them to be an idle tale, and they did not believe them" (Luke 24:10-11). No wonder they didn't believe. The sight of an empty grave wouldn't convince you or me either. Nor did the women and the apostles start believing in the Resurrection because they saw the green grass coming up. Something more than that had to happen. What happened was that Jesus himself appeared, and he was *alive*.

Like all clergy, I have sometimes been present with people at the moment of death. I don't flinch from this responsibility — it is an aspect of my calling — but given a choice, looking at dead bodies is something I prefer not to do. I didn't want to look at my father in his coffin. The look of the body imposes itself on me. I always seem to remember the look of the body dead better than I remember the look of the person alive. It's as though death has gained a sort of victory. There isn't anything we can do about death. It's so damned inexorable, and I do mean damned. People talk about what a release it is. "It was a blessing," we say. That's only so if we've been taking care of a very old or very sick person. It surely isn't a release or a blessing when you want nothing more in all the world than to have that person back again. I have never become immune to the shock of watching the appalling change in the look and feel of the body. The New Testament refers to death as an enemy (1 Cor. 15:26). Even in the case of what we call a merciful death, there is still a horrible indignity, a fearsome intrusiveness about death that causes us to feel its presence as a hostile, invading power that robs the human being of everything it was ever meant to be. Nebulous messages about religious hope for an afterlife simply do not have the power to stare down the stark ugliness of death. Such messages sound too much like wishful thinking to be convincing.[1]

At the very least, we owe it to those first Christian disciples to do our best to understand the sheer *hopelessness* of the situation they were in. They had invested their lives, their fortunes, and their sacred honor in what appeared to be a mockery. They had seen their hopes and dreams ridiculed, scorned, and spat upon by the population of the entire city. Once they had basked in the celebrity of their crowd-pleasing Master; now he had been judged a disgrace, a menace to society, a blasphemer, a pretender, and a fraud, no better than two small-time thieves. He was discredited, degraded, and dead; his once-loyal group of followers had broken ranks and deserted; there was nothing left. It is preposterous to think of them pulling themselves together, forming themselves into a mighty band and galvanizing the whole Mediterranean world with a made-up story about an empty tomb and some appearances in an upper room. Even the skeptics who want to make the Resurrection into something completely bloodless will agree that *something happened.* But what was it?

I am thinking today of a woman who is an active member in the parish that I am attending during my six-month sabbatical. She and her husband had a wonderful, rare marriage. They did everything together. They were both in good health and looking forward to celebrating their forty-ninth wedding anniversary. One month ago, with no warning whatsoever, her husband died in his sleep. She was and is devastated. I am thinking of her this morning. What message do you think will bring her true comfort this Easter Day? Will "the ancient myths of the Mediterranean imagination" do it? I had a friend whose child died in the spring; she said that the flowers and birds were agonizing for her, like a mockery. What will bring hope to that mother? What would she rather hear, a message about rebirth in nature, or this: "His soul was not left in hell, neither did his flesh see corruption; this Jesus hath God raised up, whereof we all are witnesses" (Acts 2:31-32). Would you rather hear about earth replenishing herself, or would you rather hear this: "Behold, I tell you a mystery. We shall not all sleep, but we shall all be changed, in a moment, in the twinkling of an eye, at the last trumpet: for the trumpet shall sound, and the dead shall be raised incorruptible, and we shall be changed. . . . Then shall be brought to pass the saying that is written, Death is swallowed up in victory. O death, where is thy sting? O grave, where is thy victory?" (1 Cor. 15:51-55).

A woman coming out of church on Easter Day in New York was asked about her beliefs: "Easter is when you throw off winter's robes," she said.[2] Is this enough for you? I confess it is not enough for me. If that is all there is to Easter then I would just as soon be somewhere else this morning. I didn't really want to get on a plane this week, not even to come to spectacular Colorado; I didn't want to miss the blooming cherry trees at home. But let me tell you something. The news of the Resurrection of the Lord from the dead is not something to keep to oneself. I hope you will forgive me for a self-serving remark when I say that I did succeed in becoming a Christian intellectual, after a fashion, and achieved my goal of gaining access to New York intellectuals and writers. But I would exchange it all to be with the Christian community during Holy Week and the Great Fifty Days of Easter. I am not embarrassed to tell you today that I think the Jesus Seminar is a barren and desolate enterprise. I believe the body of Jesus was in a tomb, and that it disappeared. I believe that when, a few weeks at the most after the crucifixion, the disciples began to electrify the Mediterranean world with their proclamation of a risen Lord, it was not possible for anyone to disprove their allegations by pointing to what was left of Jesus' body, not because it had been eaten by dogs but because it had simply vanished. "Why do you look for the living among the dead? He is not here; he is risen!" (Luke 24:5). It is fashionable today to deride the stories of the empty tomb. It is true that most of the Easter narratives and all of the apostle Paul's testimony focus on the appearances of the risen Jesus, but as the preeminent New Testament scholar Raymond Brown (emphatically not a member of the Jesus Seminar) has written, there is not a scintilla of evidence that any of the early Christians thought that Jesus' body was moldering somewhere.

"Go quickly," said the angel to the women, "Go quickly and tell the disciples, 'He has risen from the dead and is going ahead of you into Galilee. There you will see him.' Lo, I have told you" (Matt. 28:7). I do not believe that there is any other message on earth that could have reversed the effect of a crucifixion. I do not believe there is any other news ever uttered with human tongue that could convince us even to this present day that Death, against all the evidence and against all reason, has been driven from the field.

So this is no day for innocuous sentiments about springtime in the heart. This is the day for trumpets and timpani and organ fanfares to burst the eardrums of Satan. This is no day for wistful thoughts about the possibility of an afterlife; this is a day for Paul's cry of triumph: "If Christ is not raised, our preaching is in vain and your faith is in vain. . . . If Christ has not been raised, you are still in your sins; but in fact Christ has been raised from the dead. . . . For as by a man came death, by a man has come also the resurrection of the dead. For as in Adam all die, so also in Christ shall all be made alive!" (1 Cor. 15:14-22).

And so I am a believer. I have lived with the letters of the Apostle Paul for most of my fifty-eight years and I do not believe that he would tell a lie. I believe that the tomb was empty and that Mary Magdalene and Peter and the other disciples saw the Master alive. But it is not "my" belief. It does not belong to me. It is the church's belief, and so it belongs to you too. Jesus is the Lord of the universe and he has turned the key in the lock of the gate of Hell. Christ has won the victory over death and the devil. His promise to return and establish his Kingdom forever and ever is true, not because I am faithful but because God is faithful, and his faithfulness is powerful to break down barricades and overthrow tyrants and raise the dead to life, yes, and to give each of his children, from the least to the greatest, hope and strength and courage and defiance in daily life against everything that would ever hurt or destroy his beloved creatures.

He is risen! The Lord is risen indeed! Alleluia!

A Way Out of No Way

GRACE CHURCH AND ST. STEPHEN'S,
COLORADO SPRINGS

As a climactic ending to this glorious service on the day of our Lord's Resurrection from the dead, we are going to sing the hymn "Come, ye faithful, raise the strain of triumphant gladness!" I am going to read you the words of the first verse.

> Come, ye faithful, raise the strain of triumphant gladness!
> God has brought his Israel into joy from sadness.
> Loosed from Pharaoh's bitter yoke, Jacob's sons and daughters
> Led them with unmoistened foot through the Red Sea waters.[1]

If this was an African-American congregation, I could assume that most of the worshipers would understand the connection between Pharaoh and the empty tomb. In largely white congregations, though, there is a lot of mystification about it. During my career as a Bible teacher, I have taken quite a few informal polls and I've learned that most Episcopalians have only the vaguest idea of the connection between Exodus and Easter. So this is a wonderful day, the best day of all, to enter into the power of our Lord's Resurrection through the retelling of the story of the deliverance at the Red Sea.

The Easter story and the Exodus story are about power. Everybody is interested in power. As Henry Kissinger famously said,

"Power is the greatest aphrodisiac." Power attracts, power fascinates, power sells, power makes things happen. Powerlessness is very bad for people. The refugees in Kosovo are helpless and powerless, and we feel for them because we have some sense of how awful that is. Many, many times I have heard people say that the worst thing about a bad situation was that they couldn't do anything about it. People whose loved ones are very sick often speak of this feeling. They feel that they can't do anything to help and they feel impotent. Powerlessness paralyzes people. Many doctors curtail their visits to dying patients because they feel there is nothing more they can do.

The story of the Exodus is about the power of God. It is one of the greatest of all the Biblical narratives. All Bible stories are told with striking economy, with just a few carefully chosen words and details to make the strongest possible impression. Listen to the beginning of the Red Sea story:

> The Lord said to Moses, "Tell the people of Israel to turn back and encamp . . . between Migdol and the sea. . . . For Pharaoh will say of the people of Israel, 'They are entangled in the land; the wilderness has shut them in.'" (Exod. 14:2-3)

Now the point of this is that the Lord did not bring the Israelites out of Egypt by the normal, direct route. He brought them a roundabout way, which made no tactical sense. "They are entangled in the land; the wilderness has shut them in." We understand from this the Lord has led them to an indefensible position from which there was no way out, no escape, no exit.

The Lord did this deliberately, for a purpose. To Moses he said, "I will harden Pharaoh's heart, and he will pursue them, and I will get glory over Pharaoh and all his host; and the Egyptians shall know that I am the Lord" (v. 4). The children of Israel have been led into a cul-de-sac where the Egyptians will come after them from the land, and there is nothing at their backs but the sea.

The story continues: "When Pharaoh drew near, the people of Israel lifted up their eyes, and behold, the Egyptians were marching after them; and they were sore afraid. And the people of Israel cried out to the Lord, and they said to Moses . . . 'What have you done to us, in bringing us out of Egypt? Is not this what we said to you in Egypt, "Let us alone and let us serve the Egyptians"? For it would have been better for us to serve the Egyptians than to die in the wilderness.'" There is some degree of rueful humor here because we recognize typical human nature in the Israelites' lament. Freedom is costly. We think we want it, but we don't want to pay the price. Whenever there are great public issues to be resolved, it is easy to get people to sign up for the initial stages of an effort, but only a few will stay to do the grunt work of the next stages. Danger sounds glamorous, but after the TV cameras pack up and go home, not many will want to stay on the barricades. The idea of freedom is intoxicating, but when real enemies appear, retreat sometimes looks like a pretty good option. In this case, however, retreat is impossible. The wilderness has shut them in.

Now listen to Moses. You won't find a moment like this in any of the Exodus movies. Only in the telling of the story in the midst of the worshiping, believing community do these words come alive: "Moses said to the people, 'Fear not, stand firm, and see the salvation of the Lord, which he will work for you today; for the Egyptians whom you see today, you shall never see again. The Lord will fight for you, and you have only to be still'" (vv. 13-14).

If I stayed in this pulpit all day, I would not be able to tell you how many times I have drawn upon this verse in my own life. "The Lord will fight for you; you have only to stand your ground." In times of disappointment, in times of frustration, in times when I have failed myself, in times when I could see no way forward, I have called upon this verse. "The Lord will fight for you, and you have only to be still."

"Then Moses stretched out his hand over the sea; and the Lord drove the sea back by a strong east wind all night" (v. 21). It has often been noted that the story is a mixture of the natural and the miraculous. So there was a strong east wind; so what's the big deal? The point of the story from beginning to end, however, is that all the happenings — natural, supernatural, whatever — are the work of God. There's a song in the animated movie *Prince of Egypt,* "Miracles can happen if you believe." The Exodus story says something quite different. "It is fully clear that Israel was not saved because of her faith. Rather, Israel failed to believe right up until the moment of her deliverance."[2] Moses isn't making this happen, either; Moses is only an instrument. The power is the Lord's. God is doing this, not because Israel has earned it, but because he is a God of deliverance.

It wouldn't do any good for him to be a God of deliverance if he weren't a God of power. There are many theological disputes about this. I am not going to turn aside this Easter morning to deal with the serious theological question about why God so often withholds his power. We spent three hours with that on Good Friday; even so, we barely scratched the surface. Today is the day to glorify the mighty acts of God. Today is the day to say, as the black church does, "The Lord is able." I'll never forget the first time I heard that saying. In 1977 my father was extremely ill in the hospital. I was to be ordained to the priesthood in a few weeks. I was afraid that he would not be able to come, that he might not even live. One of his nurses took me out into the hall and said, "The Lord is able." And, yes, my father did get better, and he did come. I know that that nurse would be joyful to hear this story told twenty-two years later on Easter morning.[3]

There is something even better that the African-American church says. I have not yet had a chance to track it to its source, but Martin Luther King used to say it and Andrew Young used it as the title of his book about the civil rights movement. "God makes a way out of no way." This is the message of the Exodus.

The people of Israel went into the midst of the sea on dry ground, the waters being a wall to them on their right hand and on their left. The Egyptians pursued, and went in after them into the midst of the sea, all Pharaoh's horses, his chariots, and his horsemen. And in the morning watch the Lord in the pillar of fire and of cloud looked down upon the host of the Egyptians, and troubled the host of the Egyptians, clogging their chariot wheels so that they drove heavily; and the Egyptians said, "Let us flee from before Israel; for the Lord fights for them against the Egyptians."

Then the Lord said to Moses, "Stretch out your hand over the sea, that the water may come back upon the Egyptians, upon their chariots, and upon their horsemen." So Moses stretched forth his hand over the sea, and the sea returned to its wonted flow when the morning appeared; and the Egyptians fled into it, and the Lord routed the Egyptians in the midst of the sea. . . .

. . . And Israel saw the great work which the Lord did against the Egyptians, and the people feared the Lord; and they believed in the Lord and in his servant Moses. (vv. 22-27, 31)

My husband has given me permission to tell a story on him. Because he loves to hear Christian truth, I told him about the saying, "God makes a way out of no way," and he was greatly taken with it. He went off to a big business conference with it on his mind. Usually he is a pretty good theologian, but he really messed up this time. He came back triumphant from the meeting, saying, "I told 'em *we* had made a way out of no way!" I said, "What have I done wrong?"

Who can make a way out of no way? Only God. The American civil rights movement will live forever in the annals of the Christian church because so many of its leaders knew the power of God and depended upon it in their darkest hours. Often we do not actually see the power of God at work. We live in hope of a future we do not yet see except by faith. The exodus was "only a hint of what will come in full power at the end."[4] The church is a church of Easter faith. We have seen the evidence of the saving power of the Lord and we stand upon its promise for a future reign of God. There is more joy here than anyone who does not know God's power can possibly imagine. When the Israelites saw that they had been delivered, they broke forth into ecstatic praise:

Then Miriam, the prophetess, the sister of Aaron, took a timbrel in her hand; and all the women went out after her with timbrels and dancing. And Miriam sang to them: "Sing unto the LORD, for he has triumphed gloriously; the horse and his rider he has thrown into the sea." (15:20-21)

And even skeptical scholars agree — this should never fail to thrill us — that that fragment of poetry goes all the way back to the event itself.

Singing is empowering. Dancing is empowering. One of the most memorable news stories I ever read in my whole life was a *New York Times* report of a train ride in South Africa right after the collapse of apartheid. On the day of President Mandela's inauguration, a journalist rode from the Soweto ghetto into Pretoria. During the entire three-hour ride, the black passengers celebrated their liberation by singing and dancing in the aisles. It was obvious from the article that the reporter was completely bowled over. He called it a moment of "historic exultation."[5] Who can doubt that their song is joined to the eternal song of Miriam on the celestial shore?

Today, several years later, South Africa, as we know, has a whole new set of problems to deal with. The exodus was only the beginning of the Israelites' troubles. We still live in a world of bondage to sin, evil, and death. It has not been easy to write an Easter sermon with one eye on the televised scenes from Kosovo. I had hoped with all my heart that the allies would respond to the appeal of Pope John Paul II and other religious leaders for a symbolic Easter cease-fire. That, I believe, would have been a much more powerful thing to do than dropping more bombs. It would have been a witness for life. The bombing is piling death upon death — at little risk of American life — and it is strengthening Mr. Milosevic. The ways of Pharaoh still rule this age.

In this world, the last word for you and the last word for me will be death. All the routes of escape have been closed off. In the face of death, ultimate power lies in the hands of Dr. Kevorkian. But listen: there is another, greater Way; there is another, greater Life, there is another, greater Power. Paul proclaimed "the God who gives life to the dead and calls into existence the things that do not exist" (Rom. 4:17). He is the God who makes a way out of no way. He is the God whose power raised up Jesus from the grave as though death were shredded Kleenex. When all the ways of escape are shut off, when the whole world seems "shut up in the wilderness," when the time comes that you, too, lie helpless before the oncoming night, listen, listen, people of God, "the Lord will fight for you, you have only to be still." Listen, listen, people of God, there comes a sound of Miriam's tambourine, "Sing unto the Lord, for he has triumphed gloriously; the horse and rider he has thrown into the sea." Listen, listen, O people of God, there comes the strain of a song and the sound of a distant trumpet:

Welcome, happy morning, Age to age shall say,
Hell today is vanquished, heaven is won today!

AMEN.

Doubting and Believing

GRACE CHURCH IN NEW YORK

If Christ has not been raised, your faith is futile and you are still in your sins.

(1 COR. 15:17)

Jesus said to Thomas, "Put your finger here, and see my hands; and put out your hand, and place it in my side; do not be faithless, but believing."

(JOHN 20:27)

I cannot remember a time in my life span when Christian faith was under direct attack as much as it is today. Much of the skepticism and even ridicule is coming from within the church itself. This week I saw an English magazine, *The New Statesman,* with a cover depicting a clergyman in full vestments kneeling at the grave of God. The title of the cover story was, *O We of Little Faith.* The same thing is going on in the United States, as many of you are aware. There have been a number of news stories about the Jesus Seminar, a group of seventy-something Biblical scholars who seem to be taking great delight in showing that most of the New Testament is not true. Since those who believe in the Resurrection of Jesus have often argued that it could easily have been disproved if someone had been able to produce the body, the Jesus Seminar has come up with the imaginative suggestion that the body of Jesus was thrown into a common grave and eaten by dogs.

We can all rejoice that there has been a significant counterblast to the media-grabbing naysayers. The Easter cover story of *Newsweek* devoted six pages to the new blockbuster work by the great Roman Catholic New Testament scholar, Raymond Brown, a boxed set of two volumes called *The Death of the Messiah.* It is a unique work of research in the history of Christianity, being the first and only treatment of all four Passion narratives in a parallel fashion. His intent in doing so is not only scholarly but also pastoral, as he is a man of deep sensitivity to the needs of local believing congregations. Of the Jesus Seminar, Father Brown says acerbically, "If we ever make Christian faith totally dependent on the latest scholarly interpretation of a text, it could change each week."

Even so, it is a very comforting thing to me, in my own struggle to believe, to know that the relationship of doubt to faith is built into the Easter story. Mark, for instance, deliberately ends his Gospel on a note of doubt. Today, the first Sunday after Easter Day, the story of "Doubting Thomas" is always read. It is fascinating that it should be so. This day is popularly referred to as "Low Sunday" because the big crowds of Easter Day have vanished; the people who are in church to hear the story of *Doubting* Thomas are, for the most part, the hard-core *faithful.* What then do we have to learn from this juxtaposition of faith and doubt?

Speaking for myself, the trendy disaffections of the Jesus Seminar and the atheistic clergy are of little interest. What holds my attention is the sort of doubt that arises even in the midst of faith. This is the doubt that is on view today as we hear the story of Thomas from the Gospel of John. You know the outlines of the narrative. Thomas was not present when Jesus first appeared. When the other disciples report to him that they have seen the Lord, he says that unless he himself touches the wounds in Jesus' hands and side, he will not believe. Thomas stands for all of us here. We haven't seen the risen Lord. We have heard reports, but we don't know how reliable they are. We would like proof. We would like to see evidence that will hold up in the courts of the skeptics.

All during this past Holy Week, Southern newspapers were full of stories about the church in Piedmont, Alabama, that was destroyed by a tornado on Palm Sunday morning. Twenty people were killed, including six children. The four-year-old daughter of the pastor was killed. On Easter morning, even *The New York Times* took note of the crisis of faith that was occurring, with an article on the top of the front page. The story was filled with cries of pain. A man looked at the little patent-leather Easter shoes of the children lying in the ruins and said, "If that don't shake your faith, nothing will." A woman said, "We are trained from birth not to question God. But why? Why a church? Why those little children? Why? Why? *Why?*" The Rev. Kelly Clem, mother of the four-year-old, said, "We do not know why. I don't think 'why' is the question right now. We just have to help each other through it."[1]

Surely it is of the utmost importance that the sign demanded by Thomas was to touch the marks of Jesus' *wounds*. It was not the sign of his glory that gave proof, but the sign of his sufferings. Again and again this brings us back to the place where faith must stand — not in the place of clarity and certainty, but in the place of ambiguity and pain. Thomas's choice of signs is surely related to Jesus' amazing consent to his demand. Jesus says to Thomas, "Put your finger here, and see my hands; and put out your hand, and place it in my side; do not be faithless, but believing" (John 20:27). Interpreters tend to agree that Thomas never actually touches Jesus; the appearance of the Master, the sight of his wounds, and his word is enough. In the final analysis it is the Word of Jesus that creates faith.

I have been reading a lot of articles lately about the great popularity of New Age thinking in social circles today. Marla Maples appears this week on the cover of *New York* magazine to tout the virtues of auto-enlightenment and self-healing.[2] Says another socialite (Georgette Mosbacher), "Every morning I have a working dialogue with myself. Thank God for my inner voice." Ms. Maples adds that silent prayer offered by a New Age nurturer is "not different from what you would do in church." There is little distinction between these breathless views and that of the former priest quoted in the *New Statesman* article who said, "The idea of man-made religion isn't new. Christians always thought that Hindus and Buddhists had made up their religions. We just assumed that our own religion was an exception to the rule." This brings us to a critical point. It is quite true that Christianity stands or falls on the question of divine revelation. If we have simply made up the God who raised Jesus from the dead, then indeed, New Age prayer is no different from what we are doing in church, because then there is no God to say "Thank God" to, only an "inner voice" that changes every week according to the whims of the imaginer, like the textual interpretations of the Jesus Seminar scholars.

In the beginning of our reading for today from the Gospel of John, Thomas is in the same position that you and I are in. He has not seen the risen Lord. His reaction is one of disbelief. We are accustomed to hearing stories of Jesus turning away from people who will not believe without a sign, so it is startling when he graciously appears to Thomas and grants him the proofs that he demanded. At this climactic moment, Thomas utters a confession of faith that is the most exalted in all the New Testament. He uses words that the Old Testament reserves exclusively for the one and only Creator God of the universe, "My Lord and my God."

The story about Thomas is placed by the evangelist John at the apex of his Gospel story for a specific reason. Neither you nor I have seen the risen Lord with our own eyes as Thomas did, but our faith is founded on his Word, living and active as it is proclaimed today on the second Sunday of the Easter season. That is why Jesus says, "Blessed are they who do not see and yet believe" (John 20:29).

I read some reviews of a program about Abraham that appeared on television last week. The director was very proud of his decision to have the voice of God on the soundtrack be actually Abraham's own voice. In one stroke he has thereby undone the whole point of the Abraham saga, which is that *the Word of the Lord came to Abram*" (Gen. 15:1). When the voice of God could just as well be Abraham or Marla Maples or you or me, it is not God at all.

The voice of God in the Bible is the voice of One who comes to us from outside ourselves, the voice of the One who created the world out of nothing and raised his Son Jesus from the tomb. For that matter, the God who is really God could certainly raise a dog-eaten body, but then all four Gospels would be telling us a lie about the empty tomb, and I choose to go along with Raymond Brown in believing that the "clear and unanimous presentation" of all four evangelists that Jesus was buried in a definite, identifiable spot is the truth and not a desperate fiction.

The main body of the Gospel of John concludes with the evangelist's resounding statement of purpose: "Now Jesus did many things that are not written in this book, but these are written that you may believe that Jesus is the Christ, the Son of God, and that believing, you may have life in his name" (20:30-31). I am amused to think how different this is from the manifestos of the Jesus Seminar, of which we might say, "These things are written in order that you may *not* believe."

As many of you know, I have been dealing with a lot of death close to me lately. Yesterday afternoon when I was working on this sermon, I received another call; a close friend called to say that her husband, one of my husband's good friends, a man no older than my husband, had died in his sleep. She wanted me to assist at the funeral. This will be the third close friend in five weeks. It takes a lot of faith in the Resurrection to carry through, and I can assure you that the Jesus Seminar is no help whatsoever. The friend who just died is a person who appeared to have no faith. However, he and his wife did attend church occasionally. This means that he has heard the Word of Jesus, and the Word of Jesus can create faith where there is no faith. The power of God can, as Paul wrote, "raise the dead and call into existence the things that do not exist" (Rom. 4:17). But only a God who is really God can do this. A god that we ourselves have made up will die with us.

On Thursday night after Easter I was struggling with fresh doubts about the Resurrection. I was feeling buffeted by the skeptical articles I was reading, yet determined to work my way through no matter what it cost. I did not like the feeling of doubt that I was experiencing. As I went over to the chantry to read Evening Prayer, I felt that I was just going through the motions. My "inner voice" was saying all sorts of treacherous things: Suppose the Jesus Seminar was right? Suppose Jesus had never been buried at all? Suppose there really had never been any Resurrection? I stood at the lectern as I was assigned to do, and I began to read the lesson appointed for the Tuesday of Easter Week, the words of the Apostle Paul to the Corinthian church: "If Christ has not been raised, your faith is futile and you are still in your sins; but in fact Christ has been raised from the dead. . . . for as by a man came death, by a man has come also the resurrection of the dead. For as in Adam all die, even so in Christ shall all be made alive" (1 Cor. 15:17-22).

In that reading from the Word of God my faith was restored yet once more. I knew that the faith that I had believed since I was a small child was not founded on a lie. I knew that the countless acts of love and sacrifice that have been performed for me and for others in this part of the Body of Christ were living extensions of the wounds in his hands. I knew that Paul did not travel through great dangers and trials three times around the Mediterranean to a martyr's death in order to spread an untruth throughout the world. I knew that the families in Alabama were holding on to a crucified and risen Christ who can be trusted in spite of everything. I knew that my hope of seeing my loved ones again was not a mere projection of my own desires, but trust in the divine promise of an outcome that I had no natural right to expect.

So we have a real choice. We can choose a god who suits us in every particular because he is a projection of ourselves, whose voice is essentially our own voice magnified. This god will have no nail prints in his hands. This goddess will have no wound in her side. If we don't like the tornadoes and premature deaths and other things that happen in the world, we can absolve our man-made gods from responsibility, since they are *part of* the world and not *creators* of it. The Bible sets before us a baffling, even an infuriating God who is really God, rather than a domesticated household pet. Our God is a God who permits us to doubt, to complain, to shake our fist, to shout at him, to ask repeatedly the ultimate question, "Why?" Ultimately the divine answer does not come in the form of a "why." It comes in the form of a "Who." Even in the midst of pain, grief, and doubt, I believe we can hold on to the promise that God has entered our pain and been wounded by it, actually been killed by it, yet has been raised triumphant from the dead never to die again, having power to grant his divine life to all who come to him. And we proclaim to you today not our own voice, but the living Word of God, which is unique and trustworthy. When Thomas makes his confession, Jesus says to him, "Thomas, have you believed because you have seen me?" Then the Lord looks straight through Thomas, across and down the centuries to the believers and doubters yet to come, to you and to me: "Blessed are they who do not see and yet believe" (John 20:29).

"These things were written that you believe that Jesus is the Christ, the Son of God, and that, believing, you may have life in his name" (v. 31).

AMEN.

Jesus Will Show

ST. MARK'S, NEW CANAAN, CONNECTICUT

Come, O blessed of my Father, inherit the kingdom prepared for you from the foundation of the world.

(MATT. 25:34)

O f all days in the calendar of the Christian church, this one has the most spacious horizon. We are poised between the human past and the divine future.[1] On this last Sunday of the liturgical year we look both backward and forward. We look back over the completed story of the earthly ministry of Jesus as we have followed him all year from Christmas to Holy Week to Easter to Pentecost. That progression is relatively familiar to us. What is less well understood, even by lifelong Episcopalians, is that the end of the church year is principally the season for looking *forward* — forward to the Second Coming and the universal Reign of Christ. All three lessons today speak of this coming Rule of God. The three Sundays after All Saints and the first Sunday of Advent are entirely focused on the future of Jesus Christ, the ruler of the cosmos.

Let us not be deceived about the difficulties of this. The intellectual elite is certain to make fun of it. Some of you may have read the harrowing story of Robert Hughes's automobile accident. He is the highly respected, much admired art critic of *Time* magazine and author of the best-selling history of Australia called *The Fatal Shore.*

Last May, Hughes almost died in a head-on collision and was in a coma, on and off, for some weeks after. He wrote an essay about all this which appeared in *Time* on October 11. What happened to him, he says, was "a long way from the nice, uplifting sort of near-death experience that religious writers like to effuse about. . . . I am a skeptic to whom the idea that a benign God created us and watches over us is somewhere between a fairy tale and a poor joke. People of a religious bent are apt . . . to see the familiar images of near-death experience — the tunnel of white light with Jesus beckoning at the end. . . . Jesus must have been busy when my turn came; he didn't show." This whole mocking section of Hughes's essay is called "Jesus Didn't Show."[2]

"People of a religious bent" mean well when they use their own personal, subjective experiences as arguments for the truth of Christian faith, but personal experience is notoriously undependable and intransmissible. That is why Paul, for instance, hardly ever mentions his own conversion in his letters.[3] The Christian faith is not founded on anyone's personal or near-death experiences but on God's action in raising Jesus Christ from the dead. We cannot prove this to Robert Hughes or anyone else who does not believe it. What we do is bear our witness. The church testifies of Christ, not by telling of personal experiences, but by doing two things: serving the least of Jesus' brothers and sisters, and continuing to confess its faith.

Every third year in the lectionary cycle we read through the last days of Jesus' ministry from the Gospel of Matthew. As the curtain goes up for what seems to be the final act, the Lord is about to be betrayed. He will be arraigned, tried, and condemned as a blasphemer by the world's noblest religion and executed as an insurrectionist by the world's most powerful government. At the eleventh hour, we find him speaking privately to his disciples almost for the last time, and this is what he says: "When the Son of man comes in his glory, and all the angels with him, then he will sit on his glorious throne. Before him will be gathered all the nations, and he will separate them one from another as a shepherd separates the sheep from the goats" (Matt. 25:31-32).

Let us pause for a moment and let this incredible statement sink into our minds and hearts. Here is a man who owns nothing, who has no bank account, no resumé or portfolio, no job or house, no title or rank, a man who is about to be judged guilty and not fit to live by the highest religious and political tribunals of his time, and he is saying that he is going to come again, personally, at the end of the world, to determine the fate of all human beings who have ever been born. It should make our brains crunch just to think about it. This man Jesus is about to go on trial for his life before the judges of this world, yet he is telling us that he himself is actually the Judge. We need to pause in awe at this contradiction. When the ultimate, conclusive trial of the world takes place, the One who will preside over it is the One who was crucified.

On that last day when the Son of Man "comes again in glory to judge the quick and the dead," he will be surrounded with all the unmistakable accoutrements of majesty and dominion. He will be attended by numberless legions of angels, the heavenly host. He will sit on his throne of glory and at his feet, spread out before him, will be all of human history in unimaginable completeness. Julius Caesar and Napoleon will be there; Genghis Khan and Joan of Arc will be there; Martin Luther and Catherine the Great and Voltaire and Stalin will be there. Let us allow this awesome spectacle to penetrate our consciousness. Don't be sidetracked by literal-minded speculations about where, when, or how this is going to happen. What we are intended to feel is not intellectual curiosity but the overwhelming majesty and solemnity of the event. Paul evokes the same scene in Romans when he says, "We shall all stand before the judgment seat of God" (14:10). The impression burned into our hearts today by the passage from Matthew is this: on that climactic and final day, *we will be there.*

Jesus Christ will be the Judge, and no one else. To him "all hearts are open, all desires known, and from [him] no secrets are hid."[4] The picture is of a shepherd looking out over a vast flock of sheep, dividing them just as the prophet Ezekiel says in today's Old Testament lesson: "As for you, my flock, thus says the Lord God: Behold, I judge between sheep and sheep, rams and he-goats" (Ezek.

34:17). The Lord will put the chosen sheep at his right hand. To them he speaks words of stupendous consequence: "Come, O blessed of my Father, inherit the kingdom prepared for you from the foundation of the world" (Matt. 25:34). The goats he will place at his left hand, and to them he speaks terrible words, words that chill the heart: "Depart from me, you cursed, into the eternal fire prepared for the devil and his angels" (v. 41). To the "sheep" on his right hand he will then say, "I was hungry and you gave me food, I was thirsty and you gave me drink, I was a stranger and you welcomed me, I was naked and you clothed me, I was sick and you visited me, I was in prison and you came to me." The response comes back, "Lord, when did we do all those things?" "And the King shall answer and say unto them, 'Verily I say unto you, Inasmuch as ye have done it unto one of the least of these my brethren, ye have done it unto me'" (vv. 35-40).

We have heard these famous lines many times. Today, can we recover something of their startling originality? In the time of Jesus, the Messiah was expected to be a kingly figure, so there was nothing surprising there. What was emphatically *not* expected was that he would actually be present in the lowliest of the low. The Gospel of Matthew is known for this surprising combination of Jesus' cosmic divinity and his intimate identification with "the least" among human beings. We might have more logically expected the Judge to commend his disciples for heroic deeds, bold achievements, glorious sacrifices; instead, they are acknowledged and welcomed as those who have performed tiny, insignificant acts of charity toward people who appear to be of no account. When this story was retold by Matthew, the members of his church were asking questions about how they should conduct themselves in the lengthening period of time until Jesus would come back. Here is Jesus' own answer: it is not the moving and shaking, the "making things happen," the merging and acquiring, the wielding of power and influence that will count in the last day, but the fruits of faith in Jesus Christ — small, seemingly insignificant deeds of simple kindness on behalf of the little people who have no status in the world. With these "least" of the brothers and sisters, the Lord of the cosmos declares himself to be in solidarity.

Notice the response of those on Jesus' right hand when they are told that they are about to inherit the Kingdom. They are amazed. They did not know that they had ministered to the hidden Christ among the "least" of these his brethren. "Lord," they say, "When did we see thee hungry and feed thee?" Those who are vindicated in the judgment are those who are not even aware that they have done any good works. Notice also the response of those on the left hand. They are not aware either. Apparently they expected to be commended. It looks as though there are going to be surprises for everyone. He who congratulates himself on having done enough is precisely the one who has not. The person who trembles to think of herself before the judgment seat is closer to the Kingdom of heaven than the one who complacently assumes she is on the side of the angels. The coming of Jesus Christ as judge of the world calls every person's existence into question. There is no human merit anywhere to bail us out. We cannot rely on any known good deeds; the complete astonishment of the redeemed and the shattered confidence of the condemned are clear evidence of this.

I think of a woman I know who is always preaching about kindness and compassion. She definitely does a lot of kind deeds for people, no doubt about it. But her certainty about it is a little unnerving. There is no doubt in her mind that she is one of the anointed. It never seems to occur to her that she, too, might have something to answer for on the last day. Quite different from this woman is the one in a Barbara Pym novel who is uneasy about her standing; she says, "The trouble with doing good works is that one can never be said to have done one's share."[5] This is the beginning of wisdom.

The parable of the Last Judgment is not about totaling up one's own good deeds. It is about serving Christ the King. The teaching about the "least of these" should not be detached from the titanic figure of Christ as the final arbiter of the destiny of all creation. Without him at the center, the teaching deteriorates into moralistic pabulum along the lines of "He knows if you've been bad or good, so be good for goodness' sake." This is not what the parable means. The division of the sheep and goats is not based on who is good and who is bad. It is based on honoring Christ by serving him as he is present in the lives of those who are invisible to the world of power-mongering. If Jesus Christ is not Lord, then there is nothing here but moralism, and the Gospel of Matthew does not teach moralism. Matthew teaches Christ the Lord, which is a very different thing. It is the living presence of Christ in the midst of the community that makes the difference.

The revolutionary aspect of this would not be as obvious to us if we had no letters from Paul the Apostle. Paul helps us understand the Gospels and put them in the right perspective. In today's Epistle, appointed for Christ the King Sunday, we read these ringing words: "As in Adam all die, even so in Christ shall all be made alive" (1 Cor. 15:22). "Adam" is Paul's name for you and me under the rule of sin and death. Christian people used to understand this better than they do now; I was reminded of this the other day when a young woman told me that her grandfather used to say, when somebody misbehaved, "That's the old Adam in him." I was thrilled to be reminded of this saying. You see, it's not a matter of who's good and who's bad. We are all *both* good *and* bad. This has been noted over and over in recent years by historians and writers who have done studies of ordinary people under great stress, as in times of great social upheaval. Books and articles about the Japanese in Nanking, the French in World War II, the Americans at My Lai, the Serbs in Kosovo, and the Albanian Kosovars now that they are back home show that the old Adam is right there underneath the surface in all of us. So the division between bad people and good people is actually a division that runs through each of us, between Adam and Christ.[6]

"As in Adam all die, even so in Christ shall all be made alive." Everything depends on being *in Christ.* If Christ is going to judge me by all the things I have not done to help my neighbor who is hungry, cold, sick, or in prison, then I am doomed indeed. I cannot stand before this tribunal. I know that. But I know also that *in Christ* things can happen in me that I cannot do alone. Jesus tells the disciples that they can expect to be transformed into new people who will "bear fruit" (Matt. 3:8). They will bear fruit almost unconsciously, for it will grow organically within the community that waits faithfully for Jesus. "Our old self [Adam]," writes Paul, "was crucified with Christ in baptism so that the sinful body [Adam] might be destroyed, and we might no longer be enslaved to sin" (Rom. 6:6).

Here is another testimony. John McCain, in his book *Faith of My Fathers,* writes of his five years of solitary confinement and torture in Vietnam. After one of the many prolonged and excruciating interrogations that he endured, he was thrown into a cell he had not been in before. He writes, "I discovered scratched into one of the cell's walls the creed 'I believe in God, the Father Almighty.' There, standing witness to God's presence in a remote concealed place, [I was] recalled to my faith."[7]

This does not mean that John McCain is going to escape judgment. There is plenty of the old Adam still there, as we know. What it does mean is that the church exists in hidden places among those who suffer and that the two-thousand-year-old creed that belongs to us all still testifies to the truth. The creed continues: "I believe in his only-begotten son Jesus Christ our Lord . . . who will come again in glory to judge the living and the dead." That is why we have Christ the King Sunday. In a strange way, it is also why we have Pledge Sunday. You are being asked, today, to give a substantial amount of your money to organized religion. Organized religion takes a lot of lumps. Being full of the old Adam, it makes an easy target. But think about this: if Christians weren't organized, there wouldn't be anything left of the gospel of Jesus Christ except a lot of fairy stories. If the church weren't organized, there would be no one left to say the creed. If you understand that the church with all its many faults nevertheless exists to praise and glorify the living Lord who brings us patiently and lovingly into his divine life, if you believe and trust that you will wake up one day to find yourself "loving justice and doing mercy and walking humbly with your God" (Mic. 6:8) without even trying, then you will "rejoice and be glad" to offer up some of your substance to the Master who does a lot more than just beckon to us from a white tunnel. Those who are in Christ, who are incorporated into him, are being remade day by day into people who will some day say "When did we see thee, Lord?" in glad amazement because they did not even notice that they were ministering to him in the small actions of mercy that were performed. At the last judgment, "Adam" will disappear into outer darkness forever, and we will be refashioned in the image of him who is King of kings and Lord of lords among the least, the last, and the lost.[8]

This Master cares so much for the least, the last, and the lost that he is willing to die even for such poor specimens as you and me, covering our unrighteousness with his righteousness, offering his life to save us from death, victorious over the old Adam, the Judge judged in our place. He has compensated for our too-short list of good deeds by his one great deed. Now by his indwelling Spirit he will make us into those who will some day hear the blessed words, "Come, O blessed of my Father, inherit the kingdom prepared for you from the foundation of the world."

AMEN.

Beyond the Valley of Ashes

CHRIST CHURCH, GREENWICH, CONNECTICUT

A new opera based on F. Scott Fitzgerald's *The Great Gatsby* opens at the Met this week. Reading various articles about it got me thinking about the last sentence of that famous novel: "So we beat on, boats against the current, borne back ceaselessly into the past." As always with great fiction writing, there is a world of suggestion here, much more than I can grasp, but going back a few sentences we do find clues. We read that the future, "year by year recedes before us," and that Jay Gatsby's dream is "already behind him." As I reread these pages I felt the tension and undertow of the Advent themes. Advent is a season in which the past and the future seem to collide with one another. No other time of the church year presents us with so much contradiction. I'm not thinking so much of the contrast between the shopping mega-frenzy and the church's summons to hushed reverence. Rather, on this particular morning of Advent lessons and carols, I am thinking of the tension between looking back and looking forward, and above all the question, looking forward to what?

The closer we get to Christmas the more tempted we are to retreat to the cozy imagined world of our childhood. "I'm dreaming of a white Christmas, just like the ones I used to know." *Just like the ones I used to know* — those are the operative words. The suggestion is that the dream is behind us; the way to happiness is to return to that idealized past. Sentiment and nostalgia play a major role in our

Christmas observances. We bring out the ornaments we loved as children, we display little nineteenth-century villages with snow-covered roofs, we collect figures of carolers dressed in the style of Dickens's London. There is nothing wrong with this — I do some of it myself — but it does illustrate our tendency to romanticize the past. Popular Christmas music is popular precisely because it trades on this basic human tendency to sentimentalize. "Have yourself a merry little Christmas," goes the song, evoking the "olden days, happy golden days of yore."

Advent is exactly the opposite of all this. Nostalgia and sentiment play no part in the season. Advent, you see, is not about the past. It is about the future. It isn't a season of remembering something that happened a long time ago; it is a season of preparation for the great coming Day of the Kingdom of God. I went through the Advent section of our hymnal to make sure I hadn't made a mistake. There are twenty-four hymns in the Advent section. Twenty-three of them are about the Second Coming of Christ.[1] Think, for example, of one by Charles Wesley, one of the greatest hymnwriters of all time: "Come, thou long expected Jesus." The proximity of Advent to Christmas leads us to think this means Jesus' coming as a baby. But the hymn ends:

> By thine own eternal Spirit
> Rule in all our hearts alone;
> By thine all-sufficient merit
> Raise us to thy glorious throne.

The hymn doesn't take us back in time to pretend we are first-century Jews waiting for a Messiah who has not yet come. Advent, more than any other season of the church year, looks forward to the return of the one who was "born a child, and yet a king;/Born to reign in us for ever/Now thy gracious kingdom bring." You will notice this also in "O come, O come, Emmanuel." We are not really singing about a baby in a manger. It is a hymn of great longing for an event still in the future. It is an extended eight-part prayer to the Lord to come again. "O come, Desire of Nations, bind/in one the hearts of all mankind;/Bid thou our sad divisions cease,/and be thyself our King of Peace." These are the works of the Last Day. Peace in the world as we know it is only a hint and suggestion of the true peace in the World to Come.

Here again, though, we are capable of deceiving ourselves endlessly. There are many strange things going on around the world in the name of peace. Last Sunday an article in *The New York Times* described some truly bizarre scenes in the little Palestinian city of Bethlehem as it prepares for the millennium. The secular Muslim leader Yasir Arafat has artfully commandeered the event, staging a big rally in Manger Square, proclaiming Bethlehem as "the city of Jesus, the city where it all began," and concluding, "in the name of God, in the name of Palestine, I declare open the celebrations of the third millennium." A Peace Center has just opened in Manger Square; a local man said to a reporter that peace, for him, was "the Palestinian flag in the square and the Israelis gone."[2] In another context, it could just as well have been an Israeli speaking; the point is that peace, in this world, is often a euphemism meaning that the enemy has been displaced. This is not peace. The Kosovars are now in the process of doing to the Serbs what the Serbs did to them; it will mean a Serb-free Kosovo, but it doesn't mean peace. Just because people have withdrawn into gated communities doesn't mean peace. Cleaning all the homeless people off the streets doesn't mean peace. Recently I visited a church so split by an issue that people won't sit down and talk to each other. Right here in Greenwich people are fighting about the disposal of compost. The world-transforming peace that the angel declared to the shepherds is found only in bits and fragments now. Its eternal fulfillment is to be found only in the future of God.

So we are mistaken to look for it behind us, in an idealized past. As Scott Fitzgerald shows with such artistry in his novel, the past is a destroying current, ready to swallow us up in futility. The reader is drawn into the radiant atmosphere of the novel only to see it collapse upon itself. The symbolism of light and darkness, so central to the Advent season, is in play throughout the story. The dream world of Jay Gatsby is a world of light. Fitzgerald's book is celebrated for its glowing images of Gatsby's light-filled house, lawns, and garden. It is all deeply ironic, for immediately adjoining the mansion and bay on Long Island Sound is a valley of ashes where nothing can grow, an image of our illusions and their ultimate end, the place where Gatsby's dream dies. Similarly, we humans try to create artificial worlds of light at Christmas, hoping to stave off the darkness. Advent summons us to do exactly the opposite: to renounce the easy consolations of artificial light in order to recognize the Coming One who said, "I am the Light of the world" (John 8:12).

You understand that I am not saying, Don't have a Christmas tree. The tree, for Christians, can be a sign of our hope in Christ. Even in the very midst of the Christmas story itself, however, the expectation of the *Second* Coming is dominant. Let us listen again to the words spoken by the two angels in the readings that you just heard this morning. The first is the announcement of the birth of John the Baptist:

> The angel said to him, "Do not be afraid, Zechariah, for your prayer is heard, and your wife Elizabeth will bear you a son, and you shall call his name John. . . . And he will turn many of the children of Israel to the Lord their God, and he will go before him in the spirit and power of Elijah, to turn the hearts of the fathers to the children, and the disobedient to the wisdom of the just, to make ready for the Lord a people prepared." (Luke 1:13, 16-17)

If you know your Bible, you will recognize these references to Elijah and the turning of the hearts of the children to the parents as the last words of the Old Testament, the final section of the prophet Malachi where the focus is entirely on the future coming of the Lord, the Event to end all events. Charles Wesley has incorporated portions of Malachi into his Christmas hymn, "Hark! the herald angels sing":

> Hail the heaven-born Prince of Peace,
> Hail, the Sun of righteousness;

Light and life to all he brings,
Risen with healing in his wings.

We think of these as Christmas words, but because they are from
Malachi, they are more closely related to Advent and to the Second
Coming. Similarly, the angel Gabriel speaks to Mary:

> "Do not be afraid, Mary, for you have found favor with God. And
> behold, you will conceive in your womb and bear a son, and you
> shall call his name Jesus. He will be great, and will be called the
> Son of the Most High; and the Lord God will give to him the
> throne of his father David . . . and of his kingdom there will be no
> end." (Luke 1:30-33)

These words are familiar to us and we associate them with the
nativity, but if we take another look we will see that they are not
about an infant at all, but an adult King, one whose kingdom lies
still in the future. As the Lord himself said in the reading on the
first Sunday of Advent, "The end is not yet" (Mark 13:7).

Some of you here today are young: you are Jay Gatsby's age.
Your dreams are still alive. God rest you merry, and I mean that
with all sincerity. Others of you are middle-aged but perhaps still
deceived into thinking that it doesn't get any better than the
good life in Greenwich, Connecticut. More power to you, too.
Sooner or later, though, every person here in this church today
will find himself or herself following one of two interpretations of
life. Either you will come to a point where it will be clear to you
that life is full of disappointment, or you will settle into a pattern
of denial, bluster, and false optimism. These latter manifestations
belong to the world of the past. They may appear to give light, for
you can fool yourself and others for quite a while, but in fact they
are the "works of darkness." In the world of denial and illusion,
the future "year by year recedes before us." We are "borne back
ceaselessly into the past" where we can only brood over the loss of
a childhood that never was.

What then? In such a wilderness, what rescue? Out of such a

past, what hope of the future? Listen again to the words of the prophet Isaiah:

> In the wilderness prepare ye the way of the Lord,
>   make straight in the desert a highway for our God.
> Every valley shall be lifted up,
>   and every mountain and hill be made low;
>   the uneven ground shall become level,
>   and the rough places a plain.
> And the glory of the Lord shall be revealed,
>   and all flesh shall see it together,
>   for the mouth of the Lord has spoken it.
>
> (40:3-5)

Here is the forward thrust of Advent, the countervailing motion that lifts the boats clear, the heralding announcement of the arriving God. The note is struck; it is sounded from the future. We are not looking backward sentimentally to a baby; we are expecting the only One from whom the promise of peace will someday be fulfilled. Trusting in that promise, we can do things we thought we could not do. Relying on him, we can change our habits, confront our addictions, forgive our enemies, curb our spending, challenge our society, raise our pledge, lower our defenses — not all of them at once, to be sure, but even one break from past patterns of sin will be in its way a sign of Christ's coming. Because God is out ahead of us, we know that the cover-ups, the denials, the lies and frauds and pretenses are part of the old world that is passing away. We are not trapped in our mistakes and delusions. God is enlisting us on the side of his future.

Listen to the first lines of these Advent hymns: "Hark, a thrilling voice is sounding!" "Lo, he comes, with clouds descending!" "Sleepers, wake! a voice astounds us!" "Rejoice, rejoice, believers!" As the electrifying message reaches our ears, we recognize that we are hearing something entirely new in religion. God is on the move toward us, not the other way round. In the very midst of our confusion and incapacity, we are met by the oncoming Lord. In our valley of ashes, we are seized by hope. In the graveyard of dreams, the Holy Spirit breathes life from the dead. In the place where illusions die, the Sun rises upon us, and of his kingdom there will be no end. "Emmanuel shall come to thee, O Israel."

AMEN.

Ruth's Redeemer

ALL SAINTS CHURCH, PRINCETON, NEW JERSEY

"Blessed be the Lord, who has not left you this day without next of kin; and may his name be renowned in Israel!"

(RUTH 4:14)

If we were Jewish, we would be reading all four chapters of the book of Ruth today, as Jews do every year at Shabuot (the Feast of Weeks). The Episcopal lectionary, by contrast, is very stingy with Ruth. All we get to hear is the first half of the first chapter once every three years. I hope that, when you go home, you will want to read the whole "short story" in one sitting.[1] It may be a mistake to try to encompass the story of Ruth in the space of one sermon, but we are going to take a shot at it this morning because it is just too precious to ignore.[2]

Here are the bare bones of the story. Naomi and her husband Elimelech, who are Hebrews from the village of Bethlehem, are driven from their home by a severe famine. When I first studied this story before the age of mass media, we did not know as much as we do now about famines. All of us today have seen pictures of starving populations on the move in search of food, fighting desperately over a handful of rice. Understanding this will help us enter the world of the story.

Naomi and her husband escaped the famine by fleeing to foreign territory, the Moabite plateau east of the Dead Sea. During the years in Moab, the sons of Elimelech and Naomi married Moabite women, Orpah and Ruth. Then came a series of catastrophes. All the men, one after another, were struck down, a common occurrence in those days, for until the twentieth century death at a young age was the rule rather than the exception. Naomi is therefore left in the most vulnerable condition possible: she is a childless widow with no grandchildren. In that ancient culture, nothing could have been worse. Naomi, in fact, says a terrible thing: "It is exceedingly bitter to me . . . that the hand of the Lord has gone forth against me . . . the Lord has afflicted me and the Almighty has brought calamity upon me" (Ruth 1:13, 21). Here, at the beginning of the story, we see the greatest of all theological problems put before us. Naomi feels that she has been abandoned by God. No, it is even worse than that. She feels that God is actively *against* her. She believes that she is worse than worthless, not only to herself but also to her widowed daughters-in-law, for without husbands they are utterly unprotected in the world.

So we need to realize that the beautiful, even idyllic story of Ruth begins in the dark, with famine, death, and sexual menace. We should not overlook this latter factor. Poor women alone in the world were then, and are still, easy prey for unscrupulous men. This danger underlies the action of the story at every turn. The Old Testament takes a lot of knocks these days for being patriarchal, but I think you will see that the atmosphere of this story is galaxies away from what the Taliban is doing to women in Afghanistan, and indeed from what is often done to and with women in the corridors of power everywhere.

Naomi urges her two daughters-in-law to stay in Moab and remarry. Orpah somewhat reluctantly agrees and turns back to the land and the gods³ of Moab, but Ruth, we are told, refuses to leave. It is at this point that Ruth utters the famous words, "Entreat me not to leave thee, or to return from following after thee: for whither thou goest, I will go; and where thou lodgest, I will lodge: thy people shall be my people, and thy God my God. Where thou diest, will I die, and there will I be buried: the Lord do so to me, and more also, if ought but death part thee and me" (1:16-17). The soul is stirred by this. This is the point where the ancient storyteller really grabbed the audience. Human connectedness, human affection, human devotion, human unselfishness: these are the things that move all but the hardest hearts. From this point, we are hooked. We care about what happens to Ruth and Naomi and we follow their adventures with attention.

The two women arrive back in Judah after who knows what arduous traveling on foot. It is the time of the barley harvest, when the entire Israelite community would be eating and sleeping out in the fields in order to bring in the grain. The Lord has lifted the famine, we are told, but Naomi and Ruth have no access to the new abundance. Here for the second time we discover what an unusual person Ruth is. She proposes, fearlessly, to go into the fields to glean barley. In doing this, she is embracing the status of beggar, one who comes behind and picks up what has been discarded by the reapers. This was a rather humiliating activity, and it was also dangerous for a single woman. Here she is, obviously a gentle and virtuous young lady, out in the fields with the rough laborers and no protection of any kind.

Now we meet Boaz. Our first glimpse of him is delightful. He is the owner of the field where Ruth is gleaning. He greets his field hands, "The Lord be with you!" and they respond, "The Lord bless you." From this we rightly surmise that Boaz is a gracious and humane employer. Next we learn that he has noticed Ruth. "Who is this maiden?" (2:4-5). His men tell him that she is a Moabite woman, and that she has been gleaning since early dawn, bending over to the ground without resting. Boaz goes to her and says, "Do not go to another field or leave this one; stay close to my maidens. . . . I have charged my young men not to molest you" (v. 9). In a most charming manner, Ruth bows down respectfully and says, "How is it that I have found favor in your eyes that you should notice me, a foreigner?" (v. 10).

Now if this was a Hollywood movie, we would know the answer to that question; Boaz has noticed Ruth because she is a dish. Well, to be sure, there is no reason to think Ruth is not attractive, but this is not what the story emphasizes. Instead, Boaz says, "All that you have done for your mother-in-law since the death of your husband has been fully told me, and how you left your father and mother and your native land and came to a people that you did not know before. May the Lord recompense you for what you have done, and a full reward be given you by the Lord, the God of Israel, under whose wings you have come to take refuge!" (vv. 11-12). There are several things to notice here. Boaz is deeply impressed by Ruth's bravery and devotion. That is the kind of man he is. He recognizes the kindness of God himself at work in Ruth, the foreigner. Boaz himself lives his life — not just his personal life, but also his economic life as a landowner and manager — in the sight of God; he commits all his activities to the Lord. Thus Boaz habitually thinks in terms of a correspondence between the generosity of Israel's God and his own generosity. He is not self-conscious about it; it has become part of him. He does not simply commend Ruth to the Lord. He speaks of a reward for Ruth from God, but as we shall see, the reward from God comes through the agency of Boaz himself.

Ruth has a wonderful afternoon out in Boaz's field. Instead of being leered at and threatened, or worse, she is given choice refreshments by Boaz himself, and the reapers are ordered to drop extra grain for her to pick up. At the end of the day she has gathered a huge amount of barley to bring home to Naomi. Naomi is dumbfounded by the unlooked-for bounty. "Where did you glean today? Blessed be the man who took notice of you." Ruth replies, "His name is Boaz" (v. 19). The narrative takes a leap forward as Naomi exclaims, "Blessed be he by the Lord, whose kindness has not forsaken the living or the dead! This man is a kinsman of ours" (v. 20).[4]

Do you remember how Naomi said at the beginning that God was against her, that he had afflicted her and brought calamity upon her? Now she says, "Blessed be the Lord whose kindness has not forsaken the living or the dead!" But what has the Lord done? Nothing directly. There hasn't been any parting of the waters, or any manna; no angel has appeared; fire has not come down from heaven. The loving-kindness of God, Yahweh's covenant love, has been shown forth humbly, simply — one human being reaching out to another.

Now comes chapter three, the famous nocturnal meeting of Ruth and Boaz on the threshing floor. Naomi recognizes the unique opportunity that lies before her. Remember, in the ancient world, the extinction of the family name and bloodline was a fate worse than death. Naomi discerns that in the person of her relative, Boaz, there is a hope of redemption for herself and her dead husband's legacy. We do not use the word "redemption" lightly. The custom was that the next-of-kin was responsible for "redeeming" the property, the honor, and the family line of the deceased man. The Hebrew word "next-of-kin" *(go'el)* is the same as the word "redeemer." Naomi readily sees that Boaz might be the one to play the role of this redeemer. She proposes a most daring plan, one that even after all these thousands of years still takes the breath away. She advises Ruth to anoint herself, dress in her best clothes, and go down to the threshing floor where Boaz and his men are not only winnowing barley but also, in the age-old harvest custom, eating and drinking and making merry. Ruth is to go and observe where Boaz lies down to sleep; there she is to uncover his "feet" and lie down beside him.[5] Can you imagine a more reckless thing to urge a young woman to do? But the point is this: by performing these dramatic actions, Ruth is placing herself under the protection of Boaz — for better or for worse. It is an enormously bold and risky plan.

So our valorous heroine sets out for the threshing floor. The men are feasting and drinking. At last Boaz, "merry with wine," lies down to sleep. Ruth uncovers some part of him (we're not sure which part) and lies down. At midnight he wakes suddenly; probably he was cold! He gropes around in the dark for the covers and discovers the lovely Ruth lying near him. What a setup!

Now it must be admitted that we do not know exactly what happened that night. Many a seminary classroom has been enlivened by mildly ribald discussions concerning "the truth about Ruth" and so forth. Having read many of the available interpretations, I personally think we can conclude that Boaz did not take advantage of Ruth that night. When he says to her, "Lie here till morning," the Hebrew expression is one that is never used of sexual relations.[6] The whole point of the story is that he becomes her protector, her champion, her redeemer. Boaz does not allow Ruth's reputation to be compromised or tarnished in any way. Indeed, his behavior toward her is that of God's agent. Remember what he said to her earlier in the story, that she has come to take refuge under the *wings* of the God of Israel? It is not an accident that Ruth uses this same language in the middle of the night in the pregnant darkness of the threshing floor. "Spread your mantle [your *wing*] over your maidservant, for you are *next of kin* [which is to say, you are my *redeemer*]" (3:9). We see once again that the covenant love of God is made known through the simple, human actions of ordinary people showing kindness to one another. The wing of God is incarnate in the "wing" of Boaz.[7]

All through the story we see people facing alternatives. Ruth did not need to go with Naomi; it was not an obligation laid upon her. It was something very much more wonderful; it was, as Ephesians says, a good work that God had prepared for her to walk in. Similarly, Boaz clearly did not have to come to Ruth's rescue, let alone protect and then marry her.[8] Ruth and Boaz, by going that extra step, become bearers of the kindness and mercy of the God of Israel, who in every case does more than we either desire or deserve.

The world is indeed full of famine, death, sexual menace, and a host of other evils. Often it seems that God is absent or hostile. The story of Ruth shows us in an incomparable way that the blessings of God come to us through simple human means. When you reach out your hand to another, it is the hand of God. When you are faithful to your spouse, it is the faithfulness of God. When an employer cares for his work force, it is the care of God. When comfort and protection are offered to a stranger, or a foreigner, or an outsider of any kind, it is the protection and comfort and help of the Lord himself. His covenant love appears in human form — in the flesh.

And so we read that "Boaz took Ruth and she became his wife; and he went in to her, and the Lord gave her conception, and she bore a son. Then the women said to Naomi, 'Blessed be the Lord, who has not left you this day without next of kin; and may his name be renowned in Israel! He shall be to you a restorer of life and a nourisher of your old age; for your daughter-in-law who loves you, who is more to you than seven sons, has borne [a son].' . . . And the women of the neighborhood . . . named him Obed; he was the father of Jesse, the father of David" (4:13-15, 17). And so it was that Ruth, the foreign woman, became by the grace of God the great-grandmother of the great King David himself. And wonderful to relate, when we open our Bibles to the first page of the New Testament, there we find Ruth. The foreign maiden was the ancestor of Jesus. The story of Ruth, Naomi, and Boaz finds its fulfillment in the only begotten Son of God, who made himself to be next-of-kin for the entire human race, the Redeemer of the whole world.

AMEN.

Abigail's Strategy

GRACE CHURCH IN NEW YORK

The wonders of the Old Testament are so great that it is hard to know where to begin enumerating them. One way to begin would be to identify the cast of characters. The people of the Old Testament come in several sizes. Towering over the others are the colossi like Moses and David, Abraham and Elijah, who bestride the Hebrew Bible from one end to the other. Then there are the characters who, though they belong to just one section of the Bible, make a large impression from their respective places. Examples of these would be Joseph and Daniel, Samuel and Esther, Ruth and Jonah. Still others are stars because they are the centerpieces of the Bible's many small masterpieces of narrative art, like Naaman, Balaam, Gideon, Samson. These characters are striking and memorable enough to be routinely included in Bible story books.

Then there is another category of characters, the group that doesn't get into the storybooks and that most of us have never heard of. They flash onto the page like match lights, and after their brief moment of brilliance die away as fast as they appeared. Abigail is one of these. I had never even known that there was such a person in the Bible until I was reading 1 Samuel a few years ago in preparation for a class and she jumped off the page at me. I have never forgotten her.

Before we observe Abigail we need to remind ourselves of an overriding fact about the actors on the Biblical stage. There is just one main actor and that is God. Everyone else is there at his command. Everything that happens is according to his will or permission. Nothing occurs outside his knowledge and plan. No person is an independent operator; even the greatest villains, like Jezebel, Haman, and Belshazzar, are in God's eye and under his judgment. He raises people up and causes them to fall. Behind, beneath, above, and before every character in the Bible is the Holy One of Israel, the God of Abraham, Isaac, and Jacob, the Almighty Creator, "in the beginning, God." We need to keep this all-encompassing fact before us as we look at the various personalities that move across our field of vision, sharing the spotlight to a greater or lesser degree but always, no matter how small or huge, present because God has placed them there and holds their very existence in his hands.

And this is true of you and me also, so that we share our very essence with the people of the Bible. They are us. They are human, mortal, sinful, prideful, idiosyncratic, quirky, each of them unique and unforgettable. Each one has his "brief hour upon the stage" as Macbeth says, and then passes on. Only God remains. "All flesh is grass," we read in Isaiah; "Surely the people is grass. The grass withers, the flower fades, but the word of our God stands forever" (40:6-8). This is the setting for the Bible stories, and it is the setting for all our stories.

Now we are ready to tackle our subject. Abigail became one of King David's many wives, but she is by no means as well known as Bathsheba. Notice, however, that the only thing we remember about Bathsheba is her famous nude bathing scene, whereas Abigail emerges from the pages of Scripture as a person in her own right, a strong, self-possessed individual with guts and imagination. Her story is not introduced with fanfares or special effects. It is told as if it were the most natural thing in the world for a woman to step forward and play a prominent and decisive role. As Dorothy L. Sayers remarked, the Bible never introduces women with either "The ladies, God bless 'em" or "the women, God help us." Abigail does not appear as a mere appendage, either to her feckless first husband or to her glamorous second one, but as a specific person with her very own role to play in the drama. She plays that role brilliantly and then vanishes, having made her special, unique contribution. She is not there as a woman; she is there as a human being on the same footing as the men. This matter-of-fact even-handedness of the Bible is far more attractive in the long run than the tendentious ideologies of today.

I must admit that one of the reasons I find Abigail appealing is that she caught the eye of the sexiest man in the Old Testament. But I am getting ahead of the story. When Abigail meets David, he is not yet the King of the United Monarchy that he will later become. We take up the narrative in 1 Samuel 25 at a point when David is still on the run from King Saul, who hates him for no good reason other than jealousy and paranoia. David behaves nobly toward Saul throughout, refusing numerous opportunities to take the king's life because, as he says, "I will not put forth my hand against my lord, for he is the Lord's anointed" (24:10). David is forced to live like a sort of Robin Hood, famous throughout the area for his exploits and, no doubt, his personal charm, as he and his six hundred men act as a sort of "informal peacekeeping force" in return for their sustenance as they range throughout the territory. One commentator says that David depended on what might be called today a "protection racket." Here's where Abigail and her husband Nabal come in.

The story begins with David sending a message to Abigail's husband. The son of Jesse, we learn, has retreated to the wilderness where there was good grazing land. There he and his merry men coexisted peaceably with the flocks, herds, and shepherds of the well-to-do Nabal. At the time of the sheep-shearing, David sent messengers to Nabal full of courteous words, reminding Nabal of the security they have enjoyed during David's sojourn among them, and asking Nabal for a "protection payment" in return. (The Bible does not turn away from these facts of life, but in fairness we should note that it was necessary for David to do something of the sort in order to feed himself and his men. There is no moral judgment on it one way or the other; the story is simply told, without comment.)

Nabal and Abigail are briefly described for us. The King James Version says that Abigail was "a woman of good understanding and of a beautiful countenance," whereas Nabal was "churlish and evil in his doings." (It's one of those unequal marriages.) When Nabal hears the speech of David's men, which is very elegantly presented ("Peace be to thee, and peace be to thine house, and peace be unto all that thou hast"), he retorts, "Who is David, and who is the son of Jesse? There are many servants nowadays who are breaking away every man from their masters. Shall I take my bread and my water and my meat that I have killed for my shearers, and give it to men who come from I do not know where?" (25:10-11). You and I would no doubt say something of the sort ourselves under the circumstances, though perhaps less churlishly; the Biblical narrator, however, has a different perspective. This is not some disreputable brigand asking for tribute; this is the Once and Future King, the son of Jesse from whose house the Messiah would some day come. His life as an outlaw is not just a romantic story, but a tale of suspense on which the unfolding of God's great plan depends. What will happen to David? That is the theological question that holds the narrative together.

Abigail is several cuts above her uncouth husband. One of Nabal's shepherds, who is himself a character of note, even though like Naaman's wife's slave girl he is never named, goes to her and tells her that he is worried about what David will do when he hears Nabal's contemptuous words. He is right to be worried, as we learn, because David is furious and has told his men to gird on their swords. Nabal's young servant pleads with Abigail, knowing that she is the strong sensible one in the family: "Consider what you should do; for evil is determined against our master and against all his house, and he is so ill-natured that one cannot speak to him" (v. 17).

Our heroine wastes no time. She sees the danger. Nabal is about to get wiped out, along with all his men. This is the not-so-nice side of David, the hot-blooded, quick-tempered, impetuous side. Abigail didn't actually hear what David said about doing away with all the males in the household; nevertheless she and Nabal's young shepherd are pretty sure that something drastic is in the offing. Abigail is obviously a splendid ranch and household manager, because she is capable of rounding up, on a moment's notice, two hundred loaves, two skins of wine, five sheep ready dressed, five measures of corn, a hundred clusters of raisins, and two hundred cakes of figs and packing them up posthaste on a caravan of donkeys (v. 18). Off she went, in full mastery of herself and her retinue, saying nothing to the clueless Nabal.

Now we come to the momentous meeting of David and Abigail. You need to picture a narrow mountainous defile, winding around the rocks so that one party comes upon another quite suddenly. Abigail's donkeys and donkey drivers precede her along the narrow path, so we can imagine David, angry and full of a sense of outraged honor, bent on his bloody and vengeful mission, suddenly confronted by this rich caravan of delectable provisions followed up by a beautiful woman traveling alone.

Abigail gets off her horse and kneels on the ground at David's feet. At this point we can hear the thought police hollering, "Patriarchy! Oppression! Gynophobia!" Indeed, it is considered politically correct these days to indicate all the male chauvinist features of the Bible stories and to point out our great superiority as a culture to these benighted societies of the past. I'm not so sure about that. All civilizations have their particular horrors; generations yet to come will identify ours. The Biblical narratives live today because they transcend references to specific social customs. Clearly it is true that Abigail's place in her world was partly defined by the culture of her time. That is not what we remember about her, however. What we notice in the story is the way that Abigail uses her wits, her beauty, and her political instincts to save her husband's household and wealth, her own position, and her servants at the same time that she is risking her reputation and perhaps even her life on a hunch that God himself is mightily at work in this outlaw. What we remember, and what the Biblical writers present, is a strong, decisive woman of imagination and brains, far superior to her husband, who sees her opportunity and takes it. The story is told as if this were the most natural thing in the world for a woman to do.

Her speech to David is a long, flowery Oriental address too lengthy to repeat here, but we can highlight certain features. First she says, in the great tradition of the servants of God, "Upon me alone, my lord, be the guilt" (v. 24). This willingness to take the blame and consequences upon oneself is the central characteristic of the people of God, and its appearance, even in minor stories like this one, are miniature foreshadowings of the coming time when the One who will be called the Son of David steps forward to be the Servant of whom Isaiah will say "The Lord has laid on him the iniquity of us all" (Isa. 53:6).

Next, Abigail begs David to pay no attention to her boorish husband (1 Sam. 25:25). This could be seen as disloyal and underhanded unless we remember that the situation really is quite desperate, with many lives at stake. Most of us would be ready to use any sort of diplomacy that would work in such an extremity. Then Abigail enters upon the climactic portion of her speech, and it is so clever that one hardly knows whether to praise it most for its psychological adroitness or for its theological truth. In three or four different ways and with differing techniques she paints verbal pictures of David for him to look at as he stands there, depicting him as the person she knows he is not yet but hopes he will become. Many of you will recognize this as a forerunner of the most powerful sort of enabling exhortation, one that becomes familiar to us in the writings of Paul who says to us, in effect, "Become what you already are!"

Abigail says to David, "The Lord has restrained you from bloodguilt, and from taking vengeance with your own hand" (v. 26). This is truly audacious, because there is nothing to indicate that such a thing has happened. The Lord hasn't withheld David yet; he's still standing there with his sword at the ready and his nostrils breathing fire. Abigail is "wording" him into a new frame of mind. She says, "The Lord will certainly make my lord a sure house, because my lord is fighting the battles of the Lord; and evil shall not be found in you so long as you live" (v. 28). That's pretty clever, isn't it? David is enough of a man of God to recognize that if he is going to live up to this description of himself, he is going to have to put that sword away. And then Abigail says something that really escapes from her, becomes a prophecy, reveals to David his destiny, and becomes a part of the treasure of Israel: "The life of my lord shall be bound in the bundle of the living in the care of the Lord thy God . . . and when the Lord has done to my lord according to all the good that he has spoken concerning you, and has appointed you prince over Israel, my lord shall have no cause of grief, or pangs of conscience, for having shed blood without cause or for my lord taking vengeance himself" (vv. 29-31).

And David was touched to the heart, and David said to Abigail, "Blessed be the Lord, the God of Israel, who sent you this day to meet me . . . and blessed be you, who have kept me this day from bloodguilt and from avenging myself with my own hand! For as surely as the Lord God of Israel lives, who has restrained me from hurting you, unless you had made haste and come to meet me, truly by morning there had not been left to Nabal so much as one male" (vv. 32-34).

Thus Abigail saved the Lord's anointed, the forerunner of the Messiah of Israel, from a great evil. She went home that night to her wretched husband and found him so drunk that he was not capable of understanding anything of what had transpired. "In the morning, when the wine had gone out of Nabal, his wife told him these things"; Nabal had a heart attack and died ten days later. "When David heard that Nabal was dead, he said, 'Blessed be the Lord who has avenged the insult I received at the hand of Nabal, and has kept back his servant from evil. . . .' Then David sent and wooed Abigail, to make her his wife . . . and Abigail made haste and rose and mounted on an ass, and her five maidens attended her; she went after the messengers of David, and became his wife," and so passed into sacred history.

I am grateful for this story, as for so many other stories in the Old Testament. It teaches us many things. No one can do everything, but everyone can do something. Courage and boldness can be useful to God even if there are moral mistakes along the way. God uses men and women equally. There is a place in the providence of God for all sorts of idiosyncrasies and strategies. Women of God are real people in their own right. Even the rich are able to serve God. Jesus Christ did not come into the world in a vacuum as though he were too holy to associate with regular people; the way of the Son of David was prepared by adulterers like David and clever opportunists like Abigail, people like you and me, but people who have been given, in spite of themselves, a glimpse of what it means to know, to love, and to serve the Lord — and, in the process, to discover their true selves.

AMEN.

Lydia:
The First Christian in Europe

CHRIST CHURCH, SHEFFIELD, MASSACHUSETTS

Most churchgoing people in the mainline denominations today do not know very much about the Apostle Paul. This is rather alarming, since Paul's writings make up the largest portion of the New Testament. Paul is the person that God used to make the church happen. Without his preaching, the Christian gospel would have rapidly deteriorated into generic morality and spiritual slush.[1] Yet our knowledge of him is largely superficial and often downright wrong. One of the most well known of these misapprehensions is the widely held view that he did not like women. The persistence of this rumor is frustrating, since it is so manifestly false. This morning we are going to take a look at one of the women that Paul knew.

One thing that many people do know about Paul is that he was, in today's lingo, an "extreme" traveler. As one who has concentrated more on Paul's theology than on his itineraries, I have not always appreciated the extraordinary hardships and physical challenges that Paul undertook, covering thousands of miles; one can scarcely imagine it today. He must have had a remarkably robust constitution. We catch a glimpse of what he went through in 2 Corinthians 11:24-28:

Five times I have received . . . the forty lashes less one. Three times I have been beaten with rods; once I was stoned. Three times I have been shipwrecked; a night and a day I have been adrift at sea . . . in danger from rivers, danger from robbers, danger from my own people, danger from Gentiles, danger in the city, danger in the wilderness, danger at sea, danger from false brethren; in toil and hardship, through many a sleepless night, in hunger and thirst, often without food, in cold and exposure. And, apart from other things, there is the daily pressure upon me of my anxiety for all the churches.

We do not often think what it cost for the church to come into being. You and I sit here comfortably on Sunday morning, without a thought for the price that was paid for us to be Christians. Paul's last imprisonment was in distant Rome, the furthest point he reached, and there he was put to death by the emperor Nero. Today, however, we are joining Paul in mid-journey. He has been preaching and establishing churches in Asia Minor for several years. You will recall that Paul was appointed to be the missionary to the Gentiles, which meant that he went out from Jerusalem and Judea to the larger Mediterranean world. The distances between many towns and cities were vast and daunting even by modern standards, but nothing seems to have intimidated the apostle. He would arrive in a town, and typically would begin by going to the local Greek-speaking synagogue where there would be significant numbers of so-called "God-fearers."[2] This term was used to designate Gentiles who were attracted to Judaism and sometimes attended Jewish worship. Paul met with much success in Asia Minor, founding Christian churches in territories located in what is now modern Turkey.

At the point where our story begins, Paul is preparing to open up a new mission field in the northern regions of Asia Minor, because, as Luke tells us in the book of Acts, he and his team had been "prevented by the Holy Spirit from speaking the Word in Asia. And when they had come opposite Mysia, they attempted to go [north] into Bithynia, but the Spirit of Jesus did not allow them; so, passing by Mysia, they went down to Troas [on the Aegean Sea].

And a vision appeared to Paul in the night: a man of Macedonia was beseeching him and saying, 'Come over to Macedonia and help us'" (Acts 16:6-9). How often we have our hopes set on one direction, only to discover that God has something else in store for us! When one avenue of action is closed off to us, we may remember this experience of Paul and be alert to the voice that says, there are those who need our help in this other, unexpected direction.

Macedonia, as we all now realize with new force, is not in Asia Minor; it is in Europe. Until recently, many of us had only the vaguest notion of Macedonia, but during the terrible events in Kosovo last year, we all became acutely aware of it as that part of the former Yugoslavia which received hundreds of thousands of fleeing Kosovars. The country has presently reverted to the ancient name that made it illustrious as the homeland of Philip of Macedon, the father of Alexander the Great. Macedonia is just over the border from Kosovo; even so, as you will remember from news reports, it was not an easy crossing for the refugees. To go as Paul did from the regions of Bithynia and Mysia in Asia Minor to Macedonia in Europe was, as one commentator puts it, "an immense journey."[3] When Paul received the call, he and his mission team took a ship that sailed north from Troas and west along the Aegean coastline to the island of Samothrace and thence to Neapolis, the port city of Macedonia.[4] When the apostle Paul got off the boat in Neapolis, the Christian gospel set foot in Europe for the first time. The little team did not stop long in Neapolis, however, but headed straight to Philippi, a "leading city of Macedonia and a Roman colony" (Acts 16:12).[5]

Philippi was an old town, formerly named Krenides, that had been rebuilt and renamed by Philip of Macedon. It had a bit of a history, having been the scene of the victory of Mark Antony and Octavian (later Augustus Caesar) over Cassius and Brutus in 42 B.C., following the assassination of Julius Caesar. These were mighty events. Some sixty-five years later, nothing on that scale seemed to be happening when a little group of men, led by a Jew from Tarsus, arrived in town.[6] No one took notice of their presence. They went quietly to a local inn and began to take stock of the town, to see where they might begin their evangelistic work. After a few days, they had ascertained the lay of the land. Apparently there was no real synagogue in Philippi, for Acts tells us that on the Sabbath day, Paul went with his fellow missioner Silas to the place near the Gangites River, outside the city gate, where Jews gathered for Sabbath worship. When they arrived at the place, what did they find? A bunch of women.[7] What did that mean? It meant that there wasn't even a minyan. A minyan was then, as it remains today in orthodox Judaism, the minimum number of Jewish men that constituted a quorum for worship. No wonder there wasn't a proper synagogue in Philippi; they didn't even have ten men.[8]

Let's think about this for a moment. Here is Paul, the supposed woman-hater, newly arrived on the continent of Europe. There are no Christian congregations. There are, in fact, no Christians at all. He is the person who has been called by God to bring the gospel to the Gentile world — that is, brothers and sisters, to you and to me. He has a clear sense of his mission to evangelize the whole continent, reaching to Rome and even — he hoped — to Spain.[9] Paul was a strategic planner; we may assume that he has chosen Philippi as a place to begin because it is a Roman city of no mean distinction. However, he now finds himself outside the city walls, for Jews of the Diaspora were not always welcome to worship publicly.[10] Paul's little band goes out to this possibly bucolic but certainly off-track and non-elite spot along the river. This was definitely not a grand beginning for a new mission. It was not in the town Forum. It was not in an amphitheater. It was not even in a public space. It was off in the scrub with a handful of women. It was not an auspicious setting for a man like Paul; whatever else may be said of him, he was a man built on a heroic scale.[11] Bill Gates was never any more single-mindedly determined to build a market-dominating corporation than Paul was to bring the gospel of Jesus Christ to the whole world. How then do you think Paul felt when he saw those women? Wouldn't you think he would have turned around and said to his aides, "This isn't worth our time. Let's go back into town and find out where the powerful people are"?

Paul doesn't do that. He has placed his trust in the Lord of the gospel, and he knows that the power comes not from men but from God. He and the others go over to where the women are, sit down with them, and begin to talk to them about the One of whom they have never heard, the man of faraway Galilee who was "crucified under Pontius Pilate," put to death by "the rulers of this age," but now raised in power and alive in the Holy Spirit as his good news spreads and brings new life into being. A "God-fearer" named Lydia was among those gathered there. She felt her heart and mind being opened to the message that Paul brought (Acts 16:14). The Spirit of the Lord moved in her as she listened. Jesus Christ made himself known to her that day by the river, and she believed in him.[12] Lydia of Philippi was the first Christian in Europe.

Now who was this Lydia? Since so many of the early Christians were lower-class, poor, even slaves, it should come as good news to us relatively affluent Episcopalians to learn that Lydia was well-to-do. We are told that she was originally from Thyatira, which was known all around the Mediterranean for its purple dye. You know that this color was the most expensive of all. Prosperous Roman senators had purple borders on their togas. Emperors and kings wore purple. Lydia had come over to Macedonia as a trader in purple dye.[13] Like Paul, she had made a long, arduous journey to get to Philippi. Thyatira was far off in Asia Minor, and you had to have plenty of capital, as well as gumption, to become a purple-dye agent in Europe. Lydia was obviously a mover and a shaker. If there was any man in her life, we don't hear about him. When Lydia became a Christian, her whole household was baptized along with her — this doesn't mean her "nuclear family" such as we would have in mind; it means her servants and her business organization. This is a *woman!* One of the aspects of the story that is so striking and so significant is that all this is told as though it were the most natural thing in the world for a woman to have that much clout. Her distinction isn't commented upon. No feminist lessons are drawn. The New Testament writers don't say, Look! a new women's movement in Philippi! It just happens. It is particularly noteworthy that fifteen hundred years later, John Calvin, in his commentary on the book of Acts, praises Lydia extravagantly for her greatness. We would expect Calvin, being a man of his time, to have conservative views of male headship, but he doesn't blink at Lydia's being a woman who, as he writes approvingly, "had all her household obedient."[14] The joy of the gospel of Christ sweeps all such distinctions away.

We can readily imagine Lydia, I think. Executive women are like this — imperious, fearless, born leaders.[15] They stand out in a crowd; they take charge. Maybe they are somewhat overbearing. The next thing that happens is therefore all the more notable. After her baptism, Lydia comes to Paul and says, "Now, Paul, no more staying at that awful inn. From now on, you and Silas and the others must come and stay with *me.*" Given Paul's policies, this might not have come as a welcome invitation; it might have sounded more like an unwanted command. We know from the apostle's letters that he did not accept gifts from his congregations. In fact, he was very conscientious about earning his own living wherever he went, for two reasons: he did not want to become a burden, and he did not want anyone to be able to accuse him of turning the gospel to his own advantage (1 Thess. 2:9). Some men might be put off by having such a powerful woman come up and tell them what they are going to do next. Paul is not like that. Perhaps he demurred at first, but when he hears what more she has to say, he gives in at once. Luke puts it this way: "The Lord opened her heart to give heed to what was said by Paul. And when she was baptized, with her household, she besought us, saying, 'If you have judged me to be faithful to the Lord, come to my house and stay.' And she prevailed upon us" (Acts 16:14-15).[16] In other words, Lydia's forcefulness was subordinated to her faith. Her desire to show the earnestness of her commitment to Christ made it impossible for Paul to refuse.

Thus was born the special relationship between Paul and the Philippian church that burns in almost every word of his letter to them, words that have warmed the hearts of Christians for two thousand years to this day. It was the one church that he could always count on.[17] Their wholehearted love for him and, even more important, for the whole Christian mission gave Paul strength to the end of his life. They were the only church that he allowed to support him financially, because he knew their love for the Lord motivated them: "And you Philippians yourselves know that in the beginning of the gospel [in Europe], when I left Macedonia, no church entered into partnership with me in giving and receiving except you only; for even in Thessalonica you sent me help again and again" (Phil. 4:15). The Philippian congregation was known throughout the early church for unstinting generosity. It is the Philippian church of whom Paul later wrote to the stingy Corinthians, hoping that they would be ashamed of themselves: "We want you to know, brethren, about the grace of God which has been shown in the churches of Macedonia. . . . For they gave according to their means, as I can testify, and beyond their means, of their own free will, begging us earnestly for the favor of taking part in the relief of the saints . . . first they gave themselves to the Lord, and to us, by the will of God" (2 Cor. 8:1-5).[18] That says it all, doesn't it? Paul might as well be speaking of Lydia herself. First she gave herself to the Lord, and then, by the will of God, she gave herself to the service of the apostles. By the time we meet the Philippian church in Paul's letters, the whole congregation has taken on this character of glad giving, following the leadership of Lydia.[19]

You may remember the famous scene that takes place in Philippi shortly after the conversion of Lydia (Acts 16:16-40). Paul and Silas cause a riot and are thrown into prison and put in the stocks by the Roman authorities.[20] During the night, though they must have been frightened to death, they sang hymns and prayed aloud. Suddenly the foundations of the prison shook, and the prison doors were thrown open.[21] The chief jailer was converted and baptized that very night; the Roman magistrate let the apostles go free on the condition that they leave town at once. Paul and Silas left Philippi with glad hearts, however, for their last action before departing was to go to the house of Lydia where the brand-new Christian congregation was assembled (Acts 16:40). Again, Calvin is dazzled by Lydia's leadership; he writes that they went straight to Lydia's house because "that woman was the chief of a great number . . . all the godly were assembled in her house."[22] The most dependable of all Paul's churches was thus established, and it all came about through the leadership, gifts, and devotion of Lydia the Thyatiran.

There is a stained-glass window of Lydia nearby at Trinity Church in Lime Rock, Connecticut, the only one I have ever seen. There should be many more. She is one of those of whom we sing on All Saints Day: "She loved her Lord so dear, so dear, and his love made her strong." You might say that Lydia was strong already! Yes, but the Lord made her strong in a different way. He made her strong in the Holy Spirit. The strength of the Spirit is the strength that does not make money for itself but for "the relief of the saints." The strength of the Spirit seeks not the glory of the single believer but the good of the Body of Christ. The strength of the Spirit brings a church into being where there was no church. For as Calvin writes further, Lydia's invitation was not her inviting only, *but also God's,* to keep Paul and his companions there in Philippi. It was as though God himself laid hands upon them through the person of Lydia.

My dear friends of Christ Church, the strength of the same Spirit that can work through a tiny congregation on the riverbank two thousand years ago can work through this small congregation also. At any moment God may cause some small action of your own to become great for his service. We cannot all be Lydias, but we can all play our part by loving the Lord and serving his people. You are on the verge of a breakthrough here, with your new building plans. Just remember: "Unless the Lord builds the house, those who build it labor in vain" (Ps. 127:1). In thanksgiving for blessed Lydia and the church in her house, let us close with these wonderful words from Paul's letter to his beloved Philippian congregation:

Always in every prayer of mine for you all [I make] my prayer with joy, thankful for your partnership in the gospel from the first day until now. And I am sure that he who began a good work in you will bring it to completion at the day of Jesus Christ. It is right for me to feel thus about you all, because I hold you in my heart, for you are all partakers with me of grace, both in my imprisonment and in the defense and confirmation of the gospel.

For God is my witness, how I yearn for you all with the affection of Christ Jesus. And it is my prayer that your love may abound more and more, with knowledge and all discernment, so that you may approve what is excellent, and may be pure and blameless for the day of Christ, filled with the fruits of righteousness which come through Jesus Christ, to the glory and praise of God. (Phil. 1:4-11)

AMEN.

CODA: TWO STORIES OF
LITTLE FAITH GROWN GREAT

Gideon's Three Hundred

TRINITY CATHEDRAL, COLUMBIA, SOUTH CAROLINA

The Lord said to Gideon, "The people with you are too many for me to give the Midianites into their hand, lest Israel vaunt themselves against me, saying, 'My own hand has delivered me.'"

(JUDG. 7:2)

I nvasion by a foreign power is an exceptionally terrible thing. Modern Americans have been spared this horror, so it is very difficult for us to imagine. We do not know what it is like to be Greek when Turks are storing gunpowder in the Parthenon, or to be French when Germans are goose-stepping down the Champs Elysées, or to be Chinese when Japanese are murdering in the streets of Nanking. American Southerners talk about Sherman's men marching through Georgia, but most of us have only the vaguest idea what that was like. It is too remote from us. God's people of Old Testament times, however, knew very well what foreign invasion was like. Today let us relive the experience of the Midianite invasion of Israel and hear the great story of a young man named Gideon.

The writer of the book of Judges begins by telling us that "the Israelites did what was evil in the eyes of the Lord" (6:1), and that was the reason God allowed the Midianites to overrun them for seven years. The ancient Hebrew historians were gripped by the power of a God who had called his people to a life of obedient faithfulness to his holy commandments; it is remarkable that they did not seek to transfer the blame to the Midianites. What the Old Testament writers in fact asserted was that the nation of Israel was responsible; the people had disregarded the righteous laws of the Lord.

As our story opens, the Israelites are enduring — for the seventh summer in a row — the brutally destructive raids of the camel-mounted Midianites. (It is fascinating to note that this is the very first organized camel campaign in recorded history.) The people called "Midianites" in the Old Testament seem to have been Bedouin from the Arabian desert, who began periodically to ravage Canaan just as the crops were coming to maturity. A vivid account of Palestine under Turkish rule in the early days of our own twentieth century gives us an idea of what it must have been like three thousand years before:

> In June and July [the Bedouin] come northward . . . tens of thousands of camels . . . break through the thin ranks of soldiers, and woe unto the fields over which the hungry hordes first scatter! Not a stem, not a blade of grass is left, for what they do not devour is trampled under the broad hoofs of their camels.[1]

According to the Old Testament account, "The power of Midian was so oppressive that the Israelites prepared shelters for themselves in mountain clefts, caves, and strongholds . . . the Midianites camped on the land and ruined the crops all the way to Gaza and did not spare a living thing for Israel. . . . They came up with their livestock and their tents like swarms of locusts. It was impossible to count the men and their camels. . . . Midian so impoverished the Israelites that they cried out to the Lord for help" (Judg. 6:2-6).

During one of the Midianite raids, a young man named Gideon was attempting to thresh wheat in a winepress. This was not the proper method for such a task; ordinarily the threshing of wheat was done out on an open threshing floor, where the animals could move about freely and the wind could carry the chaff away. A method like that was out of the question with the Midianites around, so Gideon was trying rather pathetically to do the job with this little winepress, where he hoped the Midianites wouldn't see what he was up to.

Now Gideon was apparently a dutiful and hardworking young man, but we may deduce from the text that he was not a paragon of religious virtue by any means. Like most other Israelites of his day he had gone along with the trends in the Canaanite culture that were all around him. We may assume that he ogled the temple prostitutes with interest; he said a prayer now and then to the bosomy statue of the fertility goddess that his father kept in the house; and he had been known to swear by the name of Baal on occasion. He knew of his own tribal God Yahweh, of course, and he said prayers to him too; but all things considered, Yahweh was a remote figure whose impact on Gideon's daily life was minimal. Gideon had heard that God was a jealous God, but he did not really believe it; surely there were many ways to approach the divine, so one might as well try them all, just to be on the safe side.

Well, Gideon was threshing away with his winepress when suddenly a strange person materialized before him and said, "The Lord Yahweh is with you, you mighty man of valor."

Gideon's first response is skeptical. "My father told me about Yahweh, but I don't see him doing anything about these Midianites. If the Lord is with us, where are all his wonderful deeds? Why are all these things happening to us?" The angel of the Lord (for that is what he was) magnanimously overlooks Gideon's lack of theological understanding and says to him, "Go . . . and save Israel out of the hand of Midian. Am I not sending you?" (6:14).

It is one thing to be told that God is nearby. It is quite another to be told that you are going to become God's agent on a very dangerous mission. An interesting thing happens to Gideon. It is the same thing that happens to all the Biblical figures when God comes to them. Suddenly Gideon becomes acutely aware of his own smallness and inadequacy.

"But Lord," Gideon protested, "How can I save Israel? My

tribe is the weakest . . . and I am the least in my family" (v. 15). In the same way, when God appeared to Moses at the burning bush, Moses said, "Who am I that I should go to Pharaoh?" (Exod. 3:11). In the presence of God, our macho posturing, our masks of virtue, our various defenses shrivel up and fall away. How amazing, then, that God's immediate response should be one of reassurance! "The Lord answered Gideon, 'I will be with you, and you shall strike the Midianites as though they were one man'" (Judg. 6:16). Gideon wasn't in the least a mighty man of valor until God said so, but he is going to become one now. God, you see, isn't going to allow us always to keep him at a remote and pious distance to suit ourselves; God is capable of invading our lives and commandeering us into his service.

Gideon's response shows his rapid growth in faith, even as it exposes his spiritual immaturity. "Wait here," he says to the divine being; "I need a sign that what you say is true." Gideon dashes off and fetches a little offering of meat and bread, and the angel of the Lord waits patiently. Gideon bring the gifts and places them upon a flat stone; whereupon the angel sends the offerings up in flames and disappears on the instant. Gideon, overcome with awe, astonishment, and fear, cries out that he knows he is going to die because he has gotten too close to the blazing majesty of God, but the voice of God speaks gently to him: "Peace be unto thee; fear not: thou shalt not die" (v. 23). We are accustomed to hearing angels in the Bible stories say "Fear not," so we don't stop to think what it means. The sudden appearance of God in the lives of human beings is terrifying at first. We cannot stand in God's presence without his gracious permission. That is what the Lord offers to Gideon.

Strengthened by the angel's commission, the newly appointed "mighty man of valor" prepares to do the business of the Lord. The Midianites are busy too. They have crossed the Jordan River with their camels, and they have pitched their tents by the thousands in the famous Valley of Jezreel. Gideon calls up some troops from the various tribes of Israel. We can tell that Gideon is still nervous about his new calling because he keeps asking God to give him more signs. He takes his sheepskin jacket and throws it on the ground and asks God to put some dew on it, and God does, and then the next night Gideon throws it down again and asks God to put dew everywhere *but* on the sheepskin, and God goes along with all this foolishness very patiently.

Then early in the morning, we are told, "Gideon and all his [32,000] men camped at the spring of Harod . . . and the Lord said to Gideon, 'You have too many men. In order that Israel may not boast against me that her own strength has saved her, announce now to the people, "Anyone who is afraid may leave."' So thousands left and 22,000 stayed behind" (7:1-3). God reduced their numbers still further, by various interesting means that you can read about in the text, until there were only 300 left. So much for our human preoccupation with size and numbers! God works with small groups — Gideon and the three hundred, Jesus and the twelve, a few nuns in El Salvador, a handful of human-rights activists in Guatemala, a few hundred black people boycotting the buses, small prayer groups, small Bible-study groups, small bands of committed Christians. Why does God work with small groups? St. Paul wrote that God's way is to demonstrate that "His power [is] made perfect in our weakness" (2 Cor. 12:9).

God gave Gideon one more sign before the battle, in order to uphold him in his human weakness. As night fell, God said to Gideon, "Go down into the [Midianite] camp with your servant Purah and listen to what they are saying. Afterward, you will be encouraged to attack the camp" (vv. 10-11). So Gideon and his servant sneak down the hill in the dark, into the midst of the Midianites. We can visualize the valley of Jezreel, absolutely packed with men, tents, and camels. Gideon's little band are up in the hills and the Midianites are spread out below. We can imagine Gideon and Purah making their way along, trying not to trip over any tent ropes or bump into any camels, pressing their ears to the tent flaps to catch pieces of Midianite conversation. And what Gideon hears one man saying to another man is that he has had a dream — a loaf of barley bread came rolling into the Midianites' camp and knocked over one of the tents. Gideon, eavesdropping outside, knew that meant that the wheat-growing Israelites were going to get the best of the tent-dwelling Midianites.

When Gideon heard the dream, he did a noteworthy thing. He didn't turn and give Purah a high five. He didn't pump his fists in the air. He fell down on his knees right in the middle of the enemy camp and gave thanks to God. Instead of thinking of all the glory and money and endorsements he was going to get, "he worshipped God" and then "returned to the camp of Israel and called out, 'Get up! The Lord has given the Midianite camp into your hands'" (v. 15). Not a word about himself; he speaks only of God and his companions.

Stirred by the words and the conduct of their charismatic leader — for we are told the "the spirit of the Lord came upon Gideon" (6:34) — the three hundred men followed him ardently. Each carried a trumpet and a torch covered by an earthenware jar. I have always wondered how they could carry all those things at once, but never mind — it is one of the most vivid scenes in the Bible. The Midianites are asleep in the valley, expecting no trouble from the weak Israelites, when all of a sudden, on the signal from Gideon, all the three hundred broke their jars at once, so that the torches flared out like explosions in the dark, and all the trumpets sounded at the same time. From the hills around the Midianite camp the mysterious flame-lit company descended as if from the sky, accompanied by unearthly deafening blasts from the ram's horn trumpets. In that superstitious age it must have been an extraordinary sight. The terrified Midianites and their stampeding camels fled from the valley in panic, trampling on one another as they went, and the battle was won without so much as one stroke of a sword.

Now of course this story has legendary features in it, but the point is unmistakable. God is invincible. His purposes will be accomplished. Those who serve him cannot be overcome. God is not bound to the great and powerful, the mighty of the earth. God chooses to work with the small, the weak, the insignificant. What are the black children of Birmingham against the hoses and the dogs of the sheriff and police force? What is one student dancing in front of a tank in Tiananmen Square? What is Nelson Mandela alone in his prison cell? Who would have thought in their wildest imaginings that this man would become president of South Africa?

What are the torches and earthenware jars of Gideon against the Midianites?

The power of God confounds the powerful of the earth. The most striking feature in the story of Gideon is not the fairy-tale element. It is Gideon's humility before the commanding presence, power, and purpose of God. In 1933, in Germany, when the Nazis were coming to power in large numbers and the resisting Christian church was very small, there was a young Lutheran pastor/theologian named Dietrich Bonhoeffer. As you know, he became one of the greatest of twentieth-century martyrs, hanged in 1945 just before the liberation. On the day before the Reichstag fire in Berlin, he preached about Gideon, and his students never forgot it. These were his words:

> Do not desire to be strong, powerful, honored, and respected, but let God alone be your strength, your fame, and your honor. . . . Gideon, *who achieved faith in fear and doubt,* kneels with us here before the altar of the one and only Lord, and Gideon prays with us: "Our Lord on the cross, be thou our one and only Lord. Amen."[2]

Even Peter, Even Us

CHRIST CHURCH, SAVANNAH

*Jesus said, "Simon, Simon, behold, Satan demanded to have you
. . . but I have prayed for you that your faith may not fail; and
when you have turned again, strengthen your brethren." And
Peter said to him, "Lord, I am ready to go with you to prison
and to death." Jesus said, "I tell you, Peter, the cock will not
crow this day, until you three times deny that you know me."*

(LUKE 22:31-34)

The Lord turned and looked at Peter.

(LUKE 22:61)

*Go, tell his disciples and Peter that he is going before you to
Galilee; there you will see him, as he told you.*

(MARK 16:7)

Do you have any family secrets? Most families do. In fact, I
think all families do. There was a sister who was an alcoholic,
a great-grandfather who served time for tax fraud, an uncle who
committed suicide, an ancestor who had a slave mistress. Families
don't treasure stories about the failures of their members. In fact,

they usually hush them up. We don't tell the next generation about them. We throw out the incriminating documents. We certainly don't hang any plaques on the wall. When a story about the disgrace of a family member is carefully preserved, that is so unusual that it merits special notice.

Tonight we are going to ask ourselves why the church preserved and retold a terrible story about the apostle Peter.

On the last night of Jesus' life, the disciples proved themselves to be a bunch of cowards and losers. After supper, while the Lord was praying in indescribable agony in the Garden of Gethsemane, they fell asleep. When the crowd of conspirators arrived to arrest Jesus, Mark says, "they all forsook him and fled" (14:50).[1] The deplorable tale of the disciples' collapse is distilled in the story of Peter. All four evangelists tell it. Here is Luke's version:

> They seized Jesus and led him away, bringing him into the high priest's house. Peter followed at a distance; and when they had kindled a fire in the middle of the courtyard and sat down together, Peter sat among them. Then a maid, seeing him as he sat in the light and gazing at him, said, "This man also was with him." But he denied it, saying, "Woman, I do not know him." And a little later someone else saw him and said, "You also are one of them." But Peter said, "Man, I am not." And after an interval of about an hour still another insisted, saying, "Certainly this man also was with him; for he is a Galilean." [Matthew says that Peter began to curse and swear at this point.[2]] Peter said, "Man, I do not know what you are saying." And immediately, while he was still speaking, the cock crowed. And the Lord turned and looked at Peter. And Peter remembered the word of the Lord, how he had said to him, "Before the cock crows today, you will deny me three times." And he went out and wept bitterly. (Luke 22:52-62)

And the Lord turned and looked at Peter. Imagine it, if you will. Peter was the motormouth among the disciples, the one most likely to speak first and protest loudest. Peter said a number of important and good things that are preserved in the New Testament record, but he also said some very foolish things. Here is Matthew's version of what Peter said to Jesus after the Last Supper:

> When they had sung a hymn, they went out to the Mount of Olives. Then Jesus said to them, "You will all fall away because of me this night; for it is written, 'I will strike the shepherd, and the sheep of the flock will be scattered.' . . ." Peter declared to him, "Though they all fall away because of you, I will never fall away." Jesus said to him, "Truly, I say to you, this very night, before the cock crows, you will deny me three times." Peter said to him, "Even if I must die with you, I will not deny you." (Matt. 26:30-35)

Have you ever disgraced yourself like that? Of course you have; we all have. Think of all the people who have said, "For better, for worse, for richer, for poorer, in sickness and health . . . until death us do part"; they meant it at the time, but half of them are now divorced. Think of how many times you or I have said, "*I* would *never* do what that other person is doing. *I* would never lie, steal, eavesdrop, hit and run, cheat on an exam, slap my child, or drive drunk. *I* would *never* look in somebody else's medicine cabinet, accept money from a suspicious source, abandon a sinking ship, pay a nanny under the table . . . ," whatever.

So what happened to Peter, with all his fine words? Only a few hours after those passionate protestations, Peter, faced with a real live police action against Jesus, turned tail and became a traitor, just as Jesus had predicted. *And the Lord turned and looked at Peter.* Of all the looks that have ever been, this bottomless look is the one that most truly reveals us to ourselves. Here we see the wretched pretension and guilt of human beings in the light of the justice and the grace of God, his aweful love and his fearful mercy. In that moment, the abject failure of the human creature was met by the penetrating gaze of the One who was on his way to be handed over for Peter's redemption, and for ours. *And the Lord turned and looked at Peter.* In that moment, heaven and earth meet. This is the closest

[268]

anyone has ever come in this life to the truth about ourselves before God. The Judge of all the universe, going to his death, fixes his eyes upon this one wretched human being, a man who has bragged incessantly of his loyalty — and, in the space of a second, with one look, Jesus uncovers Peter's folly, his cowardice, his craven self-serving falsehoods.

Many of us will remember our parents' looks. Those looks said, "What did I tell you?" "I see what you're doing!" "Did you think you could get by with that?" "The wrath of heaven is about to fall on your head!" But the look of Jesus was not like our parents' looks. Alone of all human beings who ever lived, Jesus was able to give a pure and unmixed look of disappointed love. There were no psychological undercurrents in his look, no overtones of neurosis or displaced anger or rampant superego or need to control. The look of Jesus is the look of Peter's Creator, described in Psalm 139: "Thou didst form my inward parts, thou didst knit me together in my mother's womb. . . . My frame was not hidden from thee, when I was being made in secret." Peter tried to hide, but the Lord found him with that look. "O Lord, thou hast searched me and known me! . . . Whither shall I go from thy Spirit? Or whither shall I flee from thy presence? If I ascend to heaven, thou art there! If I make my bed in [the underworld], thou art there also! . . . Thou art acquainted with all my ways. Even before a word is on my tongue, lo, O Lord, thou knowest it altogether." Before God, there is no place to hide.

How can we stand before this kind of scrutiny? The answer is, we can't, any more than Peter could. Something has to happen, something that we do not deserve, cannot earn, and have no right to expect.

Let's make sure we have the picture right. Jesus is being led away to be scourged and crucified. Peter is not being arrested; Peter is not being tried; Peter is not being executed. He is going scot-free. He is standing by, pretending that he never saw Jesus before in his life. However, the words are hanging in the air: "Even if I must die with you, I will not deny you." . . . "Before the cock crows, you will deny me three times."

Now here is a question for us. Think for a moment about the

way in which this story of Peter's denial was transmitted. No one in the early Christian community was there when it happened. How did this episode get saved by the church? It certainly doesn't cast the leader of the apostles in a good light — to say the least. Why is this story told in all four Gospels? I wouldn't want a story like this about me to be circulated, would you? Think, for instance, about all the authorized biographies that have been published about leaders of corporations. Stories about their failures of character do not lie at the heart of these sanitized books. In contrast to that is Peter's story, right at the center of the Passion narrative. Over and over for two thousand years this tale of Peter's lying and cowardice has been re-told. It could easily have been suppressed. Why wasn't it? Here's the reason. The reason that the story of Peter's denial is at the center of the Christian tradition must be that Peter himself wanted it to be there. Peter wanted the church to remember that, at the moment when Jesus was being carried off to his horrible death, the Master caught him in the very act of betrayal that he had sworn he would never commit.[3] Without the story of Peter's failure, there is no story of Peter's restitution from beyond the grave.

"Peter went out and wept bitterly" . . . and on Friday at noon his Lord was nailed to the cross. As far as anyone knew, it was the end of the story of Jesus of Nazareth. There was nothing else to hope for. It's important for us to understand this. There was no springtime in the hearts of Jesus' disciples. It is inconceivable that mere religious imagination could have come up with the idea of a resurrection from the grave under those circumstances. There was no point in talking about preserving the Master's message; he him-self had been the message, and now he was gone — not only dead, but also debased and discredited before the whole world. As for Pe-ter, he knew himself for the first time to be a total fraud. Put your-self in Peter's place for a moment. Until the Lord looked at him, he had been able to hold on to his bluster. He was still self-deceived. You know how it is when you hear someone being critical of some-one else, and you think to yourself, "If only she knew what people are saying about *her!*" Until the cock crowed, Peter had never really looked into himself. He had never known what he was capable of.

He had not seen his own dark side clearly before. He had believed his own words when he said, "Though they all fall away because of you, I will never fall away." Now he is unmasked, not only in the sight of the Lord, but in his own sight. Peter has nowhere left to stand in all the world.

And so we come to Easter morning. This is what St. Mark says:

> Very early on the first day of the week, [the women] went to the tomb when the sun had risen. And they were saying to one another, "Who will roll away the stone for us from the door of the tomb?" And looking up, they saw that the stone was rolled back — it was very large. And entering the tomb, they saw a young man sitting on the right side, dressed in a white robe; and they were amazed. And he said to them, "Do not be amazed; you seek Jesus of Nazareth, who was crucified. He has risen, he is not here; see the place where they laid him. But go, tell his disciples and Peter that he is going before you to Galilee; there you will see him, as he told you." (Mark 16:2-7)

. . . and Peter! Have you ever heard anything more wonderful than that?[4] All the disciples, in varying degrees, had failed Jesus, but Peter had failed him the most, because he had been the biggest braggart of all. Peter's offense was the worst, and therefore Peter's restitution is the most astonishing. It is Peter who receives the message of the Resurrection specifically, by his own name. "Go and tell the disciples *and Peter!*" Interpreters of Mark's Gospel say that we can translate the Greek to read, "*even* Peter!"[5]

Some of you were here last night when we heard the story of the Emmaus Road. Here is what St. Luke says happened after the risen Lord appeared to the disciples in the breaking of the bread: "The disciples rose that same hour and returned to Jerusalem; and they found the eleven gathered together and those who were with them, who said, 'The Lord has risen indeed, and has appeared to Simon [Peter]!'" (Luke 24:33-34).

Sometimes people speak of what happened to Peter in terms of Peter's sin being forgiven. That's true, of course. But it isn't really

strong enough. St. Paul, who knew something about being confronted by Jesus in the midst of horrific sin, used a different word.
He wrote to the Christians in Rome, "God shows his love for us in
that, while we were yet sinners, Christ died for us. Since, therefore,
we are now justified by his blood, much more shall we be saved by
him from the wrath of God" (Rom. 5:8-9). Paul, instead of using
the word "forgiven," uses the word "justified" — not only *forgiven,*
but also *made right,* rectified, reconstituted to be in fellowship with
our Lord forever.[6]

Saved, furthermore, "by him from the wrath of God." Maybe
you don't want to hear about the wrath of God. The designers of the
lectionary don't want you to hear about it; they expunged it from
the cycle of readings wherever they could. But if you don't know
anything about the wrath of God, then the full dimensions of the
Resurrection will be lost to you. Do you think Jesus had a right to
be angry with Peter at that moment when he looked at him? God's
judgment fell upon Peter at that moment. But Jesus' look is not a
look of pure judgment. If it were, we could not bear it. It is also and
at the same time a look of restitution, of reconstitution, of rectification. Some years later, someone who was writing in the name and
spirit of Peter wrote these words:

> [Christ] himself bore our sins in his body on the tree, that we
> might die to sin and live to righteousness. By his wounds [we]
> have been healed. For [we] were straying like sheep, but have
> now returned to the Shepherd and Guardian of [our] souls.
> (1 Pet. 2:24-25)

There is one more text tonight. During the last supper Jesus
said to Peter, calling him by his first name, "Simon, Simon, behold,
Satan demanded to have you . . . but I have prayed for you that your
faith may not fail; and when you have turned again, strengthen your
brethren" (Luke 22:31-32). After Pentecost, Peter moved into his
destined role as leader of the apostles. How did that come to pass,
after so great a failure? Peter's faith in Jesus — the faith that caused
him to leave his fishing boat, that propelled him out onto the water

to go to Jesus, that caused him to be the first to confess Jesus as Messiah — that faith seemed to fail him at the crucial moment. But that was not the last word. Just as Jesus knew Peter would betray him, so Jesus was interceding for him. So it is with you and me. Perhaps you think you are a person of little faith, but do you realize that Christ the Lord is interceding for you that your faith may not fail? Even if your faith is no bigger than a mustard seed, it is enough, because, as Paul wrote, the Holy Spirit intercedes for us with sighs too deep for words (Rom. 8:26). How can our faith fail when we have the Holy Trinity on our side? As we sing in one of our great hymns, "Intercessor, friend of sinners, earth's redeemer, plead for me."

Think, this evening, of how "the Shepherd and Guardian of [our] souls" looks at you and me. "To him all hearts are open, all desires known, and from him no secrets are hid."[7] He sees us without our masks and pretensions. He sees the worst things that we have ever done, and the worst that we are. He sees us far more clearly than we see ourselves, because most of us live in a state of perpetual denial about our faults. In the light of the resurrection message, we may give up pretense and denial forever. He looks at us, he sees everything that there is to see, and still he says to you as he said to Peter, "I have prayed for you that your faith may not fail" (Luke 22:32). Peter's faith was no better than a castle made of sand until the risen Lord remade him. It is the same with you. No matter who you are or what you have done, he is calling you to himself and adorning you with his resurrection life. No one will ever be able to despise you or discredit you or discount you, because he has taken all the discounting and discrediting and despising unto himself. Now you are free, free to go forth and strengthen your brothers and sisters. He has paid the price and won the victory.

The Lord is risen indeed! Alleluia!

Endnotes

Preface

1. Flannery O'Connor, *The Habit of Being* (New York: Farrar Straus & Giroux, 1979), pp. 476, 452.

2. Quoted with comment from Aileen Ward's biography, *John Keats: The Making of a Poet* (New York: Viking, 1963), p. 161.

3. O'Connor, *The Habit of Being,* p. 354.

Introduction

1. Strangely, several of the American presidential candidates in 2000 made more explicit public statements about their devotion to Jesus than any candidates ever have before, including devout Christian Jimmy Carter, whose presidential speeches were carefully shorn of God-talk.

2. From my class notes, Union Theological Seminary, 1974. Dr. Steimle was a principal preacher on "The Protestant Hour" for decades.

3. William L. Lane, *The Gospel According to Mark,* New International Commentary on the New Testament (Grand Rapids: Eerdmans, 1974), p. 332.

4. Eduard Schweizer, *The Good News According to Mark* (Richmond: John Knox Press, 1970), p. 188.

5. D. E. Nineham, *St. Mark,* Pelican Commentary Series (Philadelphia: Westminster Press, 1977), p. 243.

6. This is what Jesus means when he says later that this kind [of demon] cannot be driven out except by prayer." Some copiers, thinking that prayer by itself wasn't enough, added "and fasting."

7. "Reporter at Large: Creedmoor," *The New Yorker,* June 8, 1981.

8. Nineham advocates the translation, "most people" (*St. Mark,* pp. 243-44n).

9. Schweizer, *The Good News According to Mark,* p. 189.

10. Schweizer, *The Good News According to Mark,* -p. 243-44n.

11. The work of Richard B. Hays on the faithfulness of Jesus in Paul's theology is relevant here: *The Faith of Jesus Christ: An Investigation of the Narrative Substructure of Gal. 3:1–4:11* (Chico, Calif.: Scholars Press, 1983).

Sermon 1: Moses and Monotheism: A Response to Dr. Freud

1. Henry Louis Gates, *The New Yorker,* 26 February and 4 March 1996 (double issue), p. 132.

2. Quoted in Peter Steinfels's "Beliefs" column, *The New York Times,* 11 July 1998.

3. *The New York Times,* Op-ed page, 5 March 1999.

4. Virginia Woolf, *Letters,* vol. 3 (New York: Harcourt Brace Jovanovich, 1977), pp. 457-58.

5. Peter Gomes is the distinguished preacher who ordinarily occupies the Harvard pulpit.

6. Cf. Yosef Hayim Yerushalmi, *Freud's Moses* (New Haven: Yale University Press, 1991).

7. Ludwig Feuerbach's critique of religion is similar to that of Freud at many points. Feuerbach was an important influence in the development of Karl Barth's thinking about God. I find Freud more compelling because, to me, he is both more literary and more humanistic than Feuerbach.

8. Flannery O'Connor wrote to a friend, "To religion [she means Christian orthodoxy] I think he [Freud] is much less dangerous than Jung" (*The Habit of Being* [New York: Farrar Straus & Giroux, 1979], p. 491). Philip Reiff wrote, "Theologians might well reconsider . . . who is more dangerous, Freud or Jung. Better a forthright enemy than an untrustworthy friend. Jung's psychological religiosity is too strictly for therapeutics, those for whom a god is the need of needs. . . . I am not sure whether one should not prefer Freud's strong nonexistent God to Jung's weak existent one" (*The Triumph of the Therapeutic* [New York: Harper & Row, 1968], p. 91).

9. All Freud quotations are from "The Future of an Illusion," in *The Freud Reader,* ed. Peter Gay (New York: W. W. Norton, 1989), pp. 685-722.

10. Dietrich Bonhoeffer, *Letters and Papers from Prison* (New York: Macmillan, 1972), pp. 280-81. Bonhoeffer's thinking during this period must be interpreted with care by those who know his life's work well. It is easily misunderstood and misappropriated by those who do not understand his profound commitment to the Bible and the life of the Christian community.

11. The *Time* cover was December 14, 1998. In addition, David Denby asks in a *New Yorker* essay whether Moses ever really existed, and admits that even a "secular Jew" like himself feels threatened by any suggestion to the contrary ("No Exodus," *The New Yorker,* 7 and 14 December 1998 [double issue]).

12. There is considerable scholarly disagreement about whether the name YHWH was or was not first introduced to the Hebrew people at this time. See note 24.

13. Everything becomes dated to some extent, but the four-part essay on "The Hebrews" by William A. Irwin in *The Intellectual Adventure of Ancient Man* (Chicago: University of Chicago Press, 1946) still has a lot to recommend it even after fifty years.

14. John Bright, *The Authority of the Old Testament* (Grand Rapids: Baker Book House, 1967), p. 128.

15. Thomas Cahill, *The Gifts of the Jews* (New York: Nan Talese, 1998), pp. 85-86, 93.

16. In fact, Cahill is confusing on this very point. He will suggest that what he rightly calls "the Voice" is actually from within ourselves, then on the very same page will say that it is the voice of God. There is no such ambivalence in the Bible itself. Even the famous rendering of Jesus' saying, "The Kingdom of God is within you" (Luke 17:21) is almost universally regarded as a mistranslation ("within your grasp" or "in your midst" is more like it).

17. The full passage from *The Future of an Illusion* is suggestive: "Where questions of religion are concerned, people are guilty of every possible sort of dishonesty and intellectual misdemeanor. Philosophers stretch the meaning of words until they retain scarcely anything of their original sense. They give the name of 'God' to some vague abstraction which they have created for themselves . . . and they can even boast that they have recognized a higher purer concept of God, notwithstanding that their God is now nothing more than an insubstantial shadow and no longer *the mighty personality of religious doctrines*" [emphasis added]. I mean no disrespect to Freud when I say that this last phrase can only refer to the God of the Hebrew Bible, and that the reference to a "mighty personality" comes closer than anything else he wrote that I know of to admitting that perhaps there was something more consequential here than he had otherwise allowed.

18. Nahum Sarna, *Exploring Exodus: The Heritage of Biblical Israel* (New York: Schocken, 1986), p. 41.

19. Since this sermon was preached I have been introduced by Paul Roazen to a most interesting essay written in 1928 by Oskar Pfister, a psychoanalyst and pastor, respectfully disagreeing with Freud. It is called "The Illusion of a Future," and appeared in English for the first time in 1993 (*International Journal of Psycho-Analysis* [1993]: 74, 557). It was originally published in Freud's journal *Imago*.

20. Gerhard von Rad, *God at Work in Israel* (Nashville: Abingdon, 1974), p. 132. Von Rad is somewhat out of fashion in the academy today, but it can be said of his work as of few others, "That'll preach." Far from projecting herself into a place of honor, Israel — in an arresting phrase of von Rad — *uttered a witness against herself* in faithfulness to her God. The Bible is a unique document in the history of religion because it contains *within itself* the judgment of God upon its own wishes (idols).

21. This insight is from a sermon by the great nineteenth-century preacher Alexander Maclaren (*Expositions of Holy Scripture,* 17 vols. [Grand Rapids: Baker Book House, 1974]).

22. "The being and activity of God are not played against each other, but included within the whole reality of the divine revelation. God's nature is neither static being, nor eternal presence, nor simply dynamic activity. Rather, the God of Israel makes known his being in specific historical moments . . . by redeeming a covenant people." Brevard Childs, *The Book of Exodus* (Philadelphia: Westminster, 1974), p. 88.

23. Childs, *The Book of Exodus,* p. 89.

24. Christopher R. Seitz, *Word Without End* (Grand Rapids: Eerdmans, 1998), p. 238. In order to make this point, Seitz translates the divine name as "In the manner that I will be, I am who I am."

25. Scholars disagree on whether the name YHWH was or was not first introduced at this time. The name appears frequently in Genesis, but that might be a projection back into the patriarchal period from a later perspective. Christopher Seitz reviews the discussion and comes

to the conclusion that the name was known all along *but not in the definitive way it is made known through the Exodus, which is the principal revelatory event.* Seitz concludes, *"All levels of tradition are in essential agreement here"* (p. 247, my emphasis).

26. At the time of this sermon, Rev. Sharpton was in downtown Manhattan leading demonstrations against police brutality.

27. Cahill, *The Gifts of the Jews,* p. 117.

28. Bonhoeffer, *Letters and Papers from Prison,* p. 360.

Sermon 2: Re-imagining and Revelation

1. N. H. Tur-Sinai, *The Book of Job: A New Commentary* (1957). See also Samuel Terrien, "Introduction and Exegesis to Job," *Interpreter's Bible,* vol. 3 (New York: Abingdon, 1954). It is unfortunate that this superb, universally admired commentary is entombed in the now-disused *IB.*

2. Sigmund Freud, "The Future of an Illusion," in *The Freud Reader,* ed. Peter Gay (New York: W. W. Norton, 1989), pp. 685-722.

Sermon 3: The Trinity in the Last Ditch

1. The construction of 2 Corinthians is much debated. No one knows how many letters it is or what order they were written in. It is possible that chapters 10–13 were written earlier than the preceding chapters. This unit may be the "severe letter" that Paul himself mentions in 2:3-4.

2. They are referred to as the "super-apostles" in 11:5 and 12:11. Paul seems to be quoting the Corinthians' own terminology.

3. 1 Corinthians 2:1-5.

4. Romans ends with a doxology.

5. The Galatian church probably broke his heart too, but we have only one letter to those Christians and (though it is of supreme importance theologically) it is more in the nature of a dispatch from a field marshal than a battle for the soul of a beloved child. Paul's heart is revealed in 2 Corinthians (and Philippians).

Sermon 4: Christ vs. Adam: Kosovo and Beyond

1. Peter Brown, "The New Augustine," *The New York Review of Books,* 24 June 1999.

2. All details and quotations are from the article by David Rohde, "Kosovar Attack on Gypsies Reveals Desire for Revenge," *The New York Times,* 7 June 1999.

3. "Smallpox: The Once and Future Scourge," lead article in "Science Times," *The New York Times,* 15 June 1999.

4. In the *Times* obituary on Friday for Basil Cardinal Hume, we read that in the last months of his life he "adopted as a special cause the need for prayers at midnight on December 31 to accompany the celebration of the millennium, writing newspaper articles and making appearances on television to press the point that the celebration was for the birth of Jesus Christ."

5. It is not necessary to take sides on the vexed and much-debated question about

whether Paul speaks of himself before or after conversion in order to recognize this description of the human dilemma.

6. Mark Edmundson, "Save Sigmund Freud," *New York Times Magazine,* 13 July 1999.

7. The wildly popular Foxwoods gambling casino is not far from Essex, where this sermon was preached.

8. David Firestone, "DNA Test Brings Freedom," *The New York Times,* 16 June 1999. I moved the word "just" for rhetorical purposes.

Sermon 5: Death Sentence, Life Sentence

1. Stephen Kinzer, "Tibet's Exiles Feel Forsaken," *The New York Times,* 24 June 1999, quoting Ranchen K. Chogyal, education minister for the government-in-exile.

2. *Reader's Digest.* I didn't get the date.

3. An expression made famous by former President George H. W. Bush.

4. Lance Morrow, "Something We Cannot Accept," *Time,* 8 March 1999, p. 92.

5. Sarah Lyall, "Briton Hanged in 1953 Is Finally Exonerated," *The New York Times,* 30 July 1998.

6. Carey Goldberg, "Poor Children with Bad Teeth Have Trouble Finding Dentists," *The New York Times,* 26 June 1999.

7. Robert Hanley, "Mother of Deliveryman Says Killer's Life Should Be Spared," *The New York Times,* 5 May 1999.

Sermon 7: Access to Power

1. Cal Thomas, "Graham to Clinton: Go and Sin No More," *Los Angeles Times Syndicate,* March 9, 1998.

2. This was in *The New York Review of Books.* I didn't get the date.

3. When Billy Graham made his remark the President had not yet admitted to his liaison with Monica Lewinsky.

Sermon 8: Hope among the Weeds

1. In the Episcopal Church, the governing body of laypeople is called the vestry.

2. A lot has happened to Biblical interpretation since I was in seminary. Thirty years ago, we were forbidden to allegorize the parables in any way. Now we know that there are a number of legitimate ways to proceed. Later on in the chapter, the evangelist Matthew gives us the allegorical interpretation, which actually seems pretty obvious: Jesus is the man sowing good seed and the field is his possession — the whole world.

3. A number of commentators identify this darnel as a noxious weed that looks very much like wheat until the head forms.

4. Matthew calls it the Kingdom of Heaven.

5. The "bookkeeper" idea is borrowed from Robert Farrar Capon.

6. It is not sufficiently appreciated today that Shakespeare knew the Bible intimately. What he actually *thought* about the Bible can only be inferred, but many of the plays are steeped in Biblical atmosphere.

7. J. Christiaan Beker, *Suffering and Hope* (Philadelphia: Fortress Press, 1987), p. 90.

8. Spelled thus in the program.

9. When John himself landed in Herod's prison, he was assailed by doubt. He sent messengers to Jesus, asking him if he could prove he was Messiah (Matt. 11:2-6).

Sermon 9: True Inclusiveness

1. The purpose of telling this story in this setting was that Bishop Spong and the Trinity Episcopal School for Ministry have little love for one another.

2. I tried once to tell this story to Bishop Spong and was disappointed that it did not interest him. In any event, I wrote to him later to make sure he did not mind my publishing it. Again, he showed no interest in what I had to say at what he called "the seminary in Western Pennsylvania."

3. "Sin" and "Law" are capitalized to indicate that Paul considered them to be among the Powers.

Sermon 10: Mrs. Hamer, Mrs. Durr, Brother Will, and the Word of Faith

1. "The Talk of the Town," *New Yorker,* 17 May 1999 (emphasis added).

2. "The Holy Hill" is an affectionate nickname for the area in Alexandria, Virginia, occupied by the Virginia Theological Seminary and the Episcopal High School.

3. *Outside the Magic Circle* (University of Alabama Press, 1985) is out of print, but an edition of her letters is in preparation.

4. Virginia Foster Durr, *Outside the Magic Circle,* p. 125.

5. Durr, *Magic Circle,* p. 284.

6. He believes that she is properly understood only if viewed through her Biblical faith. The otherwise reliable biography of Mrs. Hamer, *This Little Light of Mine,* is deficient in that respect.

7. I could be criticized here for failing to acknowledge that Paul is speaking of the Jews. In other places I have spoken about the meaning of Romans 9-11 as it relates specifically to the Jews. Chapter 10, however, can legitimately be understood in terms of religious people in general. As one of my longtime friends, a graduate of Virginia Seminary, used to say, "We're all Jews," meaning, we all seek to establish our own righteousness.

8. Cursillo is a very popular renewal program that emphasizes personal conversion and commitment.

9. It is a sign of how much the times have changed that this line about the Gallo wine boycott brought a big laugh in 1999. Few in the audience remembered how the charismatic leader Cesar Chavez was arousing the conscience of the nation about the plight of migrant laborers. The boycott was urgently serious during 1973 and 1974 at Union Theological Seminary

in New York. Today it seems as if there is no one to lead the migrant workers, whose predicament remains deplorable.

10. Although we could also mention the Crusades and the Inquisition.

11. Catholic writers like Flannery O'Connor and Walker Percy are more Protestant than they like to admit.

12. Cited in *Bartlett's Familiar Quotations*.

13. Quoted in *Fortune* magazine, 15 February 1999.

14. At the time of this sermon, the famous actor was president of the National Rifle Association, defending the sale of handguns and assault weapons in spite of the school shootings that had transfixed the nation.

15. 1 Corinthians 5:1-5: Paul's wording is of great importance: "You are to deliver this man to Satan for the destruction of the flesh, *that his spirit may be saved in the day of the Lord Jesus.*"

16. Matthew Shepard, a young homosexual, was beaten and left to die in sub-freezing temperatures in Laramie, Wyoming — another case that riveted the nation and caused many to rethink their attitudes.

17. One annoying thing about Will Campbell is his insistence on saying that he is not a theologian. That's equivalent to Aretha Franklin saying she is not a singer.

18. Will D. Campbell, *And Also With You: Duncan Gray and the American Dilemma* (Franklin, Tenn.: Providence House Publishers, 1997).

Sermon 11: The Faces of Love

1. I have added emphasis in order to try to reproduce the tone of the live interview, and I have made two tiny changes in the transcript to clarify Moreau's Gallicisms. But all is essentially reproduced as transcribed by CBS News.

2. Gunther Bornkamm, *Early Christian Experience* (New York: Harper & Row, 1969).

3. Karl Barth, *Church Dogmatics*, IV/2 (Edinburgh: T. & T. Clark, 1958), p. 825.

Sermon 12: Love and Power

1. In the process of streamlining this sermon, I have omitted an important part of the passage from Ezekiel. It actually reads: "I will bind up the cripples, and I will strengthen the weak, and the fat and the strong I will watch over; I will feed them in justice." In other words, not only will God care tenderly for the defenseless but also (this part might make you and me a little nervous) he will keep an eye on the fat and the strong so they won't start exploiting the weak — because, says the Lord, "I will feed [my sheep] *in justice.*"

2. Depending on how you count, there are eight or nine solemn εγώ εἰμι (I am) statements in the Fourth Gospel. If there were any doubt about the formula making Jesus equivalent to God, the saying in John 8:58 makes it clear ("Before Abraham was, I am" — I AM being the divine name in Exodus 3:14).

3. "Through the long night hours be near me,/Keep me safe till morning light."

4. *Book of Common Prayer,* Burial of the Dead [Rite I].

Sermon 13: Rewriting the Book of Love

1. The Greek word means *slave*. The word *servant* is not entirely wrong but does not convey the full contrast between the two "forms."

Sermon 15: The Once and Future Doctrine

1. I mean to suggest an era ending roughly with the date of St. Augustine of Hippo, the last and greatest of the teachers of the church on this issue until the Reformation. Paul's radical understanding of justification by grace through faith was largely though not entirely obscured during the Middle Ages — until Martin Luther produced the Ninety-Five Theses in 1517.

2. Maybe we ought to identify the meaning of "radical." The word comes from the Latin word *radix,* meaning "root." So "radical" means to get to the root, to get down to basics. Over time the word has come to mean something more extreme; it has come to mean "revolutionary," so that a person who wants to overthrow an existing set of arrangements is called a "radical." Much of Romans (especially 9–11), also by Paul, is as radical as Galatians, but because Romans is a larger, more diffuse letter, it is not readily appropriated as a single entity. Galatians, being a dispatch to the battlefront, is shorter and more concentrated.

3. The meaning of the term "apostle," from the Greek *apostolos,* is "one who is sent." The apostles were those sent directly from the Lord himself, as Paul was on the Damascus Road. Paul had to defend his apostleship repeatedly because of accusations that he had not known Christ during the Lord's lifetime on earth. When the apostles had all entered the life of the Resurrection, the "subapostolic" age began and the church became "apostolic" by derivation from the apostles' teaching.

4. A classic essay on this subject is Martin Luther's "The Bondage of the Will."

5. The character's name, interestingly, is Jean-Baptiste Clamence, which means John the Baptist crying [in the wilderness], as in chapter 1 of Mark.

6. *The New York Times,* 26 April 1997.

7. I am using J. Louis Martyn's translation. The word "rectification" is a better rendering in English than the more familiar "justification." It is too bad that there isn't a simpler English word to convey the idea of the Greek *dikaiosune.* Justification has sometimes been misinterpreted as a sort of general amnesty. *Justification* conveys the idea of the individual balance sheet being straightened out, but *rectification* encompasses a larger truth: in God's future, all wrong will be righted and those who have suffered from injustice will be vindicated.

8. It's important to understand that Flesh (*sarx* in Greek) is not a literal term, nor does it have anything specific to do with sex. It refers to the whole of human life under the dominion of sin and death, and Paul sets it over against the realm of the Spirit, which encompasses material life as well as "spiritual" life.

9. In a discussion between two theologians, the Roman Catholic Hans Küng and the Protestant Karl Barth, Küng, who admired Barth, sought to convince him that the Catholic view was not so different from the Protestant. Barth, with the mischievous humor typical of him, inquired if he would have come to that conclusion if he (Barth) had not brought the Protestant view to his attention.

10. It has been brought to my attention that this insight, so closely associated with Protes-

tantism, has sometimes been construed as anti-Judaic and even anti-Catholic. This is a perversion, however, for two reasons: (1) the critique of religion is profoundly embedded in the Hebrew Scriptures, and (2) Protestantism at its best *(semper reformanda)* is critical of itself most of all.

11. Galatians 3:10-14 explains how this came about on the Cross.

12. This is the *root,* and this is the *revolution.*

13. Since this sermon was written, numerous objections from Lutherans have indicated that the discussions still have a way to go on this crucial issue in our dialogue with the Roman Church. Protestants cannot afford to be smug, however. It is human nature to turn back to its own supposed righteousness on a daily basis.

Sermon 16: God-damned Christians

1. The historian Peter Brown has a particular insight into this. He points out that because the crucified person died of slow asphyxiation as he attempted to heave himself up on the unforgiving wood in order to draw a breath, he was forced to be his own executioner. He was not even allowed the dignity of a human executioner comparable to himself. (Conversation with Peter Brown, Princeton, January 27, 1999.)

2. Poets and novelists often understand what churchgoers do not. In Flannery O'Connor's novel, *Wise Blood,* Haze Motes is apprehended by a crazed blind man who adjures him to repent of his sins. He is asked to renounce them by name, beginning with fornication and blasphemy. "They ain't nothing but words," says Haze. *"If I was in sin I was in it before I ever committed any"* (emphasis added).

3. Dorothy Martyn, "Compulsion and Liberation: A Theological View," *Union Seminary Quarterly Review,* Winter-Spring 1981, pp. 119-29.

4. W. H. Auden, *For the Time Being: A Christmas Oratorio:* "Even in the germ-cell's primary division/Innocence is lost. . . ."

5. "A Declaration of Independence," article about Harry Merica in *The Virginia Episcopalian,* October 1995. I later learned that this remarkable young man had died at the age of 31 only two weeks before this sermon was preached, having spent much of his short life fighting for the establishment of a facility for disabled people. He lived long enough to see that dream become a reality.

6. *New York Times,* 27 January 1999.

7. The Bible teaches us that, ultimately, all sin is against God. "Against thee only, O Lord, have I sinned" (Ps. 51:4).

Sermon 17: Common Sense, or Christ Crucified?

1. Gustav Niebuhr, "Pope's Appeal Not Enough to Bridge Divide on Executions," *The New York Times,* 30 January 1999.

2. Any good commentary on 1 Corinthians will describe the spiritual arrogance, the glib enthusiasm of the Corinthian congregation. Paul struggled with it almost to the point of heartbreak in 2 Corinthians.

3. Pam Belluck, "Clemency for Killer Surprises Many Who Followed Case," *The New York Times,* 31 January 1999.

4. Looking back on this sermon, I see that it is a little like Paul's letter to Philemon. Paul never says outright that Philemon should free his slave Onesimus, but clearly that is what Paul hopes he will do. Similarly, though I do not say that the death penalty is dead in Christ, that is what I hope hearers will conclude.

Sermon 18: Steering Toward the Pain

1. *Richmond Times-Dispatch,* 24 February 1999.
2. Evelyn Nieves, "Our Towns" column, *The New York Times,* 24 July 1996.
3. Sermon by Oscar Romero in El Salvador, December 3, 1978.

Sermon 19: King, and God, and Sacrifice

1. The title of this sermon and several of the quotations are from the Epiphany hymn "We Three Kings of Orient Are."

2. It has been said that the Gospel of John is one sustained epiphany. The Fourth Gospel is known for its unambiguous setting forth of Jesus as the Christ from its very first verses. In this respect it differs from the other Gospels, which unfold his identity more gradually and with more deliberate ambiguity. Thus, in the Gospel of Matthew, John the Baptist, languishing in prison, is assailed by doubts about Jesus' identity.

4. *Pascha* is the Greek word for Passover. Hence the terms "Passover lamb" and "Paschal lamb" are interchangeable.

5. I have simplified the stipulations of Leviticus 1–6:7 considerably, but then so have the various New Testament writers.

6. Article by Suzanne Daley, *The New York Times,* 16 January 1999.

7. Article by Ginger Thompson, *The New York Times,* 23 December 1998.

8. The name of the Jesuit who is carrying out this heroic ministry is Carlos Morfín Otero.

9. Hymn, "Blessed assurance, Jesus is mine."

Sermon 20: The Resurrection Reach-Out

1. Emil Brunner.

2. The "image of God" spoken of in the creation story is essentially a relational term.

3. Always note the words "but God" where they appear in Scripture. You are about to hear the gospel.

4. Paraphrasing Graham Greene, who said that a writer should be a piece of grit in the state machinery.

5. April 28, 1999.

6. "The word of the Lord came to me again: 'What do you mean by repeating this prov-

erb concerning the land of Israel, "The fathers have eaten sour grapes, and the children's teeth are set on edge"? As I live,' says the Lord God, 'this proverb shall no more be used by you in Israel. Behold, all souls are mine; the soul of the father as well as the soul of the son is mine'" (Ezek. 18:1-4).

7. Orlando Patterson, "When 'They' Become 'Us,'" op-ed article, *The New York Times,* 30 April 1999.

Sermon 21: Money in Trust

1. Charles W. F. Smith, *The Jesus of the Parables* (Philadelphia: Pilgrim Press, 1974), pp. 11-12. Smith's book is a bit dated in some ways; he holds to an older view that leaves no room for allegory in the parables. However, his angle on the parables as weapons in Jesus' apocalyptic war is right on target.

2. The Phillips translation is fifty years old so I have multiplied the amounts accordingly. The amounts of money are supposed to be very large, fifteen years' wages in the case of the first servant.

3. C. H. Dodd, *The Parables of the Kingdom,* revised edition (New York: Scribner's, 1961).

4. Andrew Jacobs, "'Walkers' Make a Tentative Stand," *The New York Times,* 10 November 1999.

Sermon 22: Can These Bones Live?

1. Rosemary Dinnage, "Good Grief" (a review of Leon Wieseltier's *Kaddish*), *The New York Review of Books,* 4 February 1999.

2. Jay McInerney, "Naked on the Grass," *The New Yorker,* 18 January 1999.

3. What McInerney actually says is "the bullshit of Catholicism." I didn't use the first word for obvious reasons (my, how *The New Yorker* has changed!), and as for the second, I did not want to appear anti-Catholic. Protestant churches often fail to communicate the gospel, too.

4. *"C'est son métier,"* as Voltaire said.

5. Rita Dove, "Black on a Saturday Night," in *On the Bus with Rosa Parks: Poems* (New York: W. W. Norton, 1999).

6. Actually, Ezekiel has been one of my favorite Biblical books for many years. Most white folks, however, need some help in reading it.

7. I am not addressing Jay McInerney's mother's anger (and his own) at the church's teachings about sex, which is a major theme in the story, because there isn't enough time in the space of one sermon to explain that what she was taught about sex is no more Biblical than what she was taught about the path to redemption.

8. Alexander Maclaren.

Sermon 23: Nothing Virtual Tonight

1. The only information about Jesus of Nazareth that we have is in the New Testament.

That's why the Jesus Seminar scholars are having such a hard time; they don't have anything to go by except the Bible, which they don't trust. Of course there are the Gnostic gospels, but they post-date the New Testament and are informed by an almost totally non-historical perspective.

2. As this volume goes to press, this question is more urgent than ever.

3. An unarmed black man, Amadon Diallo, had just been killed by a hail of bullets from police who mistook him for a suspect.

Sermon 24: Mine Eyes Have Seen the Glory

1. One Biblical scholar has referred to God's "elusive presence" as the overarching theme of the Old Testament. See Samuel Terrien, *The Elusive Presence: Toward a New Biblical Theology* (San Francisco: Harper & Row, 1978).

2. Malcolm W. Browne, "Buried on a Hillside, Clues to Terror," Science Times in *The New York Times*, 23 February 1999.

3. This phrase describing the God of the Bible who "makes a way out of no way" has become very familiar in the black community. It is not an exact scriptural quotation but refers to the crossing at the Red Sea when the Israelites were hemmed in on every side with no means of escape. It is an apt expression of the doctrine of *creatio ex nihilo* (creation out of nothing) which was developed out of reflection on the Scriptures. Paul refers to this idea explicitly in Romans 4:17 when he speaks of the God "who gives life to the dead and calls into existence the things that do not exist."

Sermon 25: Death Shall Have No Dominion

1. Since this sermon was preached I have heard one or two deathbed stories that I found truly convincing, where devout believers seemed to fall asleep in Christ in a way that registered with all who were present. Even in such rare and radiant cases, however, the change that comes over the body cannot be loved.

2. James Feron, "In Suburbs the Resurrection Is a Personal Religious Matter," *New York Times*, 31 March 1975.

Sermon 26: A Way Out of No Way

1. The words of this hymn were written by John of Damascus in the eighth century. They were translated by John Mason Neale. The tune is by Arthur S. Sullivan (yes, that one).

2. Brevard Childs, *The Book of Exodus* (Philadelphia: Westminster, 1974), p. 239.

3. Even if my father hadn't gotten better, faith still says, "The Lord is able."

4. Childs, *Book of Exodus*, p. 239.

5. Francis X. Clines, *The New York Times*, 11 May 1994. This episode is described at more length in the sermon called "Ascension Day in Pretoria" in my first sermon collection, *The Bible and The New York Times* (Grand Rapids: Eerdmans, 1998).

Sermon 27: Doubting and Believing

1. News story, *The Atlanta Constitution,* April 1994.
2. At the time of this sermon, Ms. Maples was still Mrs. Donald Trump.

Sermon 28: Jesus Will Show

1. Christ the King Sunday positions the church on the frontier between the world's past, full of sin, evil, and death, and the coming of the Lord in glory to establish his eternal kingdom of justice, righteousness, and love. This is not to be confused with millennial hype of any kind. Jesus very specifically taught that the date and time would never be known to us. What is important for Christians in the interim — and every day is the interim — is identifying and pursuing the quality of life that is fitting for those who wait for Jesus.

2. Robert Hughes, "In Death's Throat," *Time,* 11 October 1999. This essay is well worth reading for its powerful evocation of the specter of death.

3. Paul tells the conversion story over and over in Acts, but that is Luke's version of Paul. For the more authentic voice of the Apostle we look to the letters.

4. Collect for Purity, *Book of Common Prayer,* Holy Eucharist, Rites I and II.

5. Barbara Pym, *An Academic Question* (New York: New American Library, Penguin Inc., 1986), p. 139.

6. This point is especially associated with Aleksandr Solzhenitsyn, who wrote in *The Gulag Archipelago* of the line that runs through each person. The theme has been taken up recently by Václav Havel.

7. Quoted in "The Good Soldier," a review of John McCain's *Faith of My Fathers* by Lars-Erik Nelson, *The New York Review of Books,* 21 October 1999.

8. "The least, the last, and the lost" is a phrase of Robert Farrar Capon.

Sermon 29: Beyond the Valley of Ashes

1. The sole exception is a modern carol.

2. Deborah Sontag, "Eager Palestinians Seek New Millennium's Fruits," *The New York Times,* 5 December 1999.

Sermon 30: Ruth's Redeemer

1. Many critics agree that the book of Ruth is what we today would call a *novella* or short story, not unlike the short story form that we have today, but with a concern to show forth God's working in human affairs.

2. Literary critics everywhere are agreed about the writer's genius and the perfection of the tale. I wish we had time to spend discussing all the wonderful narrative devices — for instance, the repetition of certain key words at dramatic moments to elicit surprise and joy from the listeners.

3. The principal god of Moab was called Chemosh.

4. The reader already knows that Boaz is a kinsman, though Ruth does not; this is part of the author's artistry.

5. We simply do not know exactly what is meant. "Feet" is often, but not always, used as a euphemism for the genitals. It could also mean "legs."

6. Edward F. Campbell, Jr., *Ruth: A New Translation with Introduction and Commentary,* Anchor Bible Series (New York: Doubleday, 1975), p. 138. From the perspective of today, with issues of sexual harassment and aggression so much in the news, it should be especially noted that the imbalance of power between Boaz and Ruth is vast. Boaz's respectful treatment of Ruth is therefore all the more meritorious.

7. We have skipped over another episode in the final chapter. Suffice it to say that the final chapter enlarges the character of Boaz, who unselfishly offers to stand aside for another, closer relative who has been discovered. However, this second "redeemer" withdraws, refusing his obligation to Naomi because it would cost him too much money; therefore the field is left open for Boaz.

8. Orpah and the unnamed man who was the closest next-of-kin serve as foils to Ruth and Boaz, not opposites. Neither of them behaves badly. In their prudential decisions, however, they act in a merely human way. Ruth and Boaz are human counterparts of the love of God that reaches out to do more than could have been expected.

Sermon 32: Lydia: The First Christian in Europe

1. This is not meant as caricature or exaggeration. The Galatians were on the verge of slipping back into Law, losing "the freedom we have in Christ Jesus," and the Corinthians were fast becoming spiritually vacuous.

2. Ernst Haenchen, *The Acts of the Apostles: A Commentary* (Philadelphia: Westminster, 1971), p. 486.

3. Haenchen, *The Acts of the Apostles,* p. 484.

4. Today Macedonia does not extend to the seacoast, but in Paul's time it did.

5. "The foundation of the church at Philippi introduces a new and very significant chapter in the life of Paul and the story of early Christianity." Gunther Bornkamm, *Paul* (New York: Harper & Row, 1977), p. 60.

6. Even the German scholars who are most skeptical about the historicity of Acts give credit on many points: Bornkamm writes that "Acts 16:11-40 is a typical Lukan broad-canvas picture, but some accurate information has been incorporated — the route, the city, the origin of the [Philippian] church" (*Paul,* p. 60).

7. It is generally thought that most of these women would have been Gentile "God-fearers."

8. F. F. Bruce, *Paul: Apostle of the Heart Set Free* (Grand Rapids: Eerdmans, 1990), p. 219.

9. Paul refers to his hopes for evangelizing Spain in Romans 15:24-28.

10. "The Diaspora" is the term used to denote the dispersion of Jews into Gentile territories throughout the Hellenistic world following the Babylonian Exile.

11. Donald Coggan, *Paul: Portrait of a Revolutionary* (New York: Crossroad, 1984), p. 82.

12. "Might it not have seemed that the way was stopped before Christ? But afterward there sprang a noble Church of that one small graft" (Calvin).

13. Lydia was actually from the country called Lydia, in the region of Anatolia, southwest Asia Minor (part of modern Turkey). In the fifth century B.C., Lydia was a strong, independent country; the country's most famous ruler is still remembered by us with the expression "rich as Croesus." Five centuries after Croesus, the territory of Lydia came under Roman rule and prospered. The guilds of Lydian dyers were well known. Three of the Seven Churches of Revelation are in Lydia: Thyatira, Sardis, and Philadelphia. (Information taken from the article on Lydia [the country] in *The Interpreter's Dictionary of the Bible*.)

14. Shortly after writing this sermon, I was pleased to learn that Calvin, almost alone among the Reformers, was open in principle to the ordination of women. This finding confirmed my pleasure in discovering Calvin's admiration of Lydia. The discussions of the role of women in Paul's letters, he thought, were related to congregational decency and order in that time and place, not to the essence of the Body of Christ. See Jane Dempsey Douglas, *Women, Freedom, and Calvin* (Philadephia: Westminster Press, 1985).

15. "Her faith is linked with action" (Haenchen, *The Acts of the Apostles*, p. 499).

16. Calvin says that the phrase *she besought them* has "the force of an adjuration." She says, *if you have judged me faithful to the Lord*, which makes it impossible for them to refuse. "Lydia did by such an earnest desire testify how entirely she loved the gospel." It is as though she said, "I beseech you by that faith which you have approved by [my] baptism, that you refuse not to lodge with me."

17. The conversion of Lydia and her household "formed the beginning of a church which from then on was exceptionally closely attached to the Apostle, the beginning, too, of Christianity in Europe" (Bornkamm, *Paul*, p. 61).

18. See also 2 Corinthians 11:8-9: "I robbed other churches by accepting support from them in order to serve you. And when I was with you and was in want, I did not burden any one, for my needs were supplied by the brethren who came from Macedonia."

19. The Philippian church continued to feature women in prominent positions. In his Philippian letter, Paul directly addresses two of them, Euodia and Syntyche, who have fallen out with one another. Paul's appeal to them assumes their importance to him and to the congregation (Phil. 4:2). He entreats them to resolve their differences as fellow workers who have "labored side by side with me in the service of the gospel." In an important comment, J. Hugh Michael writes that the American Standard Version and Revised Standard Version translation ("labored with me") is too weak; it "fails to bring out adequately the idea of opposition and strife involved in the [bringing of the] Word. Euodia and Syntyche had . . . been united in *strenuous service* in the face of opposition. . . . Paul says they had fought at his side in the active service of the gospel." J. Hugh Michael, *The Epistle of Paul to the Philippians*, Moffatt Commentary (New York: Harper & Row, 1927), p. 192.

20. There was local anti-Jewish feeling in Philippi (there were very few Jews there). Haenchen says that the crowd that attacked Paul and Silas were "anti-semitic" (*Paul*, p. 496). Paul was later to remember that he had been "shamefully treated in Philippi" (1 Thess. 2:2). It is interesting to read in Acts 16:36-39 about how Paul insisted on an apology from the magistrates on the strength of his (Paul's) Roman citizenship!

21. One of Raphael's most dramatic paintings in the Vatican is of this scene from Acts.

22. Similarly Haenchen: "The mission in Philippi now possessed a strong center, as 16:40 [the verse about the farewell visit to Lydia's house] confirms" (*Paul,* p. 495).

Sermon 33: Gideon's Three Hundred

1. Fleming James, *Personalities of the Old Testament* (New York: Charles Scribner's Sons, 1939), pp. 65-66.
2. Quoted in Eberhard Bethge, *Dietrich Bonhoeffer* (New York: Harper & Row, 1970), p. 197. Emphasis added.

Sermon 34: Even Peter, Even Us

1. Of the four evangelists, Mark gives us the most negative view of the disciples. In Mark there is no redeeming feature anywhere. The other three soften the picture in various ways, but the story of the threefold denial is intact in all four.
2. Some commentators think that the meaning here is that Peter actually cursed *Jesus.* See *Peter in the New Testament,* ed. Raymond E. Brown et al. (Minneapolis: Augsburg; New York: Paulist Press, 1973), pp. 61-62.
3. It should be parenthetically noted that there are scholars who think that the threefold denial is not historical and that it was invented by an anti-Peter group in the church. I find this preposterous.
4. I am indebted to Joe Alff of Grosse Pointe, Michigan, for this insight.
5. Markan specialist Donald Juel of Princeton Theological Seminary is especially good on this point.
6. We should note that St. Paul also took pains to see that his past was preserved. "For I am the least of the apostles, unfit to be called an apostle," he wrote, "because I persecuted the church of God. But by the grace of God I am what I am" (1 Cor. 15:9-10).
7. Collect for Purity, *Book of Common Prayer.*